UN Protection of
Civil and Political Rights

Volume 8, Procedural Aspects of International Law Series

The Procedural Aspects of International Law Series

Richard B. Lillich, *editor*

UN Protection of
Civil and Political Rights

JOHN CAREY

SYRACUSE UNIVERSITY PRESS

Standard Book Number 8156-2146-9

Library of Congress Catalog Card: 71-104674

FIRST EDITION 1970

To my wife, Patricia, and our children,
whose sacrifice made this study possible.

Editor's Foreword

This book, the eighth volume in the Procedural Aspects of International Law Series prepared by the Procedural Aspects of International Law Institute and published by Syracuse University Press, is the first of five studies which will be produced by the Institute's research project on "International Procedures to Protect Private Rights." This project, funded by a $160,000 grant from the Ford Foundation, has involved a four-year examination of a select number of procedural problems in three separate but interrelated areas: human rights; property rights; and, in a more limited sense, procedural rights (of aliens before national tribunals). It is especially appropriate that this first study on human rights should appear during the twenty-fifth anniversary year of the United Nations since, as Sohn has remarked, "the Charter of the United Nations was really the first international instrument in which the countries of the world agreed to promote human rights on a universal level and to try to see to it that something is done to ensure that human rights are being observed."

Any realistic evaluation of the past quarter century reveals that the progress in the area of human rights has been almost exclusively in the direction of clarifying and codifying the substantive law norms: nearly two dozen covenants and conventions, for instance, have been promulgated under the auspices of the United Nations alone. Comparatively little progress, on the other hand, has been achieved in the direction of creating effective machinery to protect the rights of individuals throughout the world. As Korey has observed, "if the United Nations has been extraordinarily successful during the past twenty years in formulating standards of conduct, it has been sadly negligent in creating institutions and procedures for translating these standards into actual observance." The International Conference on Human Rights convened by the United Nations in 1968 recognized this fact when, in its Proclamation of Teh-

viii EDITOR'S FOREWORD

eran, it acknowledged that "during this [post-Charter] period many important international instruments were adopted, but much remains to be done in regard to the implementation of those rights and freedoms. . . ."

As far back as 1965 the Institute, noting McDougal's observation that "the most difficult problem still confronting the framers of the United Nations' Human Rights Program is that of devising effective procedures for enforcement," began an examination from a procedural perspective both of the United Nations' past efforts in the field and also its potentialities as an agency for human rights enforcement in the future. Directing the study was the author of this volume, a graduate of Yale (B.A., Phi Beta Kappa), Harvard (LL.B.) and New York University (LL.M. in International Law), who is currently a partner in a leading New York firm of international lawyers and also an Adjunct Assistant Professor at New York University. With a long-standing interest in human rights recorded in numerous law review articles, plus an inside view of contemporary developments subsequently obtained while serving as Alternate United States Member and Representative to the United Nations, Sub-Commission on Prevention of Discrimination and Protection of Minorities (1966–1969) and the United Nations Commission on Human Rights (1968), he is superbly qualified to write this study, which should become the basic research tool for persons within and without the United Nations interested in increasing the effective enforcement of human rights norms.

With the exception of the first two chapters and the concluding chapter, the author eschews a theoretical or highly conceptualistic approach and concentrates primarily on the nuts and bolts of various existing and proposed implementation techniques, *e.g.*, reporting, fact-finding, sanctioning. Each technique is reviewed historically as well as from the perspective of United Nations practice. Whenever useful developments have occurred elsewhere, say for example under the practice of the International Labor Organization, they are examined in detail. Throughout the volume the author maintains a cautious and often skeptical view about the practical value of each enforcement technique, a refreshing contrast with much of the writing in the field which often tends to oversell the merits of a given device. Nor is the United Nations to him a sacred cow: when it has failed or erred the author says so, and suggests a more imaginative or prudent course, as the case may be, for the future.

Two features about the book have impressed this reader most. In the first place, it compresses within a relatively modest number of pages a vast amount of detailed analysis and constructive criticism about human rights enforcement, in a form moreover which makes this information readily available to the harried diplomat and the hard-pressed government lawyer as well as to the serious student and the general reader. It is no mere description of recent developments and future hopes, however, but an extremely analytical and systematic approach to how individuals, given the realities of international politics, actually can be protected from their own governments. Secondly, it is based almost exclusively upon original research in United Nations documents, many little known and all hard to obtain, plus the author's own personal observations over several years at the United Nations. Representing a truly original contribution to the literature on the international law of human rights, it should establish itself quickly as the leading source book in the area and a significant addition to this Series.

Richard B. Lillich

Charlottesville, Virginia
September, 1969

Preface

Writing at this moment about the UN's role in protecting civil and political rights is like stopping a moving picture in mid-reel. So much movement is going on that there is great temptation to postpone publication to see how certain trends work out.

As this Preface is written a new UN Human Rights Commission investigation has just begun, concerning alleged mistreatment of civilians in Israeli-occupied Arab areas. The same investigators are at work who in the past two years have held precedent-setting hearings on charges of violations in southern Africa. The whole world has been opened up recently to UN scrutiny, and rules for bringing it to bear are being evolved.

After two decades of inactivity in specific human rights cases, the UN is rousing itself to take what steps it can. Its early steps have faltered at times, but it is gaining assurance and now needs to re-examine and refine its methods. This volume is designed to aid in that task. The Ford Foundation has been foresighted in making possible the kind of technician's review of UN methods which this study attempts to provide.

Thanks have been expressed in a preliminary sketch of this work, published in 53 *Iowa Law Review* 291 (1967), to a number of persons who helped assemble the original materials. Thanks also are due The Association of the Bar of the City of New York, which published a 1968 summary as part of the twelfth book in its Hammarskjöld Forum series, and to the editors of the American Bar Association's publication *The International Lawyer,* of the Strasbourg-based *Human Rights Journal,* and of the *American Journal of International Law,* for permission to draw heavily on articles of mine published in their pages, as the bases for chapters IX (3 *Int'l Lawyer* 102 [1968]), X (1 *Human Rights J.* 531 [1968]), and XII (60 *Am. J. Int'l L.* 792 [1966]).

Above all I want to thank my family, who long ago got used to seeing me poring over UN documents, and Virginia Law Professor Richard B. Lillich, Director of the Procedural Aspects of International Law Institute, the intellectual entrepreneur who inspired, guided, and obtained financing for this and related projects.

John Carey

New York
July 1, 1969

Contents

UN Protection of
Civil and Political Rights

Introduction

The Need for International Protection
of the Individual

The present need for protection of individuals was plainly put by UN Secretary-General U Thant when he reminded the 1968 International Conference on Human Rights at Teheran that "independently of international and internal conflicts, any observer of present-day realities can hardly fail to be alarmed by the persistence or even the increase of violence and brutality in today's world. Massacres, tortures, arbitrary arrests, including cruel detentions of those who are already victims of various forms of discrimination, and summary executions are reported by information media so frequently that the natural human reaction of horror tends to be dulled."[1]

These observations were echoed near the end of 1968 when the UN General Assembly held a special meeting on December 9th in commemoration of the twentieth anniversary of the adoption of the Universal Declaration of Human Rights. Erik Nettel of Austria, Chairman of the Assembly's Third Committee, called 1968 "a very sad year concerning human rights," which he found in "a shabby state." Enumerating victims he would like to help, Nettel promised "anything I can do to help the Negro of America, or the unhappy intellectual of Eastern Europe, or the refugee expelled from his home and land in the Middle East or in Europe, or the exploited and downtrodden in Africa and Latin America, or the hungry and starving in Asia, or the mind shut out from light and truth and being anywhere in the world."[2]

When rampant violations of civil and political rights are joined with economic deprivation, the situation is especially explosive. The

[1] Final Act of the International Conference on Human Rights, A/Conf.32/41, at 36 (1968), Sales No.: E.68.XIV.2. United Nations documents are hereinafter cited simply by serial number and year of issue.

[2] UN Secretariat, International Year for Human Rights Newsletter, No. 8, Supp. 1, at 36 (1968).

1

Secretary-General also at Teheran called attention to "the common philosophy which has emerged within the United Nations regarding what are no longer mere aspirations, but rights, of every individual without distinction to secure respect for his dignity and essential needs as a human being. . . . The impact of inferior status, of lack of opportunity to attain adequate standards of living, of permanent humiliation of the individuals concerned, is clear to all. The consequences for humanity as a whole are no less obvious. . . . There is a clear prospect that racial conflict, if we cannot curb and finally eliminate it, will grow into a destructive monster compared to which the religious or ideological conflicts of the past and present will seem like small family quarrels." [3]

Human rights violations which threaten the peace are also especially grievous. Pope Paul VI has said that "there is a direct relationship between human rights and peace. It is impossible to have true and lasting peace where human rights are unrecognized, violated and trampled upon." [4] A European expert presumes that the drafters of the UN charter mentioned human rights, "almost for the first time in an international treaty . . . because [they] were looking behind the facts of war to its causes, . . . dictatorships which make wars possible. An international order which can effectively secure human rights is thereby taking the biggest single step towards the prevention of war." [5] Similarly, an American human rights leader has declared that "most of the trouble spots of the world are hot today because of the violation or assumed violation of some generally recognized principle of human rights." [6]

With governments committing or allowing such wrongs, the helpless individual is bound to look beyond, towards the international community. Near the end of the 1968 International Year for Human Rights, U Thant described in graphic terms the intensity of the prevailing feeling that the UN should accelerate its role in the protection of basic rights: "The need for the international community, represented by the United Nations, to state its serious preoccupation with situations implying disrespect for human rights may be

---

[3] A/Conf.32/41, at 36–37 (1968).

[4] Human Rights Newsletter, *supra* note 2, at 62.

[5] A. ROBERTSON, HUMAN RIGHTS IN EUROPE 1–2 (1963).

[6] Morris B. Abram, former United States Representative on the UN Human Rights Commission, in American Bar Association, Section of Individual Rights and Responsibilities, Monograph No. 2, at 22 (1968).

almost irresistible, but more and more clearly heard is the demand of world public opinion that the Organization play a more active role in helping to bring remedies and alleviate human suffering in spite of all existing obstacles." [7]

The UN is concerned with two broad categories of human rights, civil and political on the one hand and economic, social and cultural on the other. The two categories are treated in two covenants approved by the General Assembly in 1966. Civil and political rights, if not more important than economic, social and cultural rights, are more sharply defined in the covenants. More extensive international protection machinery is provided in the covenants for the civil and political category of rights. It is that category whose protection by the UN is the subject of this volume.

The year 1968 was celebrated as International Year for Human Rights. In that year, evaluation of the UN's protection methods was undertaken. In 1969, the International Labor Organization, pioneer in the international protection of basic rights, had its fiftieth anniversary. The year 1970 marks the UN's twenty-fifth anniversary, and provides an occasion for review of all the Organization's activities. This study is intended to help in bringing to a fruition in 1970 the evaluation commenced by the UN in 1968.

[7] A/7201/Add.1, at 43 (1968).

Chapter I

The UN Examines Its Methods of Protection

The UN began to take stock in 1968 of its methods of protecting individuals. The International Conference at Teheran in the spring was told by the Secretary-General that it had been "convened by the General Assembly because it was felt that an extraordinary event of such importance could most effectively assist in furthering the purposes of the International Year. It was undoubtedly useful to depart from the routine succession of United Nations meetings on human rights for the purpose of a detached stock-taking and long-term planning." U Thant added that "an examination of the degree of effectiveness of the methods used by the United Nations, its family of organizations and possibly of the role of existing regional organizations can lead to conclusions as to the strengthening and better functioning of competent United Nations organs, their present status within the Organization and their future needs." [1]

Included in the agenda of the Teheran Conference was an item on the "evaluation of the effectiveness of methods and techniques employed in the field of human rights at the international and regional levels: (a) International instruments: conventions, declarations and recommendations; (b) Implementation machinery and procedures; (c) Educational measures; (d) Organizational and institutional arrangements." [2] However, very little explicit evaluation of international or regional techniques took place at Teheran. While the General Assembly expressed its "satisfaction with the work of the Conference, which constitutes a solid foundation for further action and initiatives by the United Nations and other interested international bodies, as well as by the States and national organizations

[1] A/Conf.32/41, at 36 (1968).

[2] *Id.* at 3. The International Year for Human Rights was established by General Assembly resolution 2081 (XX) of 1965. Steps taken in preparation for the International Year were summarized in A/6687 (1967) and A/6866 (1967). Secretariat studies on "measures" and "methods" used by the UN in human rights matters were published in A/Conf.32/5 and 6 (1967) respectively.

concerned," [3] Jamaica commented near the end of the International Year that "owing to the fact that the methods used had been insufficiently examined and evaluated the Conference had failed to answer the question whether the human rights machinery should be expanded at the present stage or whether a more rational use should be made of the machinery now available." [4] However, certain evaluation implicit in adopted resolutions may be observed.

The unanimously-adopted Proclamation of Teheran seemed to recognize implicitly the possibility of compulsory standard-setting by the General Assembly when it asserted that "the Universal Declaration of Human Rights . . . constitutes an obligation for the members of the international community," even adding that "conventions and declarations in the field of human rights adopted under the auspices of the United Nations, the specialized agencies and the regional inter-governmental organizations, have created new standards and obligations to which States should conform." [5] Similarly revealing a belief that the General Assembly can legislate on basic rights, the Proclamation referred to the "policy of apartheid, condemned as a crime against humanity," presumably by the Assembly. [6]

International legislation to establish basic rights was by implication found to be useful but explicitly held inadequate as regards the laws of war and the newer scientific developments. As to the former, after noting shortcomings in the Hague Conventions of 1899 and

---

[3] A/Res/2442 (XXIII) (1968).

[4] A/C.3/SR.1626, at 10 (1968). The UK also found the evaluation results disappointing. *Id.* at 12. Sir Egerton Richardson, Jamaican Ambassador to the United States, has said that "the Conference failed, no doubt, for lack of time, to probe the second of its aims—the evaluation of UN methods and techniques." Human Rights, Final Report of the International NGO Conference, Paris, 16–20 September 1968, at 25.

[5] A/Conf.32/41, at 4 (1968).

[6] *Id.* "[T]he United States and Britain added to the record that the term [crime against humanity] 'constitutes an expression of moral and political opinion, not a legal categorization.'" N.Y. Times, May 14, 1968, §1, at 11, col. 1. Concerning such condemnations by the General Assembly, see Chapter VII *infra*. The Proclamation seemed itself to be attempting legislation when it declared that "parents have a basic human right to determine freely and responsibly the number and spacing of their children." A/Conf.32/41, at 4 (1968). The Teheran Conference resolution XVIII on "human rights aspects of family planning," after similar language, added the "right to adequate education and information in this respect." *Id.* at 14–15.

1907, the Geneva Protocol of 1925, and the Geneva Conventions of 1949, the Conference called for a UN Secretariat study of "(a) Steps which could be taken to secure the better application of existing humanitarian international conventions and rules in all armed conflicts; (b) The need for additional humanitarian international conventions or for possible revision of existing Conventions to ensure the better protection of civilians, prisoners and combatants in all armed conflicts and the prohibition and limitation of the use of certain methods and means of warfare." [7] As to scientific developments, the Conference urged "interdisciplinary studies at both the national and the international level, so that they may serve as a basis for drawing up appropriate standards, should the need arise." [8] Study was urged by UN agencies on human rights problems arising from such developments as recording techniques; progress in biology, medicine and biochemistry; and the uses of electronics.

Other protection techniques besides legislation that were implicitly evaluated at Teheran included investigation of alleged violations. After referring to recent UN investigations, the conference, "recognizing the importance of well defined rules of procedure" and "noting that no such procedural rules exist," urged the Economic and Social Council to ask the UN Human Rights Commission to prepare "model rules of procedure for the guidance of the United Nations bodies concerned." [9] Another technique implicitly evaluated, that of help for victims, was urged in the form of legal aid, to be provided not only by Governments acting alone or cooperatively, but also by the UN "within the limits of the human rights advisory services programme." [10]

Legislation, investigation, and help for victims, the three international protection techniques explicitly or implicitly evaluated at Teheran, are only three of the identifiable techniques that might have been examined. Others are adjudication, negotiation, publicity, and education, as well as force and coercion directed at the offending government. Since no systematic evaluation of the complete range of techniques was made at Teheran, the present volume

---

[7] *Id.* at 18.
[8] *Id.* at 12.
[9] *Id.*
[10] *Id.* at 15.

brings together under a single heading information on each of these techniques as used by a variety of international organizations. After such assembling of information, evaluation is made of the effectiveness of each of the techniques, followed at the end by proposals for practical measures in the future.

Chapter II

International Legislation to Establish Human Rights

Legislation establishing human rights may be regarded by itself, without enforcement means, as a technique for their protection, at least to the extent they are voluntarily respected. The number of legislative measures in effect or under discussion to establish human rights either world-wide or regionally has been put as high as thirty-seven.[1] Such instruments may be divided into two categories: formal agreements, which are admittedly binding, and others, like the Universal Declaration of Human Rights, which do not purport to do more than set standards but which may acquire quasi-legal status. While these instruments are not all UN products, U Thant has stressed "the importance of this norm-setting work of the Organization in the defence of human rights both by itself and in relation to the other purposes of the United Nations: the maintenance of international peace and security, the promotion of a harmonious economic and social development of humanity, and the formulation of the international law of the future." [2]

A number of formal international agreements have been concluded establishing human rights. The most widely ratified are the four Geneva Conventions of 1949 on the treatment of certain groups of persons in times of armed conflict. The widest range of rights are included in the two Covenants adopted by the UN General Assembly in 1966, one on Civil and Political Rights and the other on Economic, Social and Cultural Rights.[3] While widely signed, these

---

[1] *Situation des conventions internationales relatives aux droits de l'homme,* 1 HUMAN RIGHTS J. 315 (1968). The UN Secretariat has issued a compilation of international human rights instruments of the UN, A/Conf.32/4 (1968), and reports on the status of multilateral agreements in the field of human rights concluded under its auspices, E/CN.4/907/Rev. 5 (1969), and under the auspices of the specialized agencies, A/Conf.32/7/Add.1 (1968).

[2] A/7201/Add.1, at 41 (1968).

[3] A/Res/2200 (XXI) (1966). See *Comparative Analysis of the International Covenants on Human Rights and International Labor Conventions and Recommendations,* 52 I.L.O. OFF. BULL. No. 2, at 181 (1969).

agreements have been slow to be ratified.[4] More quickly ratified has been the more specialized Convention on the Elimination of All Forms of Racial Discrimination, approved by the General Assembly late in 1965 [5] and effective three years later, and the Convention on the Prevention and Punishment of the Crime of Genocide, approved by the General Assembly in 1948 [6] and in force since 1951.

The Racial Discrimination and Genocide Conventions illustrate a difficulty incurred by formal human rights agreements with such frequency as to render them less than adequate for dealing with the more vexatious problems. Governments frequently are reluctant to undertake binding legal obligations concerning their treatment of their own citizens, as United States experience illustrates. After President Truman submitted the Genocide Convention to the Senate in 1949, a constitutional amendment to curb the Federal Government's treaty power narrowly missed adoption in 1954.[7] The executive branch of government withdrew from participation in human rights treaty-making,[8] a position which lasted until 1963, when President Kennedy submitted to the Senate treaties on slavery, forced labor, and political rights of women. Only the first was approved by the Senate, which followed advice received from the American Bar Association.[9] Should the Senate be asked by a Presi-

[4] As of June 25, 1969, 42 signatures to the 1966 Covenant on Civil and Political Rights had been filed, 15 to its Optional Protocol, and 43 to the Covenant on Economic, Social and Cultural Rights. UN Press Release L/T/484 (1969). The Covenants had received 4 of the 35 ratifications or accessions needed for effectiveness, and the Optional Protocol to the Covenant on Civil and Political Rights had only 2 ratifications or accessions. UN Press Release L/T/437 (1969).

[5] A/Res/2106 (XX) (1965). While 27 ratifications or accessions were needed for effectiveness, and that number had been received by the end of 1968, effectiveness was delayed until January 1969 by numerous reservations, for whose approval an additional period was necessary. The 36th ratification or accession was received on May 16, 1969, by which date 71 countries had signed. UN Press Release L/T/461 (1969). Document A/6692 (1967) quotes the declarations or reservations made by some States, including those of several socialist countries excluding compulsory jurisdiction of the International Court of Justice.

[6] A/Res/260 A(III) (1948). For the ratifications and reservations to the Genocide Convention, see E/CN.4/Sub.2/302 (1969).

[7] See comment in 48 AM. J. INT'L L. at 494 (1954).

[8] The pertinent statement by Secretary of State Dulles is quoted in 47 AM. J. INT'L L. at 449 (1953).

[9] The resolution adopted by the ABA House of Delegates in August 1967 is published in 2 INT'L LAWYER 17–18 (1967). Arguments for and against ratification are published in 1 INT'L LAWYER 589 (1967).

dent for advice and consent to ratification of the 1965 Racial Discrimination Convention, equally or more vigorous resistance could be anticipated. The two-thirds Senate vote required would be even greater a hurdle than the simple majorities necessary for the several Civil Rights Acts. It is not likely that any person basically uninterested if not hostile to human equality will be moved by appeals like U Thant's that "ratifying international covenants and conventions on human rights is a true sign of devotion to international solidarity and a concrete contribution to efforts to attain the objectives of the Charter, even for those countries who may believe that it is not necessary for them to become parties to United Nations instruments because they already have adequate national guarantees." [10]

Ratification perhaps could be stimulated by international action. The UN Institute for Training and Research, known as UNITAR, has suggested that "a Committee of Experts on Ratification and Acceptance, entrusted with the task of systematic and regular review of the position of ratifications of international treaties in the field of human rights, may have a useful function to perform in the promotion of wider acceptance of these treaties. The experience of the Committee of Experts on Application of Conventions and Recommendations set up by the International Labour Organization in regard to the Conventions adopted under its aegis seems to support this suggestion." [11] Roberto Ago has cited to the same effect not only ILO experience but also that of UNESCO and WHO, whose constitutions require action within twelve and eighteen months respectively relative to acceptance of any convention adopted by the governing body of the specialized agency.[12] A Dutch proposal for a committee of experts on unratified conventions was made but not acted on at the 1968 Teheran Conference.[13]

The ratification difficulties presented by formal human rights agreements do not dictate their abandonment as one of the available techniques,[14] but they do compel increased reliance on alternative

[10] A/7201/Add.1, at 42–43 (1968).

[11] A/Conf.32/15, at 15 (1968). See generally E. LANDY, THE EFFECTIVENESS OF INTERNATIONAL SUPERVISION: THIRTY YEARS OF I.L.O. EXPERIENCE (1966).

[12] A/CN.4/205, at 7 (1968); see also A/CN.4/205/Rev. 1 (1969).

[13] A/Conf.32/41, at 48 (1968).

[14] The European Convention on Human Rights has been ratified by all but France and Switzerland of the eighteen members of the Council of Europe. In October 1968 the United States Senate readily approved the Protocol extending

techniques, including that of purportedly non-binding instruments. As the representative of a smaller country, Ambassador Richardson of Jamaica, has put it, "the value of international institutions lies mainly in their function of establishing norms and setting standards for the guidance of national authorities. I believe that the coercive powers we are attempting to give to international institutions will be of little effectiveness for a very long time to come, . . . owing to the persistence of the belief in the myth of national sovereignty and its inviolability, and owing to the persistence of the belief that outsiders who do not understand one's system and who do not accept the basic principles on which it is founded ought not to interfere." [15]

The best-known example of UN quasi-legislation by non-binding instrument is the 1948 Universal Declaration of Human Rights.[16] Three years before the Declaration was completed there had been written what U Thant has called "perhaps the boldest innovation of the Charter—the unconditional and universal obligation in regard to human rights and fundamental freedoms." [17] Human Rights are mentioned numerous times in the Charter: the provisions to which the Secretary-General doubtless referred are found in Article 56, under which "all Members pledge themselves to take joint and separate action in cooperation with the Organization for the achievement of the purposes set forth in Article 55," which in turn provides that

the Refugee Convention to persons fleeing their home countries after 1951, but this instrument may well have been considered as having little or no application to the more turgid human rights problems in the United States.

[15] Report on Annual Conference of the Non-Governmental Organizations in Co-operation with the United Nations Office of Public Information, Annex III at 7, 9 (1967).

[16] Documents A/Conf.32/6, at 114 (1967) and Add.1, at 5 (1968) list the following "declarations" on human rights adopted by the General Assembly through 1967:

> Universal Declaration of Human Rights (1948); Declaration of the Rights of the Child (1959); Declaration on the Granting of Independence to Colonial Countries and Peoples (1960); Declaration on Permanent Sovereignty over Natural Wealth and Resources (1962); United Nations Declaration on the Elimination of All Forms of Racial Discrimination (1963); Declaration on the Promotion Among Youth of the Ideals of Peace, Mutual Respect and Understanding Between Peoples (1965); Declaration on the Elimination of Discrimination Against Women (1967); Declaration on Territorial Assylum (1967).

[17] From statement at opening of 45th session of the UN Economic and Social Council, Geneva, July 8, 1968. UN Press Release SG/SM/971—ECOSOC/2474 (1968).

the United Nations shall promote "universal respect for, and observance of, human rights and fundamental freedoms for all without
distinction as to race, sex, language, or religion." Pierre Juvigny of
the French Conseil d'État has termed these clauses revolutionary:

> It was the United Nations Charter which, unlike the Covenant of the
> League of Nations—which was essentially focused on States—gave
> human rights their international recognition. The entrance of human
> rights into the sphere of international jurisdiction was really a revolu-
> tion, which perhaps astonished the jurists even more than the politi-
> cians. That revolution was more far-reaching because in addition to
> the traditional rights and freedoms, such as those of the Magna Carta,
> of the Declaration of Independence and of the Declaration of 1789,
> those of the Western constitutions of the nineteenth century, the
> Charter and then, in more specific terms, the Universal Declaration,
> gave social and cultural aspirations the character of veritable
> rights.[18]

While not by its terms binding, the Universal Declaration recites
among its purposes "a common understanding" of the rights and
freedoms to whose achievement Member States are pledged by the
Charter. During the twenty years since its adoption, the Declaration, in the view of Professor Louis B. Sohn, has become "a part of
the constitutional law of the world community; and, together with
the Charter of the United Nations, it has achieved the character of
a world law superior to all other international instruments and to
domestic laws." [19] Hence, according to the Montreal Statement of

---

[18] UN Secretariat, International Year for Human Rights Newsletter, No. 8,
Supp. No. 1, at 18 (1969). Morris B. Abram has commented that "twenty years
ago, when the Universal Declaration of Human Rights was first adopted, most
Americans had psychological difficulties with some of its concepts. The Universal Declaration seemed a startling statement because it melded the civil and
political rights—freedom of speech, of assembly, of religion, etc.—with economic and social guidelines from the labor movement and socialist movement
as well. We thought of adequate housing or sufficient leisure as very fine goals,
but we asked, 'In what sense are these rights?' Two decades later, we have
gradually accepted these as rights in the terminology of the Universal Declaration." N.Y. Times, May 25, 1969, §6 (Magazine), at 117.

[19] Sohn, *The Universal Declaration of Human Rights*, 8 J. INT'L COMP. JUR.
17, 26 (1967). See also E. SCHWELB, HUMAN RIGHTS AND THE INTERNATIONAL
COMMUNITY (1964). Carlos Romulo has called the Declaration "an authoritative interpretation of the Charter [which] strengthened the obligations of Member States by making them more precise." He considers its preparation within
three years after the UN Charter "the miraculous result of sustained co-opera-

the Assembly for Human Rights, March 22–27, 1968 "the Universal Declaration . . . has over the years become a part of customary international law. . . . Non-discrimination is a basic principle and rule of contemporary international law." The Assembly proposed that the UN "bring all the instruments adopted by it together and prepare a United Nations Human Rights Code similar to the International Labor Code developed by the International Labor Organization." [20] As noted in Chapter I, the unanimously adopted Proclamation of Teheran declared that "the Universal Declaration . . . constitutes an obligation for the members of the international community." [21]

Apart from philosophical excursions into the question of whether the Universal Declaration is "law," on which opinions differ widely, its meaning for suffering victims whose basic rights are violated was

---

tion and high resolve." UN Secretariat, *supra* note 18, at 29, 30. Charles Malik, one of the draftsmen, has recalled "1,400 votes on every comma, semicolon, word, phrase, clause, paragraph of that particular document." *Id.* at 34. Moses Moskowitz believes that, for the very reason that the Declaration "emerged from the relative calm of the conference table in a spirit of compromise and mutual accommodation," it was deprived of the "spiritual intensity and collectedness needed to command the deeds of men." THE POLITICS AND DYNAMICS OF HUMAN RIGHTS 102 (1968). A UN Secretariat description of the Declaration's influence was published in A/Conf.32/5, at 20–30 (1967) and is reproduced in Appendix A hereto.

[20] The Montreal Statement has been printed and is available in English, French, and Spanish at the office of the Assembly for Human Rights, Room 4055, 866 United Nations Plaza, New York, N.Y. 10017.

[21] See note 5, Chapter I. On the other hand, a resolution unanimously adopted by a Work Session of the World Peace Through Law Center at Geneva in September 1968 "resolved to note that the Universal Declaration of Human Rights is in fact not part of the International Law of Nations in spite of its ratification by the General Assembly of the United Nations and to reaffirm that all nations should consider the Declaration as a legal guide and that they have a moral responsibility to recognize its provisions, be they personal, political, economic or social, and to implement them, where appropriate, by just national legislation or administrative measures." World Peace Through Law Center, The International Observance, World Law Day Human Rights 1968, Pamphlet Series No. 12, at 34 (1969). The French version involves greater difficulty: "Prend acte du fait que la déclaration . . . ne fait pas effectivement partie du droit des gens, . . . et réaffirme que la reconnaissance de ses dispositions . . . est un devoir juridique aussi bien que moral pour tous les pays, . . ." Letter from the Director of Programs of the World Peace Through Law Center to the author, March 6, 1969.

testified to by one of the witnesses before the UN Human Rights Commission's *Ad Hoc* Group of Experts at its August 1968 hearings in Conakry when he stated that "the value of that Declaration for us has been that—as stated in the operative part of that historic document—we have learnt through it, as have all men, those rights which are ours to demand, as men or as women, in our own country." [22]

Further international human rights legislation is planned. The General Assembly late in 1968 invited the Secretary-General, "in consultation with the International Committee of the Red Cross and other appropriate international organizations, to study: (a) Steps which could be taken to secure the better application of existing humanitarian international conventions and rules in all armed conflicts; (b) The need for additional humanitarian international conventions or for other appropriate legal instruments to ensure the better protection of civilians, prisoners and combatants in all armed conflicts and the prohibition and limitation of the use of certain methods and means of warfare." [23] Furthermore, the United Kingdom has proposed a draft convention on biological warfare.[24]

At the regional level, the existing European Convention on Human Rights and Fundamental Freedoms soon may be matched in the Western Hemisphere. A Draft Inter-American Convention on Protection of Human Rights has been prepared by the Inter-American Commission on Human Rights at the request of the Council of the Organization of American States.[25] The Inter-American Convention is an outgrowth of the American Declaration of the Rights and Duties of Man, which was approved by the Ninth International Conference of American States in 1948, a few months before completion of the Universal Declaration.[26]

The establishment of standards, whether or not theoretically binding on governments, concerning their treatment of their own nationals is helpful both directly and indirectly in protecting human

[22] E/CN.4/AC.22/RT.28, at 4 (1969).

[23] A/Res/2444 (XXIII) (1968).

[24] N.Y. Times, July 3, 1969, §1, at 10, col. 2.

[25] OEA/Ser.L/V/II.19/Doc. 48 (1968).

[26] The American Declaration is included in a publication of the Organization of American States, Inter-American Commission on Human Rights, Basic Documents, OEA/Ser.L/V/I.4, Rev. (1963).

rights. Directly, such standards merely by existing promote their own enjoyment, wherever governments have the means and will. Indirectly, standards are essential for the application of enforcement measures, in providing the goals towards which such measures are invoked.

Chapter III

Education: Long-Range Protection

The Universal Declaration of Human Rights calls for "teaching and education to promote respect for these rights and freedoms." In the opinion of former Cabinet Minister Brohi of Pakistan, who submitted a paper at the 1968 Teheran International Conference on Human Rights, "no more effective procedure for implementation of human rights could be conceived." [1] He added that "a worldwide campaign conducted by the United Nations in the manner of a diligent crusader for the cause of protecting human rights will be far more decisive in shaping the course of the future than the mere securing of signatures of various Member States to the Covenants on Human Rights." [2]

A long-term and indirect method of international protection of human rights through a program of seminars and fellowships has been carried on in recent years by the UN under the title of "advisory services in the field of human rights." [3] In 1966 seminars were held in Dakar on "Human Rights in Developing Countries," [4] in Budapest on "Participation in Local Administration as a Means of Promoting Human Rights," [5] and in Brasilia on "Apartheid." [6] In

[1] A/Conf.32/L.4, at 58 (1968).

[2] *Id.* at 78. To be truly world-wide, such a campaign would in some areas depend on methods suggested by Saudi Arabian Ambassador Baroody: "Why do not those states that have planes capable of flying over every part of the world without being chased away . . . drop educational leaflets . . . to the peoples of Zimbabwe and Namibia, telling them of their rights as decent human beings entitled to political, economic and social rights like any other people in the world?" S/PV.1478, at 27–28 (1969).

[3] These programs are described in E/CN.4/896—E/CN.6/452 (1966), E/CN.4/897–E/CN.6/453 (1966), and A/Conf.32/6, at 173–84, 213–17 (1967). The entire UN work program on human rights is described in E/4463/Add.16—E/AC.51/16/Add.16 and Corr.1 (1968).

[4] ST/TAO/HR/25 (1966). For reports of earlier seminars, see ST/TAA/HR/2 (1958), ST/TAO/HR/7 (1960), ST/TAO/HR/8 (1961), ST/TAO/HR/21 (1964), ST/TAO/HR/22 (1965), ST/TAO/HR/23 (1965).

[5] ST/TAO/HR/26 (1966).

[6] ST/TAO/HR/27 (1966).

1967 regional seminars were held in Jamaica on "The Effective Realization of Civil and Political Rights at the National Level," [7] and in Poland on "The Realization of Economic and Social Rights Contained in the Universal Declaration of Human Rights," [8] while in Finland a seminar was conducted on the "Civic and Political Education of Women." [9] The year 1968 saw not only the International Conference on Human Rights at Teheran [10] and a Seminar in London on "Freedom of Association,[11] but also a Seminar in India on "The Elimination of All Forms of Racial Discrimination" [12] and another in Accra on "The Civic and Political Education of Women," for African participants.[13] In 1969 seminars were held on the special problems relating to human rights in developing countries (Cyprus, world-wide) [14] and scheduled on the establishment of regional commissions on human rights (Cairo, for African participants), while Rumania offered to host a 1969 seminar concerning the status of women.[15]

One only can speculate about the possible usefulness of such seminars as a technique for even the long-range international protection of basic rights. The London Seminar on Freedom of Association provides an instance from which conclusions can be drawn because of its direct relevance to the range of human rights issues then (June 1968) current in Czechoslovakia. While that country was not represented at the seminar, her fluid status regarding the political aspects of freedom of association was doubtless in the minds of all participants, especially the Soviets. The Czech trend away from monopolization of ideas and methods had two months left to flourish before being choked off. That the Kremlin still may have doubted

---

[7] ST/TAO/HR/29 (1967).
[8] ST/TAO/HR/31 (1967).
[9] ST/TAO/HR/30 (1968).
[10] A/Conf.32/4 (1968).
[11] ST/TAO/HR/32 (1968).
[12] ST/TAO/HR/34 (1968).
[13] ST/TAO/HR/35 (1968).
[14] UN Press Release HR/304 (1969). Cyprus anticipated a "glow from the Seminar, radiating respect for human rights in Cyprus and the area around it." S/9241 (1969).
[15] E/CN.4/995—E/CN.6/522, at 9–10 (1969). The Soviet Union was reported to have invited the holding of a 1970 seminar on the status of women in economic development. UN Press Release ECOSOC/2651 (1969).

what course to follow is confirmed by the statement of the chief Soviet Participant that

> Marxist-Leninist doctrine and the practise of socialist and communist construction have never denied and do not deny the possibility of founding various associations for political purposes under socialism, particularly political parties. Other political associations are possible —for example, the Popular Front, unifying a number of political parties and other social organizations (women's, youth, etc.).
>
> The claim that Marxists always and everywhere stand for the existence of a single party in a socialist society—Communist Party—is, either slanderous or the result of ignorance of the actual state of affairs.
>
> Historically it has so happened that in our country one party only has existed—the Communist Party of the Soviet Union.
>
> But it is precisely for historical reasons, because of the collapse of other political parties, their discredit in the eyes of the people, their self-disbandonment or total disintegration, and not as a result of any outlawing, that only one party exists.[16]

Although this viewpoint appears to have been rejected when the Soviet forces occupied Czechoslovakia in August, one may speculate that the holding of the London Seminar might have had some slight liberalizing influence on the Kremlin, which was under pressure at the seminar to produce a formulation on freedom of association which would allay as much as possible the other participants' suspicions. Any other results of such seminars are even more speculative, depending as they do upon the extent to which participants are influenced by ideas or information which they encounter and upon the extent to which the same are conveyed by participants to their governments and compatriots. All in all, seminars hardly can be considered as more than a peripheral device even for the long-range protection of human rights through education.

The other aspect of the UN's "advisory services in the field of human rights," that of fellowships, is similarly speculative as to its effectiveness. From 1962 to 1965 a total of 158 such fellowships were awarded, 42 to Africans, 60 to persons from Asia and the Far East, 28 to Europeans, 20 to the Americas (including two Canadians,

---

[16] Professor Trukanovsky, Head of the Department of History of International Relations and Foreign Policy of the USSR, Institute of International Relations, Moscow, Working Paper at 5 (1968).

but no United States citizen), and 8 to persons from the Middle East. The total rose each year, from 21 in 1962 to 54 in 1965. In 1968 fellowships were awarded to 47 persons from 26 countries.[17] The UN believes that "an important indication that the fellowships have proved useful lies in the continued demand for such awards from Member States at all stages of economic development, in the high level of the candidates proposed, and in the improved quality of the applications received." [18] Group training of fellows, begun in 1967 with a program in Tokyo studying ways of protecting human rights in the administration of criminal justice, was continued in 1968 with a project at Warsaw for ten prominent Africans on the rights of the child under Polish law and procedures.[19]

Both the seminar and the fellowship programs have the disadvantage of being confined in their direct effects to a relatively small number of participants. A program which would affect directly a far greater number and have a proportionately more substantial educational impact was approved late in 1968 by the UN General Assembly, which

> conscious of the fact that young people cannot receive training which meets the requirements of a world increasingly characterized by the interdependence of peoples if educators do not themselves receive special instruction in international organization,
>
> 1. Requests the States Members of the United Nations and members of the specialized agencies and of the International Atomic Energy Agency to take steps, as appropriate and according to the scholastic system of each State, to introduce or encourage:
>
>> (a) The regular study of the United Nations and the specialized agencies and of the principles proclaimed in the Universal Declaration of Human Rights and in other declarations on human rights, in the training of teaching staff for primary and secondary schools;
>>
>> (b) Progressive instruction on the subject in question in the curricula of primary and secondary schools, inviting teachers to seize the opportunities provided by teaching of [sic] drawing the attention of their pupils to the increasing role of the United Nations system in peaceful co-operation among nations

[17] E/CN.4/995—E/CN.6/522, at 12 (1969).
[18] E/CN.4/897—E/CN.6/453, at 17 (1966).
[19] E/CN.4/995—E/CN.6/522, at 13–14 (1969).

and in joint efforts to promote social justice and economic and social progress in the world.[20]

Without doubt all the international educational measures described above are of some effect—sufficient to justify their use—in preventing government oppression, at least by well-intentioned governments, just as is the case with international standard-setting by convention or declaration. However, where governments cannot be influenced on behalf of human rights, enforcement is required. The measures heretofore attempted for enforcement of human rights protection are discussed in succeeding chapters.

[20] A/Res/2445 (XXIII) (1969). The Assembly also endorsed "the appeal made by the International Conference on Human Rights to States to ensure that all means of education should be employed so that youth may grow up and develop in a spirit of respect for human dignity and equal rights of man without discrimination as to race, colour, language, sex, or faith." A/Res/2447 (XXIII) (1969). See the UNESCO publication "Some Suggestions on Teaching About Human Rights." Another form of education whose impact might be greater than seminars or fellowships is technical assistance, whose use to help Governments eliminate slavery and slave trade was suggested by ECOSOC in resolution 1330 (XLIV) (1968). Seminars on this topic were also requested by ECOSOC, in resolution 1331 (XLIV) (1968). Technical assistance in providing legal aid was urged by the 1968 International Conference on Human Rights, resolution XIX, and requested by the General Assembly in resolution 2449 (XXIII) (1969). An expert was sent in 1968 to Cameroon at Government request to advise on promotion of participation of women in national affairs and development. E/CN.4/995—E/CN.6/522, at 16 (1969). The dissemination of UN information, including much on human rights, to the trust territories is described in T/1695 (1969). It also should be noted that the UN, primarily through its Sub-Commission on Prevention of Discrimination and Protection of Minorities, has made a series of studies in the human rights area. The technique is described in A/Conf.32/6, at 46–50 (1967), and the subjects are listed in E/CN.4/Sub.2/276, at 134 (1967). Other studies are described in A/Conf.32/6, at 168–72 (1967).

Chapter IV

Coercing Governments to Respect Basic Rights

Under the rubric of "humanitarian intervention" the military power of single nations, or of several acting jointly, once was considered by some authorities as proper for succoring groups oppressed by their own government.[1] Since the coming of the UN Charter, articles 2, 42, and 51 of which forbid the use of force except in self-defense or on orders of the Security Council, far less can be said for the validity of humanitarian intervention.[2]

Unilateral use of force having been greatly restricted, Great Britain was on firm ground in declining since 1965, though not perhaps for legal reasons alone, the General Assembly's pleas to use her military power to overthrow the discriminatory Ian Smith regime in Rhodesia.[3] Whether or not Britain had the legal right to quell rebellion there, she clearly had no legal duty to do so, with or without the General Assembly's urging. Britain's contrasting readiness to use force in Anguilla, although for political rather than humanitarian purposes, drew scornful comment.[4]

[1] See Lillich, *Forcible Self-Help by States to Protect Human Rights*, 53 Iowa L. Rev. 325 (1967); M. Ganji, International Protection of Human Rights 9–43 (1962), quoted in Chapter VI at notes 29–31. Echoes of this notion were heard in recent times when Belgian and British troops in the Congo and American Marines in the Dominican Republic were used to rescue not only their own compatriots but other aliens too. However, there was no need to justify either use under the humanitarian intervention principle, since the Congo's consent had been given and in neither case were local nationals being rescued.

[2] This is the view set forth in A. Thomas & A. Thomas, Non-Intervention 384 (1956). However, Lillich, "in view of the present state of the international legal order, . . . is prepared to argue the legitimacy of a limited right of forcible self-help by states, collectively or individually, as a minimum enforcement measure to protect human rights." Lillich, *Intervention to Protect Human Rights*, 15 McGill L. J. 205, 207 (1969).

[3] See for example A/C.4/SR.1544 (1965).

[4] For example, the Epsom, Leatherhead and Districts Anti-Apartheid Committee, of Surrey, United Kingdom, declared: "This Committee, noting the courage and determination of Her Majesty's Government in invading Anguilla, ostensibly to restore law and order, urges that this new resolution to establish

While refusing to send her troops to Rhodesia, Britain gave her full approval to three Security Council mandates designed to stifle Rhodesia's trade, a lesser form of coercion whose efficacy remains to be judged.[5] The Secretary-General considers it

> evident that no conclusions on the effects of the measures recommended by the Security Council can be reached unless all countries and, in particular, all the traditional trading partners of Southern Rhodesia, make available to the Secretary-General complete information on the measures they have taken in accordance with the provisions of the resolution adopted by the Security Council.[6]

Significantly, the Secretary-General added in a later report that

> as to petroleum supplies to Southern Rhodesia, no meaningful evaluation of the status is possible from the data reported by the reporting countries listed in the annex. The reason for this is that the traditional suppliers were countries in the Middle East region, none of which has as yet reported its data to the Secretary-General.[7]

To boost enforcement, the Security Council in May 1968 established a Committee to examine governments' reports and to seek from them "further information regarding the trade of that State . . . or regarding any activities by any nationals of that State or in its territories that may constitute an evasion of the measures decided upon. . . ."[8] The Committee's first report stated that 85 governments had reported and that "besides South Africa and Por-

---

legal and democratic government should be employed with equal fearlessness in Rhodesia to safeguard the lives and liberty of four and a half million British citizens." A/AC.109/PET.1077 (1969).

[5] S/Res/221 (1966), S/Res/232 (1966), and S/Res/253 (1968). Concerning the results, see S/7781/Add.3, at 1 (1967) and S/7781/Add.5, at 2–6 (1968).

[6] S/7781/Add.3, at 1 (1967). The Christian Science Monitor noted: "stagnation . . . spreading," Nov. 29, 1968, at B 18, col. 3, and a report of "marked economic deterioration," Dec. 6, 1968, at 7, col. 4.

[7] S/7781/Add.5, at 6 (1968).

[8] S/Res/253 (1968). Appointed to the Committee were Algeria, France, India, Paraguay, USSR, UK, and US. See S/8786, at 6 (1968), containing Governments' responses to resolution 253. Pakistan replaced India early in 1969 after the expiration of India's Security Council term. S/8697/Add.1 (1969). Poland reported having taken no action as depository of the 1955 Protocol to the 1929 Convention for the Unification of Certain Rules Relating to International Carriage by Air with respect to a notice of adherence to the Protocol received from the "Ministry of Foreign Affairs of Southern Rhodesia." S/8786, at 6–7 (1969).

tugal there are some countries which continued to have trade with Southern Rhodesia." [9] A United Kingdom assessment of the effects of sanctions up to mid-1968 concluded that

> the crucial question for the success of comprehensive mandatory sanctions in 1969 is the willingness of the United Nations Member States who are co-operating over sanctions to close the existing sanctions gaps, under which Rhodesian exports worth some £R30 million are still being imported into their countries.[10]

The United States noted that

> many Member States . . . have not yet supplied the Secretary-General with information on specific measures taken to implement Security Council resolution 253 (1968). It appears that thirty-nine Members have not replied in any way to inquiries from the Secretary-General. Of the ninety-one Members who have replied, twenty-nine merely stated that they have no relations with Southern Rhodesia or merely that they condemn the illegal regime and/or racism, colonialism, etc. None of those replies gives any definite indication of the action taken by the Member. It is impossible for the Security Council Sanctions Committee to have an accurate understanding of the implementation of resolution 253 (1968) or to properly perform its functions if it is not kept adequately informed by Member States.[11]

---

[9] S/8954, at 4–5 (1968). The second report discussed "specific cases of suspected violations" brought to the attention of the Committee, S/9252, at 13 (1969), and set forth details of Rhodesian trade with various countries, S/9252/Add.1 (1969).

[10] *Id.* at 102.

[11] S/8786/Add.7, at 25 (1969). A UN Office of Public Information release in the spring of 1969 held that the effect of sanctions on Southern Rhodesia's economy was "measurable" and stated that:

> Apart from South Africa's own expanded trade with Southern Rhodesia, it has been persistently reported that South Africa has provided cover for clandestine trade between third countries and parties and Southern Rhodesia; goods marked for South African destinations are said to find their way to Southern Rhodesia through prearranged contracts, while Rhodesian exports move through South African ports. Portugal also has been reported to provide an outlet for re-exporting embargoed Rhodesian commodities, primarily tobacco and sugar.

UN Reference Paper No. 3/Add.2 (1969). A witness told the General Assembly's Apartheid Committee in early 1969 that "so many African countries were now trading with South Africa that others had come to regard it as meaningless and self-destructive to take a firm moral stand on commercial policy." A/AC.115/SR.106, at 5 (1969).

Whether effective or not, these measures are of such a nature that the first of them was called by US Ambassador Arthur J. Goldberg, who voted for it,

> one of the gravest and most far-reaching proposals that has been made to this Council. . . . We are asked . . . to put our sanction upon what will be a rule of international law—that when this Council acts vessels on the high seas can be arrested and detained. . . . It is not an easy decision for my Government to give its support to a resolution of this character, both in the light of our history and traditions and in the light of all the far-reaching implications that such a step as we are asked to take may envisage.[12]

How far-reaching the implications are of the Security Council's having applied its Charter Chapter VII law-making powers to a basically human rights problem may be seen by examining the basis for using Chapter VII. Fundamental to such use is a Council determination under Article 39 of "the existence of any threat to the peace, breach of the peace, or act of aggression." Thereupon, either recommendations, or "measures not involving the use of armed force" under Article 41, or "action by air, sea or land forces" under Article 42, may be employed. Armed force can be used only if "measures provided for in Article 41 would be inadequate or have proved to be inadequate." Should the trade restrictions now in force be found not to suffice, the legal basis would exist, but for the veto, for a call to arms, made compulsory by Article 49.

The threat to international peace posed by the Rhodesian regime bears examination. Since the regime was threatening no one outside Rhodesia, the threat must have been against it, a "boot-strap" situation whereby seemingly a country could by its own remonstrance convert its neighbor's otherwise internal affairs into threats to the peace warranting Chapter VII measures. Goldberg explained that "the Security Council is authorized to order sanctions without the necessity of determining which party to a dispute is the source of a threat. . . ." In any event, said the Ambassador, the "threat to the peace inherent in the Rhodesian situation is the seizure of power by the Smith regime rather than the potential response to it." [13]

[12] S/PV.1276, at 15 (1966).
[13] US Dep't State Press Release No. 304, at 6 (1966). The right of the UN to use coercion is debated in McDougal & Reisman, *Rhodesia and the*

The Security Council's actions on Rhodesia have serious implications regarding the Republic of South Africa, where it also has been urged that human rights problems threaten international peace.[14] With this argument the United States has not agreed,[15] although former US Ambassador to the United Nations Francis T. P. Plimpton, more recently the President of The Association of the Bar of the City of New York, has publicly dissented:

> There are those (South Africans, of course), who say that it is the neighboring states who are creating the threat to international peace and security, because they are determined, in the last analysis, to invade South Africa to get rid of South Africa's racial policies. But the fact does remain that there is a threat to international security which grows out of South Africa's racial policies. . . . South Africa's policies do constitute a threat, a factual threat, to the peace of that continent, if not of the world.[16]

Short of the Chapter VII measures for which a Security Council finding of threat to the peace would lay the basis, there have been numerous but unsuccessful efforts by the UN Security Council and General Assembly to deter South Africa from its policies of apartheid by coercing it in various ways. At least 29 resolutions have been adopted by the General Assembly and 5 by the Security Council with regard to that Government's racial policies.[17]

As if to punctuate the close of Human Rights Year, a General Assembly majority late in 1968 engaged in a drastic but fruitless coer-

---

United Nations: The Lawfulness of International Concern, 62 AM. J. INT'L L. 1 (1968); Acheson, *The Arrogance of International Lawyers,* 2 INT'L LAWYER 591 (1968); and *Response by Professors McDougal and Reisman,* 3 INT'L LAWYER 438 (1969).

[14] For example, resolution III of the Teheran Conference "declares that the policy of *apartheid* is a threat to international peace and security." A/Conf.32/41, at 6 (1968).

[15] See for example position taken at UN International Seminar on Apartheid, Racial Discrimination and Colonialism in Southern Africa, held in Zambia in 1967. A/6818, at 28 (1967).

[16] THE ASSOCIATION OF THE BAR OF THE CITY OF NEW YORK, INTERNATIONAL PROTECTION OF HUMAN RIGHTS 49–50 (J. Carey ed. 1968).

[17] Review of United Nations Consideration of Apartheid, ST/PSCA/SER.A/2, at 27 (1967). The General Assembly Resolutions, as well as reports regarding South Africa's racial policies, are listed in S/8172 (1967). The UN's efforts are described in MacDonald, *The Resort to Economic Coercion by International Political Organizations,* 17 U. TORONTO L.J. 86, 106–34 (1967). Regarding UN measures on apartheid, see A/Conf.32/5, at 69–80 (1967).

cion attempt. The object was South Africa, and the device expulsion from UNCTAD, the UN Conference on Trade and Development. Despite contrary legal advice, 55 members voted to expel, while 33 voted against and 28 abstained. The measure was defeated only because of a prior ruling requiring for expulsion a two-thirds majority.

The expulsion proposal came from the Assembly's Second Committee, in which it had been proposed by 39 Members, mostly from Africa, Asia and the Caribbean area.[18] The draft resolution recited that South Africa already had been expelled from ECA (the UN Economic Commission for Africa), endorsed a March 1968 UNCTAD resolution urging expulsion by the Assembly, and decided that UNCTAD's members should be the members of the UN, the specialized agencies, and the International Atomic Energy Agency, "with the exception of South Africa until it shall have terminated its policy of racial discrimination and until that fact has been duly confirmed by the General Assembly."

The Second Committee had before it a formal, written opinion from the UN Legal Adviser, which noted earlier advice to UNCTAD itself "that the Conference was not empowered to suspend or exclude any member from participation in the Conference."[19] South Africa's having been barred by ECOSOC from participation in ECA in 1963, when Portugal actually was expelled, was described as the only precedent for expulsion or suspension of Member States from a permanent UN subsidiary organ. Noted the Legal Counsel, "this decision does not, therefore, provide a precedent consonant with the views set forth in the present note."[20] Constitutional amendments by the World Health Assembly and the International Labor Organization for the purpose of exclusion were held to be more persuasive than the "precedents both ways in relation to Conferences convened by the specialized agencies."[21] The opinion concluded that suspension from organs open to UN Members generally can be accomplished only by joint Assembly-Security Council action under Article 5.

In a General Assembly plenary session, Hungary tried to water down the expulsion into mere Assembly agreement with UNCTAD's

[18] A/7383 (1968).
[19] A/C.2/L.1030 (1968).
[20] *Id.* at 7.
[21] *Id.* at 8.

opinion that South Africa should not participate until it mended its ways. This proposal was rejected by a vote of 73–11–29, with only Guatemala and Malaysia joining the socialist countries.[22] The United States' opposition to expulsion was based on defense of the law of the Charter:

> When we seek to deny to any Member any of the rights that flow from Membership in the United Nations, we thereby put in jeopardy all the rights of all the Members. An unlawful act against my neighbour, be he guilty or not, is an act against each Member of the whole community. If we are to live together with one another in anything but chaos, we must have reliable safeguards of law and of due process by which each may be protected against the hostility of the others.
>
> All of the nations we represent look to the United Nations as a great instrument of peace and justice. It is sometimes a weak instrument because it cannot go faster than the concerted will of its Members will permit it to go; and yet it has done noble service to both peace and justice. Among those services, none is nobler than the assistance the United Nations has rendered to the cause of independence, self-determination and human rights for a thousand million beings inhabiting the former colonial areas of the world.
>
> That work is not finished. We are facing now some of its last and most difficult chapters. Together, we of the United Nations can and will finish that work. But if we are to fall apart, if the law which is so essential to this community of ours is so weakened by arbitrary exceptions that no Member, strong or weak, dare depend upon it, then I fear we shall be able to do little together; it will be a matter of each nation for itself, and the future will look very dark indeed.
>
> If this draft resolution is adopted, the General Assembly will be telling the world what the world already knows: that it detests and deplores *apartheid*. But, sadly and ominously, it will also be telling the world that in the United Nations General Assembly there is no law, no provision in the Charter, no guarantee of the legal rights of any nation that may not be overridden if it obstructs the majority will.[23]

The ineffectiveness of the expulsion proposal, apart from its illegality, also was argued in the Assembly. Australia noted that "the reasons advanced for the proposed suspension of South Africa from

[22] A/PV.1741, at 63–64 (1968).
[23] *Id.* at 45–46.

UNCTAD are irrelevant to the functions of UNCTAD, as a technical organ with important economic and commercial purposes." [24] Malawi was more penetrating in its reasons why expulsion would be self-defeating:

[T]he policy of seeking to isolate the Republic from the rest of the international community is a wholly misguided one. . . . Far from encouraging South Africa to give up *apartheid,* it is merely reinforcing their defiant attitude. . . . Indeed, it is the international bodies themselves—all of which were created for the purpose of furthering technical cooperation for the benefit of the entire international community—that have necessarily suffered by the absence of so wealthy and populous a nation.

And in the case of UNCTAD, the exclusion of South Africa will have particularly grievous consequences for the developing countries that fought so long and hard to get the Assembly to establish a world trade organization as a permanent subsidiary organ. As the representative of South Africa himself remarked in the Second Committee, it is both ironic and tragic that all the sponsors of the present draft resolution are representatives of developing countries, which stand to lose the most from the expulsion of the Republic. For like the developing countries, South Africa is heavily dependent upon the sale of exports of basic commodities: not just of gold, but also agricultural products. Its trading interests therefore at least partially coincide with those of the developing nations. But because it is much wealthier than some of the members of the Group of Seventy-seven and possesses the gold so ardently desired by most of the industrialized manufacturing nations, its voice is especially influential when it comes to negotiating international commodity agreements or favourable terms for the producer countries. For this reason, I confess I was considerably astonished to hear one of the sponsors of the draft resolution declare in the Second Committee that there was no reason to suppose that South Africa's participation in UNCTAD is likely to promote relations between the Republic and the developing nations. . . .

One of the chief values of the organization lies precisely in the fact that it serves as a centre of contact for all countries regardless of differences of individual ideologies or temporary disputes. At present the United Nations embraces several nations which have no direct diplomatic relations with certain other nations. Yet because they are also Members of this body they are compelled to sit down side by side, to observe elementary courtesies and to publicly share common friends

[24] *Id.* at 36.

and political liaisons. All these types of indirect contact are very useful in helping to maintain and develop peaceful international relations in general. But the ability of the United Nations to provide outlets for indirect contact at several different organizational levels could be badly eroded by the illegal expulsion of Member States from subsidiary bodies.[25]

Besides the efforts by the Security Council and General Assembly to force change in southern Africa's racial policies, other attempts have involved UN specialized agencies, some of which have been reluctant while others like UNCTAD have readily participated. In either case results have been hardly perceptible. The specialized agencies generally were invited by the General Assembly in 1965 "to take the necessary steps to deny technical and economic assistance to the Government of South Africa" and "to take active measures, within their fields of competence, to compel . . . [it] to abandon its racial policies." [26] The response of the International Bank for Reconstruction and Development (IBRD) and the International Monetary Fund (IMF) disappointed some parties. The Assembly's Special Committee of 24 on Decolonization expressed "deep disappointment at the granting of new loans and the extension of credits" to South Africa and Portugal by the IBRD and IMF.[27] When the IBRD General Counsel argued that the Bank could not look legally beyond economic considerations into political factors,[28] the Assembly appealed again in 1966 to all the specialized agencies, particularly IBRD and IMF, to refrain from aiding Portugal, and asked the Secretary-General to consult with IBRD "to secure its compliance." [29] After the consultation,[30] the Assembly in 1967

[25] A/PV.1740, at 60, 61, 67 (1968).

[26] A/Res/2054A (XX) (1965).

[27] A/AC.109/206 (1966). The IBRD and IMF were urged to cooperate in implementing General Assembly Resolutions 2105 (XX) and 2107 (XX).

[28] A/C.4/SR.1645, at 317–25 (1966).

[29] A/Res/2184 (XXI) (1966). The Committee of 24 in 1968 "reiterate[d] its appeal to all the specialized agencies, in particular the [IBRD and IMF], to refrain from granting Portugal any financial, economic or technical assistance as long as the Government of Portugal fails to implement General Assembly resolution 1514 (XV)." A/AC.109/292 (1968).

[30] The Secretary-General issued a report on his consultation with the IBRD. A/6825 (1967). The IBRD's Executive Directors, "with some dissents, endorsed the position taken by the Bank's General Counsel." A/AC.109/333, at 9 (1969).

reiterate[d] its request to the International Bank for Reconstruction and Development to deny financial, economic and technical assistance to the Government of South Africa and, in this connexion, expresse[d] the hope that the Bank will stand by its assurance that it will avoid any action that might run counter to the fulfilment of the great purposes of the United Nations.[31]

Other UN specialized agencies have been readier than the IBRD to deprive human rights offenders of available benefits.[32] UNESCO has authorized its Director-General to withhold from Portugal, South Africa, and Southern Rhodesia assistance as well as invitations to participate in UNESCO activities.[33] Deprivation of membership in the World Health Organization for any nation which "ignores the humanitarian principles and the objectives laid down in the Constitution by deliberately practising a policy of racial discrimination" is proposed in a constitutional amendment approved in 1965 by the WHO Assembly.[34] Moreover, the International Labor Organization has pledged continued cooperation

> within the limits of its competence and by its established procedures, in ensuring general respect for the principles of equal rights and self-determination of peoples as essential human rights. . . . In the specific case of Portugal no aid or co-operation has been granted at any time in respect of territory outside Europe and no such aid or cooperation has been granted in Europe since January 1966 and the question therefore does not arise at the present time.[35]

[31] A/Res/2307 (XXII) (1967).

[32] A/AC.109/276 (1967) contains requests to and replies from specialized agencies and international institutions.

[33] A/AS.109/L.388, para. 40 (1966). UNESCO's Executive Board had decided in 1965 not to invite Portugal to UNESCO meetings, pending a study on education in African territories it administers. A/6300/Add.3, part I, para. 41 (1966). Portugal's request that the International Court of Justice be asked for an advisory opinion on the validity of this decision was voted down 60–38–4 in the November 1966 meeting of UNESCO's General Conference.

[34] As of February 7, 1968, 36 countries had accepted of the 82 ($\frac{2}{3}$ of 123 members) needed to give the amendment effect. UN Press Release L/T 195–H/2010 (1968). For a descripion of WHO measures against South Africa, see A/AC.115/SR.112, at 10–11 (1969). In 1966, WHO had adopted a resolution which "suspends the right of Portugal to participate in the Regional Committee for Africa" and "suspends, pursuant to article 7 of the Constitution, technical assistance to Portugal. . . ." A/AC.109/194, at 9 (1966). For description of measures taken against Portugal, see UN Office of Public Information, Reference Paper No. 8 (1969).

[35] E/4603, at 1, 3 (1968).

Possible counter-productivity of such measures was indicated by WHO when it reported to the Secretary-General concerning South West Africa that

> following a decision of the World Health Assembly to suspend the voting privileges of South Africa, the Government of that country has virtually interrupted contacts with this organization. Even in the technical medical field our relations with the South African Government have been reduced to a minimum so that, in the circumstances, you will certainly understand that the organization has little hope of being able to use its influence in the matter.[36]

Similarly, Mexico has stated that "by virtue of the fact that [it] has no diplomatic or trade relations with the Republic of South Africa, . . . it is not in a position to influence that country. . . ."[37] As Bilder has pointed out, expulsions and diplomatic boycotts, while possibly "useful in expressing a moral stance" or furnishing "an emotional outlet," have produced little change in the policies objected to and "have simply further isolated the target country from the potential influence of international opinion."[38]

The aid of specialized agencies, or even membership in them, may not be important enough to respondent governments for their denial to affect objectionable human rights policies. After ECOSOC in 1963 barred South Africa from the UN Economic Commission for Africa until ECOSOC, "on the recommendation of the Economic Commission for Africa, shall find that conditions for constructive co-operation have been restored by a change in its racial policy,"[39]

---

[36] A/7045/Add.7, at 8 (1968). Nevertheless, the 21st World Health Assembly's Committee on Administration, Finance and Legal Matters in May 1968 recommended that no assistance to Portugal be considered until it renounced its policy of colonial domination.

[37] S/8506/Add.1 (1968). "Kuwait has no diplomatic or other relations with the Government of South Africa and, therefore, is unable to exert any influence with that Government to obtain compliance with the provisions of resolution 264 (1969), adopted by the Security Council at its 1465th meeting." S/9204, Ann. II (1969).

[38] Bilder, *Rethinking International Human Rights: Some Basic Questions*, 1969 WIS. L. REV. 171, 200 (1969). He cites experience with the expulsion of the USSR from the League of Nations; exclusion of Communist China and for a time Spain from the UN; suspension of Cuban participation in the OAS; and "the forcing of South African withdrawal from the International Labor Organization and certain other international bodies."

[39] E/Res/974 D (XXXVI). Similarly the Economic Commission for Africa (ECA) recommended that the Organization for African Unity determine the

South Africa itself notified ILO in 1964 of its withdrawal from the organization, which could not become effective until March 1966.[40] A threat of deprivation of representation in the UN itself might have greater weight, but efforts to deprive the South African Government of representation in the General Assembly have not succeeded.[41]

Those who promote UN efforts to compel governments to observe basic rights can so far draw scant encouragement from regional experience. The consequences of the 1967 military coup in Greece have been dealt with to little avail in the Council of Europe. In a resolution of September 1968 the Council's Consultative Assembly decided "to consider, at its session in January 1969, in the light of a new report of its Rapporteur concerning the progress made towards the restoration of democracy in Greece, whether to recommend to the Committee of Ministers to suspend the Greek Government from its right of representation in the Council of Europe, in accordance with Article 8 of the Statute." [42] Article 8 provides for suspension of any member which has "seriously violated" Article 3, whose terms require acceptance of "the principles of the rule of law and of the enjoyment by all persons within its jurisdiction of human rights and fundamental freedoms."

The Assembly in early 1969, declaring the Greek regime "in serious violation" of Article 3, suggested it withdraw from the Council and recommended that the Committee of Ministers "take such action, within a specified period, as is appropriate." [43] The Committee, at the Council's twentieth anniversary meeting in May 1969, postponed the decision on suspension until December, by which time it appeared that the European Human Rights Commission

---

conditions under which the peoples of Angola, Mozambique, so-called Portuguese Guinea, and South West Africa would be represented. E/Res/151 (VIII). The UN Council for South West Africa reported in November 1967 that it had been considering "the question of the participation of representatives of South West Africa in the work of the Economic Commission for Africa, which has been under consideration by the Economic and Social Council and by the Economic Commission for Africa since 1964." A/6897, at 6 (1967).

[40] E/4305, Ann. I, at 5 (1967).

[41] See, for example, Report of the Credentials Committee of the 22nd Session, A/6990 (1967).

[42] Proceedings summarized in Forward in Europe, I/1969, at 5.

[43] *Id.*

might have completed the investigation described in Chapter IX. One observer attributed the delay in part to a desire, in the optimistic post-de Gaulle atmosphere, "not to take action that would rupture European harmony." [44] Another observer felt that "the aim is not to isolate Greece," despite "socialist and Communist demands for abrupt action." [45]

The political factor deterring Greece's suspension from the Council of Europe illustrates a crucial difficulty in using coercion as a means of protecting basic rights. Coercion is unreliable not just because it usually fails to compel but also because states fail to use it fully. Too many influences affect third-party governments besides the plight of the victims. West Europeans tread softly with Greece because of the East European threat. America, France, and the United Kingdom value too highly their trade and investment in South Africa to join wholeheartedly in efforts to mobilize economic sanctions against apartheid. Besides the loss of trade and investment, larger perils flowing from mandatory sanctions against South Africa have been envisaged by former US Ambassador Francis T. P. Plimpton:

> The Security Council made a special study about two years ago as to sanctions against South Africa, and it came to the conclusion that it was possible that sanctions might work after quite a long time, but that sanctions would have to involve, almost certainly, a naval blockade because virtually the only economic weakness of South Africa is in petroleum and, particularly, heavy lubricants. Now, if economic sanctions were imposed on South Africa they would first have to be enforced by a navy, and second they would most certainly involve counter-sanctions against the United Kingdom, and that is where I think the difficulty arises. One has to assume for the purpose of argument that the United Kingdom would be willing to impose sanctions and of course if they were to be imposed mandatorily, United Kingdom consent would be necessary in the Security Council. Calculations vary, but it's quite clear, I think, that if sanctions were imposed by Great Britain against South Africa—the loss in foreign exchange to the United Kingdom would be almost astronomical, and that in turn

[44] Drew Middleton, N.Y. Times, May 7, 1969, §1, at 4, col. 5.

[45] John Allen May, Christian Science Monitor, May 8, 1969, §1, at 16, col. 1, 3. May reported an instant though limited response; Greece "promised a new appeals system for persons sentenced by military courts, fresh hearings if necessary, and a new press law to institute a form of what was called 'self-censorship'." *Id.*

would almost certainly result in the devaluation of the English pound and worldwide currency chaos.[46]

Morris B. Abram, in the light of his experience as United States Representative in the UN Human Rights Commission, has called for his own country to set an example of putting aside political considerations when it comes to human rights:

> It is also true that the U.S. rarely criticizes the human rights practices of a friendly nation whether it be Greece, whether it be Haiti, or whether it be Great Britain, which this year did something in Kenya that wasn't exactly in accord with the principles of the Declaration of Human Rights.
>
> I often have felt that we in the United States have a tremendous opportunity probably not possessed by any other state. I have wondered why we, for the first time in human history, couldn't adopt a policy which says in effect: we value freedom so much, we place such a high value on human rights, that we are never going to deal politically with these matters in any world forum. We therefore will criticize our friend and our foe alike. The fact that we may criticize our closest ally on a human rights matter, has nothing to do with whether or not we continue the alliance or even furnish articles of trade, or continue a military association. When we criticize, we criticize from principle, and we welcome the criticism of others from principle, as well.[47]

[46] THE ASSOCIATION OF THE BAR OF THE CITY OF NEW YORK, RACE, PEACE, LAW, AND SOUTHERN AFRICA 192 (J. Carey ed. 1968). Elsewhere in the same volume, Professor and Mrs. Howard Taubenfeld speculated about the make-up of a military force sufficient to compel an end of South African apartheid:

> For the African states the key question clearly is which Major or Middle Powers would be their best ally. . . . [W]e will confine ourselves to presenting a suggestive list of some apparently feasible alternative coalitions inside and outside the UN, which could presumably rely on the African states to furnish the bulk of the fighting men: . . . I a) Africa plus China; b) Africa plus China and Communist bloc countries; II a) Africa plus U.S. or/and U.S.S.R. with possible parallel Chinese-aided insurgency. . . . [T]o overthrow this government for these stakes, which amount in the eyes of the defenders to total capitulation and suicide, would probably require a large military expedition.

Id. at 109–10, 120. According to a May 1969 Reuters dispatch, "South Africa is planning a big buildup of its military striking power to protect itself against sea and air attacks and guerilla incursions from black Africa." Christian Science Monitor, May 12, 1969, §1, at 13, col. 3. Foreign sources of South African arms are noted in A/AC.115/L.252 (1969).

[47] American Bar Association, Section of Individual Rights and Responsibilities, Monograph No. 2, at 24–25 (1968).

With its twin drawbacks of ineffectiveness and political sensitivity, coercion by UN bodies seems to have little promise as a means of protecting basic rights. A variation was attempted in the spring of 1969—the use of UN facilities to embarrass not just governments but private parties as well if they dealt with South Africa. In April the General Assembly's Apartheid Committee published a proposal by an officer of the American Committee on Africa for a "disengagement policy" whereby, for example, the US Government would discourage trade and increased investments in South Africa, end its sugar quota, and remove its South African space tracking stations.[48] The Apartheid Committee then published the same author's suggestion of a way to "diversify the strategy of pressure," whereby dozens of named companies with property elsewhere in Africa would be put under pressure by African host governments to curtail their South African activities.[49] Simultaneously the Committee published his proposal that it follow up on the opening provided by some executives' attempt to justify their South African operations "by calling together international businessmen to discuss with them the effect of their involvement in the South African economy." [50]

Pressure exerted by an international organization directly on private parties, bypassing their government, would doubtless be resented, and would be attacked on legal grounds under UN Charter article 2(7), which forbids intervention in internal affairs not threatening the peace. This form of coercion would be more effective if freed from these hindrances by being carried out through acts by local pressure groups, such as the Episcopal Church threat to withdraw funds from three New York banks if they continued extending credits to South Africa.[51] Coercion of private parties by local private groups might well prove more effective than UN coercion of governments.

[48] A/AC.115/L.244, at 9 (1969).

[49] A/AC.115/L.245, at 2 (1969).

[50] A/AC.115/L.246, at 3 (1969).

[51] N.Y. Times, May 25, 1969, §2, at 67, col. 3. The tactics of the Episcopal Church on South Africa are set forth in A/AC.115/L.250 (1969); those of the United Methodist Church in A/AC.115/L.248 (1969), A/AC.115/SR.109, at 13 (1969), and A/AC.115/SR.110, at 8 (1969); and those of the United Church of Christ in A/AC.115/SR.112, at 2 (1969).

Chapter V

Protection Through Non-Criminal Adjudication

To lawyers, accustomed as they are to the judicial process, adjudication often seems the most natural procedure for resolving disputes, including those between governments and individuals they allegedly oppress. Ambassador Goldberg expressed such a view in March 1967: "the ideal way [to enforce nations' human rights obligations] would be through the international judicial powers, such as the international writ of habeas corpus advocated by my former colleague, Mr. Justice Brennan. I supported this long before coming to the United Nations. . . . And my view has not changed. . . ."[1]

In 1965 Justice Goldberg had proposed fact-finding by a UN commission, rather than a court, to investigate religious discrimination.[2] In 1967 he had urged "world-wide habeas corpus."[3] To similar effect, the Montreal Statement of the Assembly for Human Rights of March 22–27, 1968, considered that "international implementation measures, like national measures that must be based on the rule of law, require the existence and accessibility of judicial remedies." The Statement recommended considering "the establishment of further regional courts of human rights, and possibly, a universal court of human rights."[4] Later in 1968 Sean MacBride, Secretary-General of the International Commission of Jurists, asked an international conference of non-governmental organizations whether the time had not come to "envisage the establishment of a Universal Court of Human Rights analogous to the European Court of Human Rights. . . . Even if initially its judgments were to be

---

[1] Press Release USUN–27, at 2 (1967). See Brennan, *International Due Process and the Law*, 48 VA. L. REV. 1258 (1962).

[2] N.Y. Times, May 3, 1965, §1, at 37, col. 1.

[3] Letter to Editor of American Bar Association Journal, 53 A.B.A.J. 586 (1967). See Kutner, *World Habeas Corpus: The Legal Ultimate for the Unity of Mankind*, 40 NOTRE DAME LAWYER 570 (1965), and other writings.

[4] See Chapter II, at note 20.

only declaratory, they would be of considerable moral value and would help to create standards in the field of human rights." [5]

An opposite view on the use of judicial process in human rights matters was expressed by one of the persons invited to submit a study to the Teheran International Conference on Human Rights, A. K. Brohi, Jurist and former Cabinet Minister of Pakistan: "It is not possible at the current stage of development of international law to insist that there be an effective international rule of law capable of being enforced by some forum like the International Court of Justice." [6] Mr. Brohi went further and said that "too much reliance should not, in the considered opinion of the present writer, be placed on securing the enforcement of human rights by means of the law-applying organs, whether these be established by national or international law." [7]

Actual use of adjudication of human rights cases has taken two general forms, non-criminal and criminal. The best known instances of the former are the European Court of Human Rights proceedings and the South West Africa Cases before the International Court of Justice, while the Nuremburg trials illustrate the criminal type of human rights adjudication. These and other precedents described below indicate the extent to which confidence may justifiably be reposed in the judicial process when used in the international human rights context.

The only existing international court specializing in human rights cases is the one established by the Council of Europe's 1950 Convention for the Protection of Human Rights and Fundamental Freedoms.[8] The Convention now binds all but two (France and Switzerland) of the 18 Member States of the Council of Europe.

---

[5] Human Rights: Final Report of the International NGO Conference, Paris, 16–20 September 1968, at 64.

[6] A/Conf.32/L.4, at 19 (1968).

[7] *Id.* at 45.

[8] 213 U.N.T.S. 221. The Court was constituted in 1959. One of its presiding judges was René Cassin, who was awarded the Nobel Peace Prize in 1968 for his work in the human rights field. The Fourth Protocol to the Convention came into force in May 1968 after its fifth ratification; it deals with imprisonment for debts, exile, expulsion of aliens, free movement, and choice of residence. Council of Europe Press Release C (68) 10 (1968). Eleven States also have accepted the optional right of individual petition against themselves provided for in Article 25 of the Convention, such petitions being considered initially not by the Court but by the European Commission of Human Rights.

The Court's jurisdiction has been accepted by Austria, Belgium, Denmark, the German Federal Republic, Iceland, Ireland, Luxembourg, the Netherlands, Norway, Sweden, and the United Kingdom. Not only the European Court of Human Rights but also the Committee of Ministers of the Council of Europe "has judicial functions conferred on it by the Convention on Human Rights," in the view of A. H. Robertson, Head of the Directorate of Human Rights of the Council of Europe.[9] The Committee decides cases not brought before the Court by the Commission or the State concerned. One authority has stated that, "avec 'l'avis' de la Commission, 'l'arrêt' de la Cour ou la 'décision' du Comité des Ministres, toute requête, étatique ou individuelle, est, dans le vrai sens du terme, 'jugeé.' "[10] The Deputy Secretary General of the Council declared that "at Strasbourg, an application lodged by a Contracting Party or an individual person leads to an opinion of the European Commission, followed by a judgment of the European Court or a decision of the Committee of Ministers. Under the European system each complaint is investigated and judged."[11]

Access to the European Court is limited to States Parties and the European Commission of Human Rights. The Court's jurisprudence, thus far limited to Commission-instituted actions,[12] consists of five completed matters, the *Lawless, De Becker, Neumeister,* and *Wemhoff* cases, and the group of *Belgian Linguistic* cases. The

[9] THE INTERNATIONAL PROTECTION OF HUMAN RIGHTS 212 (E. Luard ed. 1967). These functions of the Committee of Ministers are described in K. VASAK, LA CONVENTION EUROPÉENNE DES DROITS DE L'HOMME 193–218 (1964). See also Wiebringhaus, *Jurisprudence et procédure du comité des Ministres du Conseil de l'Europe en vertu du premier paragraphe de l'article 32 de la Convention Européenne des Droits de l'Homme,* in MELANGES OFFERTS À POLYS MODINOS 454 (1968). In June 1968 the Council of Ministers decided that the Federal Republic of Germany had not violated the European Convention by mistreating a prisoner named Zeidler-Kornmann, and authorized publication of the Commission's report. Council of Europe Press Release C (68) 18 (1968). In May 1969 the Council decided the "Rudolf Köplinger Case," holding, as had the Commission, that Austria had not violated the Convention in its treatment of him. Council of Europe Press Release C (69) 14 (1969).

[10] Modinos, *Coexistence de la Convention Européenne des Droits de l'Homme et du Pacte des Droits Civils et Politiques des Nations Unies,* 1 HUMAN RIGHTS J. 41, 63 (1968).

[11] E/CN.4/975, at 22 (1968).

[12] The *Neumeister, Stögmuller,* and *Matznetter* cases were referred to the Court not only by the Commission but also by the Austrian Government. Council of Europe Press Release B (69) 12 (1969).

Stögmuller and *Matznetter* cases, concerning like *Neumeister* and *Wemhoff* the right to trial in a reasonable time or release pending trial, remain to be decided. A further case, *Delcourt,* was referred to the Court by the Commission in February 1969, raising the propriety of a prosecutor's presence at a court's deliberations.

Of the European Court's completed cases, *De Becker,* involving charges of suppression of free expression, was stricken by the Court after amendatory action by the Belgian Parliament.[13] The others were decided on the merits. In *Lawless* the Court held that a member of the Irish Republic Army had been validly detained without trial in view of the Irish Government's having duly exercised the right of derogation provided for in Article 15 of the European Convention.[14] *Neumeister* was held to have been detained by Austria overly long pending trial, while no such offence was found as to *Wemhoff.*[15] In the *Belgian Linguistic* cases, based on complaints by 327 French-speaking Belgians about laws requiring education of their children in Flemish, the Court in 1967 affirmed its jurisdiction,[16] and in 1968 ruled 8 to 7 that the legislation breached Article 14 of the Convention, which forbids discrimination in the enjoyment of rights like education, while unanimously ruling out five other types of alleged violation.[17] Without doubt this case was the Court's most difficult one to date because of the intense feelings of a large number of the persons involved.

The added burden imposed on the judicial process by human rights problems involving numerous rather than single complaints also is illustrated in the *South West Africa Cases* of 1966.[18] The International Court of Justice, after lengthy arguments on whether apartheid breached South Africa's Mandate duty to "promote to the utmost the material and moral well-being of the inhabitants," disposed of the cases on a quite different ground. Ethiopia and Liberia were held by an evenly divided Court (the President having in that event an extra deciding vote) to lack sufficient interest in South West Africa's people to be entitled to a ruling on their behalf, de-

---

[13] De Becker Case, Judgment of 27th March, 1962.
[14] Lawless Case (Merits), Judgment of 1st July, 1961.
[15] Council of Europe Press Releases C (68) 19 and 20 (1968).
[16] Council of Europe Press Release C (67) 4 (1967).
[17] Council of Europe Press Release C (68) 27 (1968).
[18] South West Africa, Second Phase, Judgment, [1966] I.C.J. 6.

spite the Mandate's grant of World Court jurisdiction over "any dispute whatever . . . between the Mandatory [i.e, South Africa] and another Member of the League of Nations [e.g., Ethiopia and Liberia] relating to the interpretation of the application of the provisions of the Mandate." [19]

Not only League of Nations Mandates but a number of specialized human rights treaties provide World Court jurisdiction over disputes.[20] Five such treaties that have at various times been presented for United States Senate approval deal with Genocide, Practices Akin to Slavery, Political Rights of Women, Forced Labor, Employment Policy, and the Status of Refugees, the second of which was ratified in 1967 and the last in 1968.[21] The first three and the last contain compromissory clauses not unlike that in the South West Africa Mandate. The fourth and fifth derive compulsory ICJ jurisdiction from the Constitution of the International Labor Organization, under whose auspices they were written.[22]

The treaties noted allow for ICJ access only by States Parties (the ICJ being in all contentious matters open only to states), not by injured individuals nor by any quasi-executive body like the European Commission on Human Rights. Advisory, rather than adversary, opinions from the ICJ, however, can be sought by UN organs under Article 96 of the UN Charter, as occurred several times regarding South West Africa.[23] Furthermore, the Conciliation and

[19] So great was the outcry in the UN over this ruling that the Court in 1968, "conscious of the need for closer co-operation with the other organs of the United Nations," obtained permission to submit a 1967–68 annual report to the General Assembly. A/7181 (1968). Fawcett has identified several ICJ cases in which "human rights as set out in the Draft Covenant [on Civil and Political Rights] were directly in issue or the problem of their implementation is, in one form or another, raised." HUMAN RIGHTS IN NATIONAL AND INTERNATIONAL LAW 292–93 (A. Robertson ed. 1968).

[20] The following such treaties are listed by the Secretariat in A/Conf.32/6 at 95 (1967): Genocide, Status of Refugees, International Right of Correction, Political Rights of Women, Slavery, Nationality of Married Women, Status of Stateless Persons, Reduction of Statelessness, Elimination of All Forms of Racial Discrimination.

[21] See Chapter II, at note 9.

[22] Also included in the more than 120 ILO Conventions subject to ICJ jurisdiction are the treaties on Discrimination in Respect of Employment and Occupation and on Remuneration for Men and Women Workers for Work of Equal Value.

[23] See Chapter VI, at notes 44–46.

Good Offices Commission established by the 1962 Protocol [24] to the UNESCO Convention against Discrimination in Education could recommend to the UNESCO Executive Board or General Conference that an ICJ advisory opinion be sought on any legal question before the Commission.[25]

Without quasi-executive bodies empowered to initiate adversary actions, non-criminal adjudication of human rights problems is of little value. The alternative of allowing individuals to bring international court proceedings against governments is not permitted even by the relatively advanced European system; individuals may complain to the European Human Rights Commission, which in any court appeal becomes the party opposing the government concerned. State versus state court actions have little appeal for governments, reluctant as they normally are to damage relations with sister governments by formally charging them with misconduct towards their own citizens. No state versus state case has reached the ICJ under any ILO Convention. In nearly a half century of ILO experience only two such complaints have even been filed, both charging forced labor and both settled without judicial process.[26] State versus state complaints under the European system, such as those complaints pending against the current Greek regime, have not reached the judicial stage. The usefulness of non-criminal adjudication in human rights matters would seem clearly to depend on procedures for non-governmental initiation, either by organizations or individuals.

[24] The Protocol became effective in October 1968. E/CN.4/Sub.2/292/Add.1, at 3 (1968).

[25] Yearbook on Human Rights for 1962 (Sales No. 65.XIV.1), at 400. See E/4133, at 7–8 (1965).

[26] 45 I.L.O. OFF. BULL. No. 2, Supp. II (1962); 46 I.L.O. OFF. BULL. No. 2, Supp. II (1963); see White, *The Ploughing of Two Furrows: The International Labour Organization (I.L.O.) Commissions of Inquiry of 1961 and 1962*, AUSTRALIAN Y.B. INT'L L. 1966, at 47.

Chapter VI

The Problem of Enforcing Judgments Against Governments

Non-criminal adjudication depends for its effectiveness on compliance by defeated parties. The most elaborate judicial machinery would afford no protection for victims of oppression if governments found to be oppressors ignored instructions to desist. In considering the problem of compliance, it is useful to examine initially the degree of need for enforcement, as judged by the past record of voluntary compliance with decisions of international courts and other tribunals, then to evaluate enforcement measures previously employed, and finally to speculate on the usefulness of enforcement possibilities which have little or no precedent.

THE RECORD OF COMPLIANCE

Elation existed shortly after World War II concerning voluntary compliance by nations with adverse judicial decisions. At the U.S. Senate hearings on the Statute of the International Court of Justice, an American Bar Association representative supported the new Court by stressing the effectiveness of the Permanent Court of International Justice from 1920 to World War II. Comparing the PCIJ with the US Supreme Court in inter-state disputes, he pointed out that "all manner of questions affecting the sovereignty of the parties have been peaceably settled by the judgments of the World Court. In no case has the losing party failed to comply with the judgment." [1] Dean Acheson, then Under Secretary of State, while stating the view that "in international relations, enforcement measures are greatly lacking, and the force and effect of decisions depend in the main upon the good faith of the parties involved," felt it "important to note that all decisions of the Permanent Court of International Justice were carried out. . . ." [2] However, when Sena-

[1] Hearings on S. 196 before a Subcom. of the Senate Committee on Foreign Relations, 79th Cong., 2d Sess., at 59 (1946).
[2] *Id.* at 127.

tor Austin claimed that the moral power of the US Supreme Court, which also has no sheriff or execution, "has never failed," Secretary Acheson called attention to the years taken by states in accepting certain adverse money judgments.[3]

Those witnesses who testified to the effectiveness of the PCIJ had the authority of Judge Manley O. Hudson behind them. He had written in 1944 that "in no case did a State refuse to carry out a judgment of the Court." Each of its judgments "was promptly complied with, some under dramatic circumstances." [4] Nevertheless, the new version of the Court for which they were testifying was at that very moment in the early stages of a litigation that was to chill the elation over voluntary compliance. This litigation was the *Corfu Channel* case, in which two years later Albania became, in one view, "the first state in history to refuse in principle to comply with a decision of the Court in a contentious proceeding to which it was a party." [5] It may be argued that Albania did not refuse "in principle" to comply, since it took the stand that a money judgment was *excès de pouvoir*,[6] the submission having asked only "is there any duty to pay compensation?" Still a trend was set, so that ten years after the Senate hearings Shabtai Rosenne, Israeli Ambassador, Foreign Affairs Ministry Legal Adviser, and International Law Commission member, wrote of both the contentious and advisory jurisdiction that "since 1947 there have occurred a number of serious instances of failure, both on the part of the States concerned to comply with, and on the part of the international Organization to enforce, decisions of the Court." The first ten years of the ICJ were

---

[3] *Id.* at 130–31.

[4] M. HUDSON, INTERNATIONAL TRIBUNALS 129 (1944). He pointed out, however, the "relatively few cases" of non-compliance with decisions of other international tribunals, including US refusal to accept the awards in the *Northeastern Boundary Case* (1831) and in the *Chamizal* dispute with Mexico (1911). *Id.* at 130. The latter award finally was complied with by President Kennedy. Professor Hans Morgenthau found "fewer than ten cases" of non-compliance out of the thousands of decisions of mixed arbitral boards and special international courts in the last century and a half. POLITICS AMONG NATIONS 230 (3d ed. 1948).

[5] O. LISSITZYN, THE INTERNATIONAL COURT 80 (1951).

[6] The "stock excuse," according to Hudson, *supra* note 4, at 131, and the type of reason given for United States non-compliance with the *Chamizal* award.

"dominated by this novel and unwelcome phenomenon of the non-implementation of several of its decisions." [7]

A more recent study by Jenks of the ICJ's compliance record lists as "ineffective in practice": the advisory opinion on Conditions of Admission of a State to Membership in the United Nations; the *Corfu Channel* decision; the advisory opinion on the Interpretation of Peace Treaties with Bulgaria, Hungary, and Romania (first phase); the 1950 advisory opinion on the International Status of South West Africa; and the interim measures aspect of the Anglo-Iranian Oil Company Case.[8] The record of non-compliance, however, is not complete without stressing the *Assessments* case, respecting which the Soviet Union contended that "the International Court is not an organ that has the right to issue binding interpretations of the Charter" and still dismisses as "unlawful [the] expenses arising from operations in the Near East and in the Congo which could not be considered as a component and integral part of the regular budget of the Organization." [9]

Jenks has asked whether it is "possible to conceive of procedures of execution analogous to judicious proceedings *in rem* against foreign property, or proceedings for the execution of foreign judgments and foreign arbitral awards, or proceedings for the execution of judgments in federal states." His objective would be to "remove the execution of international decisions and awards from the political sphere to that of recognized legal procedures." [10] While implementation methods might gain sustenance through adaptation of domestic procedures, it seems too much to ask that an intensely political dispute be shorn by any device of its turgid aspects at the very moment of final confrontation, namely, when enforcement is attempted. Rather it seems that enforcement methods must be devised that can withstand the buffets of politics. The more contentious the case, the more difficult the enforcement, particularly where jurisdiction is founded on prior obligation and not on *ad hoc* submission. Oscar

[7] S. ROSENNE, THE INTERNATIONAL COURT OF JUSTICE 74 (1957). See also 2d rev. ed. (1963).

[8] C. JENKS, PROSPECTS OF INTERNATIONAL ADJUDICATION 9 (1964).

[9] A/AC.121/PV.15, at 31, 37 (1965). Examining this advisory opinion for compliance, despite its not qualifying as "binding" under Article 59 of the Court's Statute, is consistent with Jenks' analysis.

[10] C. JENKS, *supra* note 8, at 10.

Schachter has predicted that "should there be a wider acceptance of compulsory jurisdiction . . . the chances of non-performance would almost certainly increase. . . ."[11] Such a development would be tragic, since, as Hambro has put it, "Rien ne peut être plus dangereux pour la communauté internationale que les sentences qui restent lettre morte."[12]

ENFORCEMENT METHODS ATTEMPTED

Schachter has classified enforcement methods into measures "by the successful party" and measures "through international organization."[13] The same scheme will be followed here, using the terms "self-help" and "UN help." To these two a third category will be added, designated "judicial help." The precedents for this category are found in enforcement attempts against sovereign states in the US Supreme Court, as well as in enforcement attempts in the World Court.

SELF-HELP

Because of the absence of an "international sovereign concerned to ensure compliance . . . , the role of self-help in the enforcement of international judgments is accordingly very prominent," reasons Rosenne, who feels that "in international law, execution by the parties concerned is the rule. . . ."[14] The range of self-help measures open to the winning party is as broad as those open to a State to right any international wrong, for non-compliance is but the wrongful breach of a duty under law, i.e., UN Charter Article 94(1), giving the party wronged the same recourse to coercive steps as are given by many other types of wrong. Such steps include classical protest and breach of diplomatic relations, plus those economic pressures which may be available.[15]

---

[11] O. Schachter, *The Enforcement of International Judicial and Arbitral Decisions,* 54 AM. J. INT'L L. 1, 5 (1960).

[12] E. HAMBRO, L'EXECUTION DES SENTENCES INTERNATIONALES 70 (1936).

[13] O. Schachter, *supra* note 11, at 6, 17.

[14] S. ROSENNE, *supra* note 7, at 79.

[15] O. Schachter, *supra* note 11, at 7, cites the example of the UK's linking of the USSR's payment of the *Lena Goldfields* arbitral award to the UK–USSR trade agreement talks. He also discusses action in domestic courts as a means of enforcing an international decision.

The legal limits on self-help for enforcement should possess, both Schachter and Rosenne believe, the same flexibility as normally results from the concepts of retorsion and reprisal.[16] A respondent's property therefore may be unilaterally applied to a judgment debt, as Great Britain attempted to do following the *Corfu Channel* decision. In that case, a 1948 judgment upholding the Court's jurisdiction was followed by a 1949 judgment that Albania was legally responsible for mine explosions in her waters and for the resulting damage to British warships and loss of life. The Court held that the damaged ships were legally in Albanian waters by virtue of innocent passage, but that later British minesweeping was illegal. In a third judgment the Court set money damages.

When Albania did not pay, the UK turned to self-help and announced that it would apply to the judgment certain monetary gold removed by the Germans from Rome in 1943 and found to belong to Albania, unless Albania or Italy, which wanted the gold applied to a claim of its own, asked the ICJ to judge the various claims. This announcement was made jointly with France and the United States, the three countries having responsibility for distribution of the gold as reparations. Albania did not act, but Italy took advantage of this advance offer to accept suit. The UK's self-help effort foundered on the technicality that priority between its claim and that of Italy would not be judged without deciding whether Italy had a claim against Albania, which the Court could not do without Albania's being a party.

While the judgment remained unpaid, new ground was broken on enforcement by self-help. Rosenne concluded that, despite its failure, "the incident as a whole has lost nothing of its value as a diplomatic precedent for the development of this branch of the law. . . ."[17] At least it may be said that the opinion seems to have advanced, since the *Corfu* case, beyond the view stated in 1944 by Judge Hudson, that "international law confers on a State no powers to enforce execution of a decision against another State," and that "the authoritative formulation of international law has stopped short of adopting such concepts" as retorsion, retaliation, and reprisals.[18]

[16] *Id*. See also S. ROSENNE, *supra* note 7, at 92–95.
[17] *Id*. at 102.
[18] M. HUDSON, *supra* note 4, at 131.

Since France and the United States abetted the British attempt at self-help against Albania, the legality of their participation should be considered. Schachter discusses this issue in the light of the *Corfu-Monetary Gold* situation, noting that third-State participation was "regarded by the three governments as consistent with the requirements of international law." [19] Rosenne's view is that "the way is open for other States to associate themselves" with the judgment creditors' self-help attempts, and even "to do so independently and on their own account." [20]

The crucial question whether self-help may legally include the use of force has no clear answer. Schachter has concluded that UN Charter Article 2(3) and Article 2(4) preclude forcible action to vindicate a legal right.[21] He does admit, however, of a possible exception where "a state would use armed force to prevent the carrying out of an international decision recognizing substantial territorial rights or a vital right of passage, and where counter-measures of a forcible nature by the aggrieved state could be validly justified as self-defense in response to armed attack." [22] To the same effect, Lissitzyn, after labeling as unanswered the questions whether Articles 1(1) and 2(3) and 2(4) preclude the threat or use of force to compel compliance with ICJ decisions, and whether there is any rule outside the Charter "limiting the freedom of states to use force to maintain their rights under international law as determined by the Court," suggests that Article 51 "could on occasion serve to justify the use of force to carry out a judgment of the Court. For example, the forcible occupation of a territory by the state entitled to its possession under a judgment of the Court might be regarded as a lawful exercise of authority, armed resistance to which by another state would constitute an 'armed attack' within the meaning of Article 51." [23]

Rosenne, too, visualizes self-help enforcement through self-defense. Armed force to compel compliance with a money judgment, he believes, could be justified only if the consequences of non-com-

[19] O. Schachter, *supra* note 11, at 12.

[20] S. ROSENNE, *supra* note 7, at 97. Joint action to enforce a judgment would seem consistent with the principle of UN Charter Article 51 allowing "collective self-defense if an armed attack occurs against a Member of the United Nations."

[21] O. Schachter, *supra* note 11, at 14–15.

[22] *Id.* at 16–17.

[23] O. LISSITZYN, *supra* note 5, at 76.

pliance were of a "very broad scope." [24] But he points to "a world of difference" between the money judgments in the *Wimbledon* and *Corfu Channel* cases "and a judgment deciding the question of sovereignty over disputed territory—as in the *Eastern Greenland, Fisheries* and *Minquiers* and *Ecrehos* cases. If non-compliance with a decision of this latter category involves infringement of rights of sovereignty upon which the Court has adjudicated, it may well constitute an act of aggression, . . . as such non-compliance is liable to lead to an infringement of territorial integrity in the teeth of a judicial decision establishing that territorial integrity." [25]

While these views are reminiscent of the argument that India, in taking over Goa, was defending itself against Portuguese attack in the form of armed occupation of Indian territory, one difference is that India had no Court decision in its favor. Yet any action proper in the absence of court decision should be all the more proper in its presence. With this fact in mind, one might consider a final form of self-help, involving not the seizure of property to satisfy a money judgment, nor the seizure of territory to vindicate rights of sovereignty, but entry into a State to protect a group of persons, the so-called humanitarian intervention referred to in Chapter IV.

The history of humanitarian intervention was summarized in 1956 by Professor and Mrs. Thomas as follows:

> England, France, and Russia intervened to end the atrocities in the Greco-Turkish warfare in 1827. President Van Buren intervened with the Sultan of Turkey in 1840 in behalf of the persecuted Jews of Damascus and Rhodes. The French intervened and by force checked religious atrocities in Lebanon in 1861. Various nations directed protests to the governments of Russia and Rumania with respect to pogroms and atrocities against Jews. Similar protests were made to the government of Turkey in behalf of the persecuted Christian minorities in 1915.[26]

The Thomases conclude, however, that "humanitarian intervention in the twentieth century . . . retains but little vigor" in view of its disuse against the dictators in the 1930's.[27] The UN Charter, they feel, has barred the use of force for this purpose.[28]

[24] S. Rosenne, *supra* note 7, at 94.
[25] *Id.* at 91.
[26] A. & A. Thomas, Non-Intervention 373 (1956).
[27] *Id.* at 374.
[28] *Id.* at 384. But see Lillich, *supra* Chapter IV, at notes 1, 2.

Manouchehr Ganji of Iran has reviewed in greater detail the history of humanitarian intervention, together with opinions of writers on its existence and extent.[29] He concluded that "in almost all cases, while the actions of the intervening powers were motivated by humanitarian considerations, they were justified on the basis of treaty stipulations." [30] In no case, apparently, had such rights and obligations been passed upon by a court or arbitral board before the intervenors acted. Gangi also concluded that "the doctrine of humanitarian intervention does not seem to claim the authority of a customary rule of international law. . . ." In any event, "in an organized international community, as we have today under the aegis of the United Nations, the act of intervention must be the result of a decision of the Organization." [31]

UN HELP

The Charter has machinery for enforcement. Article 94(2) says the injured party may "have recourse to the Security Council, which may, if it deems necessary, make recommendations or decide upon measures to be taken to give effect to the judgment." Schachter has contrasted this provision with the language of Article 13(4) of the League of Nations Covenant, requiring the League Council to "propose what steps should be taken to give effect" to an award or decision.[32] He also has treated the questions whether Security Council action under Article 94(2) presupposes a threat to peace and security (he believes not) and whether the veto applies (he thinks it does).[33]

Use of the Charter and Covenant enforcement machinery has been extremely limited. Lissitzyn wrote in 1951 that neither the

[29] M. GANJI, INTERNATIONAL PROTECTION OF HUMAN RIGHTS 9–43 (1962).

[30] *Id.* at 37.

[31] *Id.* at 43–44. Recent efforts to resurrect the doctrine of humanitarian intervention, motivated largely by the Biafra tragedy, are referred to in Chapter IV.

[32] O. Schachter, *supra* note 11, at 17–18.

[33] *Id.* at 19–22. In the Council of Europe human rights system, Article 54 of the Convention provides that "the judgment of the Court shall be transmitted to the Committee of Ministers which shall supervise its execution." Robertson has noted that "the Committee does not, of course, have power to force a State into compliance but it would undoubtedly, if the need arose, have strong persuasive authority backed, in the last resort, by the power of suspension from membership of the Council of Europe under Article 8 of the Statute." A. ROBERTSON, HUMAN RIGHTS IN EUROPE 105 (1963).

League Council nor the Security Council had yet been asked to enforce a judgment of the Court.[34] Judge Hudson, writing before the UN Charter, cited only one case in the twenty years of the League Council where it was asked to "propose . . . steps," when Bulgaria failed to execute a 1933 award to Greece concerning the forest of Rhodope, which matter was settled shortly thereafter.[35] Rosenne credits the public airing of this case in the League Council with inducing Bulgaria to "come to terms with the judgment creditor without more ado." [36]

Turning from the League to the UN, no instance is found where the Security Council, strictly speaking, has been asked to secure compliance with a judgment by using its power under Charter Article 94(2) to "make recommendations or decide upon measures to be taken to give effect to the judgment." Rosenne points out that this article "was invoked, in 1951, by the United Kingdom in an attempt to secure compliance by Iran with the interim measures of protection [the international term for interim injunction] indicated by the Court, in the early stages of the Anglo-Iranian dispute, in order to preserve the object of the litigation pending its outcome. However, the Security Council showed little enthusiasm for this procedure, which led to no concrete result." [37] While the Court is to inform the Security Council of its interim measures of protection under Article 41, such measures are hardly a "judgment" such as to bring Article 94(2) into play. Schachter believes it "likely that the indecision of the Council was attributable to the doubts which several Members had regarding the competence of the Court on the merits of the case." [38] He concludes, citing Rosenne, that the General Assembly as well could act, under Article 10, to discuss noncompliance or make recommendations. In any event, UN help in enforcing judgments, whether through the Security Council or the General Assembly, remains untested.

[34] O. LISSITZYN, *supra* note 5, at 75.

[35] M. HUDSON, *supra* note 4, at 133.

[36] S. ROSENNE, *supra* note 7, at 109. He also considered that "the role of self-help in the enforcement of international judgments received implicit recognition in Article 13 of the League Covenant. . . ." *Id.* at 93. Presumably he referred to the obligation of League Members not to "resort to war against a Member of the League which complies" with an award or decision.

[37] S. ROSENNE, THE WORLD COURT 43 (1962).

[38] O. Schachter, *supra* note 11, at 23–24.

JUDICIAL HELP

Have courts the power to bend slowly a sovereign power that armies cannot break? A glimpse of what is possible is seen in Article 60 of the World Court's Statute: "The judgment is final and without appeal. In the event of dispute as to the meaning or scope of the judgment, the Court shall construe it upon the request of any party." It is submitted that the Court's power to construe its own prior judgments may be regarded quite rightly under certain circumstances as enforcement through judicial supervision. Several ICJ cases must be examined to test this proposition, followed by a look at some recent practice of the US Supreme Court in curbing sovereign states of the Union.

The first two of the ICJ cases are the *Colombian-Peruvian Asylum Case* [39] and the *Haya de la Torre Case.* [40] The ICJ was presented by Colombia and Peru in October 1949 with a submission concerning the legality of asylum granted a Peruvian in the Colombian Embassy at Lima. The Court issued judgment in November 1950, declaring that the urgency necessary to make asylum legal was not present. Immediately Colombia put questions to the Court by way of interpretation of its judgment, asking whether Colombia was required to surrender the refugee to Peru. One week after its judgment the Court rejected this request for interpretation, partly because no "dispute" had been shown. The next day Peru demanded Haya de la Torre. Colombia declined, and then asked the Court whether the judgment required it to surrender him. Peru requested the Court to say how Colombia should execute the judgment. This opinion the Court declined to give, saying it was not a judicial function to choose among ways of terminating the asylum. Further, the Court said Colombia was not obliged to turn the man over, although the asylum should have ceased upon the judgment.

These decisions, delivered in June 1951, were followed in March 1954 by announcement at the tenth International Conference of American States of a settlement by which Haya de la Torre left Lima for Mexico. What emerges from this experience is that the parties were kept engaged, by protraction of the litigation through interpretation of the Court's first judgment, allowing time for events

[39] [1950] I.C.J. 266.
[40] [1951] I.C.J. 71.

to take their course and compliance to be worked out by the parties. In this case interpretation involved but little judicial supervision.

The second ICJ problem to examine for evidence of attempted enforcement by judicial supervision is the Advisory Opinion on Interpretation of Peace Treaties with Bulgaria, Hungary, and Romania.[41] After the UN General Assembly in 1949 had drawn the attention of these governments, to no avail, to their treaty obligations regarding human rights, the Court was asked several questions. The first was whether a dispute existed under the treaties. The second was whether, if there were a dispute, the three governments were obliged to nominate representatives to a commission provided for in the treaties for settling disputes. At this point the General Assembly resolution called for a pause: "In the event of an affirmative reply to question II and if within thirty days from the date when the Court delivers its opinion, the Governments concerned have not notified the Secretary-General that they have appointed their representatives to the Treaty Commissions . . ." then question (3) should be considered, whether the Secretary-General could appoint the third commission member if they failed to do so.[42] The Court held in March 1950 that a dispute did exist, allowing thirty days for the three governments' appointments. After the time was up, the Court in July said the Secretary-General could not appoint the third member, furthermore holding that it need not answer the fourth question, whether a Commission of only two members could act.

Was the second phase of the Peace Treaties case an attempt by the General Assembly, albeit unsuccessful, to enforce the first? Judge Azevedo, who believed it was, expressed his view in these terms:

> But the request is not content with indirectly transmitting a dispute between Member States and States which are not members to the Court, against the will of some of the parties. It goes further and attempts to attribute material effects to the opinion.
>
> Thus, the Assembly lays down that, if the Court replies in the affirmative to the first two Questions, a period of grace will automatically begin to run so as to allow the recalcitrant States to make good the time they had lost, as in a case of *emendatio morae*.

[41] [1950] I.C.J. 65.
[42] *Id*. at 67–68.

The Court's opinion will thus possess an enforceability *sui generis* somewhat in the nature of an interdict or a writ. It is tantamount to a summons which is addressed to the above-mentioned States without even waiting till the requesting organ has received the Court's opinion and deliberated on it.

This opinion will therefore produce more impressive effects than many judgments in contentious cases. There will be a sanction, resembling a daily fine, suspended over the heads of the States which are opposing the application of the Treaties. And finally, the usefulness of this formal summons will be apparent if, for example, the Court replies in the negative to the other questions which constitute the last links in the chain.[43]

The final group of ICJ cases to be examined for evidence of attempted enforcement by judicial supervision is the South West Africa series of advisory opinions. The Court in 1950 said in part that the need for supervision of the Mandate continued despite the demise of the original League of Nations supervisory organ, that the General Assembly was competent to supervise, and that South Africa was required to report to the Assembly and submit to the Court's compulsory jurisdiction.[44] In 1954, the Court was asked whether a two-thirds vote requirement was a correct interpretation of the 1950 opinion and, if not, what voting procedure should be followed. The Court approved the two-thirds rule, on the ground that its earlier opinion had not even touched such matters.[45] In 1955, the Court was asked whether oral hearings could be granted petitioners consistently with the first opinion. The Court approved the hearings, since the first opinion held the UN had the same supervisory powers as those of the League, which could have allowed its Permanent Mandates Commission to grant hearings even though in fact it had not done so.[46]

In the South West Africa advisory opinions, as in the Peace Treaties case, the General Assembly was trying to push a heavy stone uphill in seeking enforcement by judicial supervision over a party not before the court. The efficacy of enforcement by both self-help and judicial supervision should not be judged by any case where this defect existed.

[43] *Id.* at 86–87.
[44] [1950] I.C.J. 128.
[45] [1955] I.C.J. 67.
[46] [1956] I.C.J. 23.

Turning now from the attempts that have been made to enforce some of the rulings of the ICJ through judicial supervision, the United States Supreme Court's handling of the school integration cases should be examined. There the Court was ordering sovereign states to alter deeply entrenched customs of long standing, and doing so without a sheriff or other coercive means at its disposal. Only rarely in the early days, such as at Little Rock, Arkansas, was the Court backed up by force. The parallel between the ICJ and the Supreme Court was made by Rosenne when he remarked that the situation where the ICJ's decree would be backed up by the Security Council acting under Article 94(2) "would not be unlike that which a few years ago confronted the Federal authorities in Little Rock." [47] A 1957 observation noted that "so far the national effort for racial integration in the public schools has been left almost solely to the judiciary, traditionally weakest of the three departments of government. . . . Vastly greater exercises of power could occur, but unless they do the role of the courts is a lonely one." [48]

The role of the ICJ is also a lonely one. There is no legislature like the Congress, nor any executive with a popular mandate to put its shoulder to the wheel beside the Court. So what was done before these allies came to join the US Supreme Court may show what the World Court could do, or what it could be asked to do, in human rights and other cases.

The five US Supreme Court segregation cases jointly known today by the name of the first of them, *Brown v. Board of Education,* were argued in December 1952. The Court then propounded certain questions around which the cases were reargued in December 1953. In the words of the Chief Justice, "reargument was largely devoted to the circumstances surrounding the adoption of the Fourteenth Amendment in 1868. It covered exhaustively consideration of the Amendment in Congress, ratification by the states, the existing practices in racial segregation, and the views of proponents and opponents of the Amendment. This discussion and our own investigation convince us that, although these sources cast some light,

[47] S. ROSENNE, *supra* note 37, at 43.
[48] Leflar, *Law of the Land,* in WITH ALL DELIBERATE SPEED 14 (D. Shoemaker ed. 1957). For the record of subsequent events, see THE CIVIL RIGHTS READER: BASIC DOCUMENTS OF THE CIVIL RIGHTS MOVEMENT (L. Friedman rev. ed. 1968).

it is not enough to resolve the problem with which we are faced. At best, they are inconclusive." [49] However, the Court found "so little in the history of the Fourteenth Amendment relating to its intended effect on public education" [50] that it felt it could not "turn the clock back to 1868 when the Amendment was adopted, or even to 1896 when *Plessy v. Ferguson* [approving "separate but equal" facilities] was written. We must consider public education in the light of its full development and its present place in American life through the Nation. Only in this way can it be determined if segregation in public schools deprives these plaintiffs of the equal protection of the laws." [51]

These words, so similar to the argument heard in the ICJ a decade later that South Africa's duties towards the South West Africans under the Mandate must be read to have a contemporary meaning and not confined within 1920 concepts, were followed by the ringing holding that "the plaintiffs and others similarly situated for whom the actions have been brought are . . . deprived of the equal protection of the laws," since "in the field of public education the doctrine of 'separate but equal' has no place. Separate educational facilities are inherently unequal." [52]

Having so held, the Supreme Court did not pass on to other problems and allow the losing parties to sulk while doing nothing to comply. With masterful finesse, the unanimous Court in the next breath called on the parties to assist the Court to fashion their own compliance:

> [T]he formulation of decrees in these cases presents problems of considerable complexity. . . . In order that we may have the full assistance of the parties in formulating decrees, the cases will be restored to the docket, and the parties are requested to present further argument on Questions 4 and 5 previously propounded by the Court for the reargument this Term. The Attorney General of the United States is again invited to participate. The Attorneys General of the states requiring or permitting segregation in public education will also be permitted to appear as *amici curiae*.[53]

[49] 347 U.S. 483, 498 (1954).
[50] *Id.* at 490.
[51] *Id.* at 492–93.
[52] *Id.* at 495.
[53] *Id.* at 495–96.

How reminiscent of the *Peace Treaties* case four years before. There as here the second set of questions dealt with remedies in case the Court first held against Respondents.

The following year the segregation cases were again before the Supreme Court. A still-unanimous bench, speaking again through the Chief Justice, stated that "there remains for consideration the manner in which relief is to be accorded." [54] Praising as "informative and helpful" the briefs and arguments of six states besides the parties and Attorney General, the Court noted that "substantial steps . . . have already been taken. . . ." [55] The Court then set the areas of responsibility for implementation. The judiciary was not to take over and administer compliance. Respondents were responsible to take the initiative. However, the judiciary would continue supervision, with patience and forebearance, for as long as might be needed, brooking no delay or avoidance. Thus dextrously did the Supreme Court fashion its handiwork. The process is full of differences from the international judiciary, but just as full of similarities.

Application to Human Rights Cases

Which, if any, of the previously attempted enforcement methods might be appropriate where human rights matters are adjudicated? A case in point would have arisen if the *South West Africa* decision of 1966 had gone against South Africa. There were various possible ICJ decisions other than the Court's denial of the standing of Ethiopia and Liberia to obtain decisions on the merits. Among the possible outcomes, the ones raising enforcement problems would have been decisions (1) requiring South African departure from South West Africa, (2) requiring UN supervision, and (3) confirming duties under the Mandate or UN Article 73 but requiring no UN supervision.

If the ICJ had ordered South Africa to depart and compliance had been refused, forcible self-help enforcement, even if available, would have been doubtful legally since the UN Charter forbids force except in self-defense or proper collective action. Non-forcible self-help sufficient to oust South Africa would have been most unlikely, as would UN help involving force. As to economic sanctions,

[54] 349 U.S. 294, 298 (1955).
[55] *Id.* at 299.

a UN Expert Committee in an early-1965 report listed the various ineffectual measures referred to in prior resolutions of the Security Council and General Assembly, as well as those of the Organization for African Unity and Conference of Non-Aligned Countries, since 1960.[56] The Expert Committee stated cautiously that "it was not possible to draw precise conclusions as to the degree to which these measures [embargo on petroleum and its products, cessation of emigration into South Africa, and banning of financial transactions] or a combination of them might affect South Africa's economic activity, or as to the length of time it would take for their effects to be felt." [57]

If self-help and UN help would have seemed unlikely means of getting South Africa to comply with an ICJ decree to leave South West Africa, what of judicial help? Is there any guidance to be found in the US Supreme Court's handling of the segregation cases? Could the ICJ by keeping jurisdiction and relying on Statute Article 60 as needed have held South Africa in the court room and induced it to participate in the implementation process, thus obligating itself at least to move gradually in the desired direction? Such protraction of the case would have disappointed many persons like the African leaders who wrote Mr. Ernest Gross, Agent for Ethiopia and Liberia, that "the non-whites in this country rejected the application to the International Court of Justice by the South African Government that the Court or a Commission of the Court should visit South West Africa for on the spot investigation. To our view the application . . . was made only to delay the proceedings of the International Court." [58] However, their disappointment hardly could have been greater than it was in the actual case.

In the event that the Court, rather than ordering South Africa out of South West Africa, had required UN supervision, or simply confirmed that South Africa had duties under the Mandate or UN Charter Article 73, enforcement by self-help or UN help would have become only remotely relevant. To gain the goal of final freedom, South West Africa would have needed most desperately the Court's continuing surveillance. The Court would have been better suited than any other UN body, because of its opportunity for deep inves-

---

[56] S/6210, Ann. VI (1965).
[57] *Id.* at 7.
[58] A/AC.109/PET.371/Add.2, at 1 (1965).

tigation which Lissitzyn has pointed out in contrast to the Security Council's shallower facilities in the *Corfu Channel* case.[59]

Ways have been worked out by the UN to administer the emergence into freedom of former colonial territories. The UN Temporary Executive Authority (UNTEA) was created to bridge the gap between Dutch and Indonesian rule in West New Guinea, or West Irian. On October 1, 1962, the UN flag was hoisted beside the Dutch, which was lowered December 31st when the Indonesian was raised. The UN flag came down May 1, 1963, and international civil servants of 32 nationalities departed. UN participation recurred, in West Irian's 1969 "act of free choice." UN supervision of the Cook Islands elections, whereby the inhabitants passed from colonialism into voluntary association with New Zealand under UN aegis, affords additional precedent for executive assistance in bringing forth a nation. Of course, South West Africa did not enjoy such compliant administering authorities, and therefore needed supervision by an organ whose jurisdiction did not turn on consent of that authority. UNTEA and the Cook Islands supervision had such consent. Only the ICJ had consent from South Africa to its jurisdiction, thanks to the compromissory clause in the 45-year-old Mandate.[60]

Judicial supervision appeared to concern South Africa's counsel. At the arguments in April 1965 they urged that it would be a most unusual function for the Court to inquire into the political and technical questions raised by Article 2 of the Mandate, which required the Mandatory to "promote to the utmost the material and moral well-being and the social progress of the inhabitants. . . ."[61] The Mandatory, they argued, had discretion in exercising its powers, which powers must be judged by 1920 standards. The Court, they claimed, could not substitute its judgment for that of the Mandatory, only see whether the limit of good faith had been transgressed. As long as the Mandatory honestly sought the right result, it could not be in breach, they contended.[62] Application of a current "so-called legal norm of non-discrimination" which would lead to chaotic results would be judicial legislation, they claimed.

[59] O. LISSITZYN, *supra* note 5, at 80.

[60] No UN "presence" in South West Africa, however brief, has been permitted since 1962, when the Chairman and Vice-Chairman of the Assembly's Special Committee for South West Africa spent 23 days there.

[61] UN Press Release I.C.J./231, at 2 (1965).

[62] UN Press Release I.C.J./233, at 2 (1965).

All these arguments, or some like them, surely were raised about the US Supreme Court's role before it resolved the segregation cases, so perhaps some guidance in enforcement by judicial supervision could have been gained from that source, as well as from the ICJ's own precedents. The fact that the ICJ resolved the matter in such a way as to avoid all compliance problems merely means that such problems remain to be confronted in some other international adjudication involving human rights.

Chapter VII

Protection by Criminal Adjudication

Criminal adjudication of human rights cases has been sporadic. *Ad hoc* tribunals like those at Nuremberg and Tokyo have adjudged charges encompassing governmental oppression of individuals. At Nuremberg crimes against humanity as well as war crimes and crimes against peace were covered by the London Agreement for the Prosecution and Punishment of the Major War Criminals of the European Axis.[1] Crimes against humanity, defined as involving "inhuman acts committed against any civilian population, before or during the war," were limited by the London Charter to acts connected with crimes against peace or war crimes.

Since Nuremberg efforts have been made to free the concept of crimes against humanity from the limits then imposed on it, and to evolve a definition broadly applicable to large-scale human rights offences. The earlier post-Nuremberg years saw the General Assembly's adoption of the Genocide Convention in 1948,[2] followed by the International Law Commission's formulation of the Nuremberg Principles [3] and the Draft Code of Offences Against the Peace and Security of Mankind.[4] More recently, the General Assembly has branded as "crimes against humanity" such offenses as "the practice of apartheid, as well as all forms of racial discrimination," [5] and "the policies of apartheid practised by the Government of South Africa." [6] An unadopted proposal by 61 Afro-Asian Members in

[1] 82 U.N.T.S. 279.
[2] 78 U.N.T.S. 277.
[3] A/1316 (1950).
[4] A/2693 (1954).
[5] A/Res/2189 (XXI) (1966).
[6] A/Res/2202 (XXI) (1966). This "condemnation" was reiterated by the Assembly in 1967, A/Res/2307 (XXII), at the adoption of which, according to a UN report, "there was no discussion of this particular item, the debate in the General Assembly and its subsidiary bodies centering heavily on other questions. Therefore, it was not specified which of its elements made *apartheid* a crime against humanity." E/CN.4/984/Add.18, at 3 (1969). The Ukraine has asserted that "the South African racists are guilty of the crime of genocide. . . .

1966 would have had the Assembly condemn as such a crime "the violation, wherever it occurs, of any of the rights and freedoms set forth in the Universal Declaration of Human Rights." [7]

The drive towards a broader scope of "crimes against humanity" was encouraged by the Secretariat in 1967 when it suggested that the Human Rights Commission might consider using a treaty on statutory limitation to add to the definition "such crimes against humanity, comprising the elements mentioned in the Charter of the International Tribunal of Nuremberg, whether perpetrated in time of war or in time of peace, as are the consequence of the policy of apartheid." [8] The following year the General Assembly adopted a draft convention on non-applicability of statutory limitation to prosecutions of "war crimes," as defined, and

> crimes against humanity whether committed in time of war or in time of peace as they are defined in the Charter of the International Military Tribunal, Nürnberg, of 8 August 1945 and confirmed by resolutions 3(I) of 13 February 1946 and 95(I) of 11 December 1946 of the General Assembly of the United Nations, eviction by armed attack or occupation and inhuman acts resulting from the policy of

---

The General Assembly, in resolutions 2022 (XX), 2074 (XX), 2105 (XX) and 2189 (XXI) has described the policy of apartheid as a 'crime against humanity.' And international law, as is well known, unequivocally requires the prosecution and punishment of persons who have committed such a crime." A/6688/Add.1 (1967). The "Committee of 24" (decolonization) "strongly condemns the colonial war being waged by the Government of Portugal against the peoples of the Territories under its domination, which constitutes a crime against humanity. . . ." A/AC.109/292 (1968). The Committee in a 1967 resolution "condemns as a crime against humanity the . . . [Portuguese] settlement of foreign immigrants in the territories and . . . the exporting of African workers to South Africa." A/AC.109/251 (1967). ECOSOC has condemned "the criminal policy of apartheid." E/Res/1216 (XLII) (1967). The General Assembly has declared "that the practice of using mercenaries against movements for national liberation and independence is punishable as a criminal act and that the mercenaries themselves are outlaws." A/Res/2465 (XXIII) (1968). The vote was 87 to 7, with 17 abstentions.

[7] A/C.3/L.1340 (1966). See also A/C.3/L.1336 (1966).

[8] E/CN.4/928, at 12 (1967). "The Ministry of Foreign Affairs of the German Democratic Republic shares the view expressed in the study of the Secretary General that the Convention [on non-applicability of statutory limitation to war crimes and crimes against humanity] should take account of the fact that crimes against humanity ought to be regarded as separate crimes rather than a category of offenses accessory to crimes against peace and war crimes. . . ." E/CN.4/L.901, at 6 (1967).

apartheid, and the crime of genocide as defined in the 1948 Convention on the Prevention and Punishment of the Crime of Genocide, even if such acts do not constitute a violation of the domestic law of the country in which they were committed.[9]

Thus, while definitions were tending to broaden, ideas were being presented for procedures of enforcement. In 1967 Sean MacBride, Secretary-General of the International Commission of Jurists, speaking for his own and other non-governmental organizations, proposed at the UN Seminar in Zambia on apartheid, racial discrimination and colonialism in southern Africa

> that a register or record office be established at United Nations Headquarters for the purpose of registering all complaints of acts of brutality and other acts amounting to crimes against humanity committed in South Africa, South West Africa, Southern Rhodesia, Angola and Mozambique . . . by anyone in these territories purporting to act in pursuance of the racial or colonial laws or practices being applied in these areas.[10]

The British author Colin Legum proposed that Mr. MacBride's own organization

> open a register of people accused of committing atrocities in defiance of [a Convention on Crimes Against Humanity]. Men like Inspector Lambron, head of the Greek security police, Asphalia, and the torturers in South Africa, Portugal and other countries, should have dossiers on them prepared against the day when conditions change and they become available for prosecution. The mere threat of such a possibil-

---

[9] A/Res/2391 (XXIII) (1968). "Unfortunately, the results of the work of the United Nations in this field are considered unsatisfactory by the great majority of Council of Europe States," according to Council of Europe Press Release R (69) 5 (1969). "[T]he Council of Europe member states not voting for the United Nations Convention . . . were prompted . . . by certain legal imperfections, especially in respect of the definition of crimes against humanity." Council of Europe Doc. 2506, at 16 (1969). The European Consultative Assembly recommended the drafting of a European convention on the non-applicability of statutory limitations to crimes against humanity, taking into account the criticism raised against the United Nations Convention by the representatives of several European States. Forward in Europe 1/1969, at 16.

[10] A/6818, at 38 (1967). Mr. MacBride made similar suggestions in July 1967 to a Sub-Committee of the General Assembly's Committee on Apartheid, A/AC.115/L.206, at 12 (1967), as did Zambian President Kaunda in September 1968 to a non-governmental organization group. Human Rights: Final Report of the International NGO Conference, Paris, 16–20 Sept. 1968, at 18.

ity might make torturers think twice before they commit their loathsome brutalities.[11]

Mr. MacBride later proposed a Universal Court of Human Rights to deal with crimes against humanity.

> For a start, violations of the United Nations and the Red Cross Conventions could be made indictable offences before an International Tribunal to punish crimes against humanity. Such a Tribunal could, in addition, be given general power to pass judgment on crimes that violate ". . . the law of nations, the laws of humanity and the dictates of the public conscience." Gradually, later, a code of Crimes against Humanity could be evolved and embodied in an international convention, but the Tribunal with the jurisdiction indicated could be set up now.[12]

A geographically narrower proposal appeared in the Montreal Statement of the Assembly for Human Rights on March 22–27, 1968, which concluded that "criminal courts and procedures might be established for dealing with gross violation of human rights" in South West Africa, whose "unique status provides a special opportunity to experiment with further implementation procedures." [13]

The pace of proposals for criminal jurisdiction was escalated

[11] Reprinted from The Observer (London) by Vista, March–April 1968, at 72. The Second International Conference of the International Association for the Prevention of Crime adopted a resolution in 1967 recommending, to deal with genocide, "that an International Criminal Court should be set up, to which actions might be brought by a State, by the United Nations Organization, by international organizations having consultative status with the United Nations, by any group that is victimized, or by the Centre that it is decided to establish. This court should have jurisdiction to give opinions, to impose penalties and to order reparation. . . ." The Association decided to establish a "Centre of Observation, Information and Study on Genocide." Levasseur, *The Prevention of Genocide*, 8 J. INT'L COMM. JURISTS 74, 81 (1967).

[12] MacBride, *The New Frontiers of International Law*, UNESCO COURIER 26, 28–29 (Jan. 1968).

[13] Chaper II, at note 20. See similar proposals of Amnesty International, a non-governmental organization in consultative status with ECOSOC, A/AC.-115/L.225 (1967). The Soviet Association of International Law, in the name of its President, Professor Gregory Tunkin, sent to the UN in March 1968 a statement that "South Africa refuses to grant independence to the South West African people, practises racial discrimination and completely denies them the basic human rights and freedoms. These actions of the South African government on South West Africa's territory were rightly described as a crime against humanity. This was stated by the United Nations General Assembly in its resolution 2145 (XXI)." A/AC.109/Pet.990 (1968).

when the UN Human Rights Commission's Special Rapporteur on apartheid and racial discrimination suggested to the Commission in early 1968 that it recommend to the Assembly asking the South African Government to repeal its discriminatory laws:

> In case the present situation continues to prevail, the General Assembly would declare the leaders and responsible officials of the South African Government criminals at large who could be apprehended and tried by the courts of any State under the charge of the commission of crimes against humanity. In case of conviction the penalty would be the severest (penalty) which could be imposed under the laws of the country concerned.[14]

This proposal was not dealt with explicitly by the Commission. The Special Rapporteur went further with his proposal for a Grand Jury of Legal Experts for South West Africa:

> The Commission could recommend to the General Assembly that it establish, in connection with the Assembly's decisions to administer South West Africa (Resolutions 2145 (XXI) and 2248 (SV)), a Grand Jury of Legal Experts for South West Africa for the protection of the life, personal safety and rights of the inhabitants of the Territory. Such a body of legal experts would determine *prima facie* violations of international law, crimes against humanity and other serious offenses committed by individual South African Government officials against the inhabitants of the territory for which the Assembly has assumed special responsibility. It could be given a variety of police powers including the powers to issue arrest warrants, lists of wanted men and requests that they be brought to justice by Member States of the United Nations. By acting *in personam* it could have some deterrent effect on South African officialdom in so far as torture, brutality and the execution of death sentences are concerned. Later the terms of reference of this same body may be extended to cover Southern Rhodesia and South Africa as well, in case the Assembly's call for repeal, amendment and replacement of legislation is not heeded.[15]

An American viewpoint on the usefulness of international criminal proceedings was expressed by the Human Rights Committee of

[14] E/CN.4/949/Add.4, at 510 (1968).

[15] *Id.* at 515. The Commission in resolution 3 (XXIV) asked for further study of this proposal. The proposal was refined in E/CN.4/979/Add.5, at 12 (1969). ECOSOC requested Member States' views. E/Res/1415 (XLVI) §13 (1969). For South Africa's position on UN jurisdiction over Namibia (South West Africa), see S/9204 (1969).

the American Branch of the International Law Association, which reached the following conclusions:

Prima Facie Findings Without Trial

Grand-jury-type proceedings might be useful in cases where the accused were not available to be tried. The spotlight of public opinion could be focused sharply through orderly measures taken in the drastic context of criminality. Those accused might feel compelled to respond, with public statements if not formal appearance, where the spotlight shone from an impartial source, depoliticized as far as possible.

Criminal "Trials" Without Presence of Defendants

The reasons for *prima facie* findings apply even more strongly in favor of proceedings in which such findings are subjected to "trial." A greater impact on public opinion should result from facts found after hearing both sides. If the accused neither appeared nor submitted statements, a hearing of sorts for both sides could be obtained through an active tribunal seeking evidence on its own, on the order of an American administrative body or European *"juge d'instruction."* [16]

Such recent proposals for international criminal courts and related facilities are not the first to be made since Nuremberg. The Genocide Convention, written in 1948, referred expectantly to proceedings in "such international penal tribunal as may have jurisdiction with respect to those Contracting Parties which shall have accepted its jurisdiction." [17] But a UN Committee's Draft Statute for an International Criminal Court, prepared in 1951 and revised in 1953,[18] was shelved to await, so far to no avail,[19] agreement on the meaning of "aggression."

[16] AMERICAN BRANCH, INTERNATIONAL LAW ASSOCIATION, PROCEEDINGS AND COMMITTEE REPORTS, at 43–44, 1967–68.

[17] 78 U.N.T.S. 277, art. VI.

[18] A/2645, at 23–26 (1954). See A/Conf.32/5, at 197 (1967).

[19] A committee established by A/Res/1181 (XII), which had last met in April 1964, held its fourth session in April 1967. In September 1967 the USSR requested inclusion in the General Assembly's agenda of an item entitled "Need for accelerating the definition of aggression in the light of the present international situation." A/6833 (1967). In December 1967 the General Assembly adopted A/Res/2330 (XXII) which stated that "there is a widespread conviction of the need to expedite the definition of aggression" and which established a new Special Committee, the fourth on defining aggression, whose first meeting was held in June–July 1968. In September the Assembly took note of its General Committee's decision that it would not be desirable, prior to com-

While international criminal jurisdiction lagged, the practice of national prosecution of crimes of "universal jurisdiction" was used occasionally to fill the gap. Building on the long-standing precedent subjecting pirates to punishment by any state,[20] other serious wrongs have been made universally punishable by convention. Chief among these are the four 1949 Geneva Conventions for the protection of war victims, to which the United States is one of many parties.[21] Typical of the universal jurisdiction provisions in the 1949 Geneva Conventions is that in the Convention for the Protection of Civilian Persons in Time of War, not only authorizing but actually obligating "each High Contracting Party . . . to search for persons alleged to have committed, or to have ordered to be committed, such grave offenses [as defined therein], and [to] bring such persons, regardless of their nationality, before its own courts." [22] Such procedures for national prosecution of international crimes have lain idle for the twenty years they have existed.

With respect to the relative merits of international and national courts for prosecution of international crimes, the Human Rights Committee of the International Law Association's American Branch concluded that

> while universal criminal jurisdiction has been widely accepted, not only in the four 1949 Geneva Conventions but also in the 1958 Convention on the High Seas (for piracy), its lack of use causes concern. Like state vs. state complaints, found in I.L.O. experience to be seldom used and then most likely for political purposes, universal criminal jurisdiction may be a rusty tool, seized at times in haste and crudely wielded. Unilateral prosecution of offenses against the whole international community would seem less desirable than machinery whose guidance is multilateral. Politically motivated prosecutions could then be better controlled. Political prevention of otherwise desir-

pletion of the definition, to include in the Assembly's agenda the items "Draft code of offences against the peace and security of mankind" and "International Criminal Jurisdiction." A/PV.1676, at 41 (1968). A survey of UN action on the subject appears in A/AC.134/1 (1968).

[20] Universal jurisdiction over acts of piracy was confirmed in Article 19 of the 1958 Convention on the High Seas. A/Conf.13/38, at 135 (1958).

[21] "The Geneva Conventions are pre-eminently treaties open to all. Today they are formally binding on 117 States and are among the treaties with the most universal participation." A/CN.4/200, at 79 (1968).

[22] 75 U.N.T.S. 287, art. 146.

able prosecutions, which might occur, would be a lesser evil than uncontrolled political prosecution.[23]

The growing interest in criminal process to protect basic rights, matched in the United States by concern over personal accountability for international crimes connected with the Viet Nam conflict,[24] is not difficult to comprehend. Frustration at the impregnability of white supremacy bastions like South Africa, or even Rhodesia, is bound to add appeal to the notion of punishing apartheid's individual practitioners who, though presently immune through safe location, would, if ever caught, be as subject to punishment as are their own present victims. The actual capture of Adolph Eichmann encourages speculation about others accused of human rights crimes. Names of such persons are being listed, as shown in Chapter X.

Can it be wrong, in the light of Nuremberg, to plan for prosecution on international authority of today's oppressors? The answer is not categorical but qualified. The qualifications concern geographical jurisdiction, the nature of the tribunal, the type of findings made, and the consequence for the accused.

Geographical jurisdiction is better founded in Namibia (South West Africa) than it would be for South Africa itself. As mentioned, a special rapporteur of the UN Human Rights Commission has argued for UN criminal accusation based on jurisdiction gained by General Assembly action in 1967 declaring South Africa's Mandate ended and the UN responsible. While one may differ with the Assembly's right to end the Mandate, its end is hardly disputed, leaving a jurisdictional vacuum in which the UN's authority can be disputed only by South Africa, based on its having conquered

[23] *Supra* note 16, at 44.

[24] See generally Clergy and Laymen Concerned About Vietnam, In the Name of America: The record of U.S. military behavior in Vietnam compared with the laws of war which are binding on all Americans (1968). A number of attempts have been made to defend against charges of refusing to cooperate with the armed forces on the ground that such cooperation would result in personal guilt for war crimes or crimes against peace. The attempts have not succeeded in producing a ruling on whether United States participation in the war is legal, let alone a ruling on the legality of individual actions on its fringes. The report of a conference at George Washington University in June 1968, sponsored by the American Veterans Committee states: "with particular reference to the present situation whereby some young men are refusing to serve in Vietnam, it was pointed out that a man cannot refuse to serve, but only to carry out an illegal order." J. WILLENZ, HUMAN RIGHTS OF THE MAN IN UNIFORM 11 (1968).

the area fifty years before. In its own territory, however, South Africa could assert its lack of consent to international prosecution, a far more potent objection not available at Nuremberg where the Allied Powers spoke as successor sovereigns to the beaten Reich.

The nature of the tribunal, as between the national type of court which sentenced Eichmann and the jointly formed Nuremberg tribunal, should be determined—apart from the legal requirement of an injured sovereign—by the test of wide acceptability. The Nuremberg Tribunal would have been less acceptable if constituted by but one of the victorious states. The injured sovereign requirement would loom less large if, for the normal arrest-trial-punishment sequence, there were substituted less complete criminal proceedings. Prima facie findings like indictments could be made without arrest and with far lighter legal foundation. The body making the findings would rely on public opinion, not on legal jurisdiction to punish, for its sanction. Trial of indictments could be held, again without arrest so long as punishment was not the goal, and the truth-seeking machinery of the normal trial could be supplied through an official designated either to cross examine and argue the accused's case or, alternatively, to interrogate all witnesses like a European *juge d'instruction*.

In short, criminal-type proceedings can be conceived of in forms suitable for UN protection of civil and political rights today and tomorrow.

Chapter VIII

International Negotiation to Assist Victims

The prospect of an international "ombudsman" [1] with the official title of UN High Commissioner for Human Rights calls attention to negotiation or persuasion as a method of international protection of individuals.[2] The need was explained in the Montreal Statement of the Assembly for Human Rights of March 22–27, 1968, which concluded that "in every country . . . some specialized institution needs to be established by law, in addition to the courts, to which a citizen who considers himself deprived of his rights may turn. . . . It may be of the type of the ombudsman or the procurator general, or an administrative tribunal such as the Conseil d'État, or it may be a national human rights committee or commission." [3]

The High Commissioner proposal was first formally introduced at the UN by Costa Rica in 1965.[4] ECOSOC in June 1967 by a vote

[1] See W. GELLHORN, OMBUDSMEN AND OTHERS: CITIZENS' PROTECTORS IN NINE COUNTRIES (1967); OMBUDSMEN FOR AMERICAN GOVERNMENT? (S. Anderson ed. 1968); Gellhorn, *The Ombudsman's Relevance to American Municipal Affairs,* 54 A.B.A.J. 134 (1968).

[2] See Bissell, *Negotiation By International Bodies and the Protection of Human Rights,* 7 COLUM. J. TRANSNAT'L L. 90 (1968). At the 1968 session of the UN Commission on Human Rights, the "negotiation" proposal described at note 36 *infra* was objected to by some on the ground that the word implied the possibility of the negotiator's dealing away rights belonging to third-party victims. As used herein, "negotiation" is intended to be synonymous with "persuasion," which has no such connotation.

[3] Chapter II, at note 20. Such institutions, as well as the Japanese Civil Liberties Bureau and Commissioners, are described in ST/TAO/HR/33 (1967). Canada reported to the 1968 Teheran Conference on Human Rights that two of its Provinces had appointed Ombudsmen in 1967. Hawaii adopted an Ombudsman Act in April 1967, while many other states and a few local governments have been considering such an institution. N.Y. Times, Oct. 30, 1967, §1, at 25, col. 3. It has been estimated that 20 to 30 American colleges have tried ombudsmen, some of whom are students. Brann, *The Campus Ombudsman: College Student Defender,* The Chronicle of Higher Education, Nov. 11, 1968, vol. III, no. 5, p. 1, col. 2.

[4] The history of the proposal is summarized in A/7170 (1968). See Report of the Working Group to Study the Proposal to Create the Institution of a

of 17–4–5 recommended that the General Assembly "establish a United Nations High Commissioner's Office for Human Rights," with certain defined powers including negotiation, and "establish a panel of expert consultants to advise and assist the High Commissioner . . . having regard to the equitable representation of the principal legal systems and of geographical regions. . . ." [5] The General Assembly in 1967 and 1968 postponed decision on the High Commissioner proposal.[6]

National positions on the proposal vary greatly. The United States favors the creation of such a post.[7] Japan has been opposed on various grounds, including the argument that "the adoption by the Assembly of the International Covenants on Human Rights with a moderate implementation system by a unanimous vote should be interpreted as the final decision of the Assembly on the question of setting up international machinery to ensure respect for fundamental freedoms and human rights." [8] The Netherlands, on the other hand, believes that "the functions of a High Commissioner can be distinguished from implementation machineries provided for in international conventions with a view to the protection of human rights." [9]

Uruguay, in registering its approval, recalled its similar proposal at the fifth session of the General Assembly.[10] The most vigorous opposition to such a High Commissioner comes from the socialist countries.[11] The opposition may be appraised in the light of the precedents for negotiation with governments by intergovernmental agencies on behalf of individuals.

United Nations High Commissioner for Human Rights, E/CN.4/934 (1967); Analytical and Technical Study prepared by the Secretary-General under paragraph 3 of resolution 4 (XXII) of the Commission on Human Rights, E/CN.4/AC.21/L.1 (1966), USSR objections to which were reproduced in E/AC.7/L.529 (1967). See also Etra, *International Protection of Human Rights: The Proposal for a U.N. High Commissioner*, 5 COLUM. J. TRANSNAT'L L. 150 (1966); MacDonald, *The United Nations High Commissioner for Human Rights*, 1967 CANADIAN YB. INT'L L. 84.

[5] E/Res/1237 (XLII). ECOSOC also requested comments from Member States, ILO and UNESCO. E/Res/1238 (XLII).

[6] A/Res/2333 (XXII) (1967); A/Res/2437 (XXIII) (1968).

[7] A/6699/Add.7 (1967), noting detailed US recommendations.

[8] A/6699/Add.6 (1967).

[9] A/6699/Add.5 (1967).

[10] A/6699/Add.9 (1967).

[11] See, for example, E/AC.7/L.529 (1967); A/6699/Add.6 and 7 (1967).

One negotiation precedent is the "international protection" function of the UN High Commissioner for Refugees.[12] This office, established 17 years ago, succeeded earlier institutions which started in 1921 with appointment of a League of Nations High Commissioner for Refugees. The precedent is based on more than the similarity of names. One of the present High Commissioner's functions is negotiation with the refugee's former government respecting repatriation under conditions feasible for the refugee.[13] Only the circumstance of the refugee's having left his country differentiates his case from that of the oppressed person still in his own country, on whose behalf the new High Commissioner for Human Rights might negotiate.[14] For example, the High Commissioner for Refugees declared himself unable to aid Biafrans in Nigeria, a group for whom a great deal more could have been done by an official with broader jurisdiction. U.S. Senator Edward Kennedy, who has proposed a UN emergency relief force to bring aid to Biafra, is said to favor expanding the UN Refugee Commissioner's authority and putting him in charge.[15]

[12] See P. Weis, *The Office of the United Nations High Commissioner for Refugees and Human Rights,* 1 HUMAN RIGHTS J. 243 (1968). The UNHCR's Statute is quoted in A/Conf.32/6 at 61–62 (1967). "[T]he most important preoccupation of UNHCR [is] that of international protection." A/AC.96/352 App. I, at 4 (1966). In thus commenting, the High Commissioner cited his "negotiations with the German Federal Government on the establishment of an additional fund for persons persecuted for reasons of nationality. . . ." In December 1966, UNHCR announced a formal agreement with such government. A/Conf.32/5, at 201 (1967). See also A/7211, at 15–16 (1968). UNHCR and West Germany agreed that "a person is damaged by reason of his nationality . . . (b) who would not have been damaged if he had not been a national of a foreign State or if he had not been of non-German ethnic origin." E/CN.4/983, at 135 (1969).

[13] Even persons not refugees at all have been given the High Commissioner's protection through "U.N. interagency action in settling about seven million Andean Indians in six Latin American Countries. Although these . . . were technically not refugees, the problems raised in their settlement tended to be analogous to those of refugees in developing countries." A/AC.96/343, at 4 (1966).

[14] Both the Council of Europe and the Inter-American Commission on Human Rights illustrated the blending together of refugees' problems and other human rights matters when they told the May 1967 session of the Executive Committee of the High Commissioner's Programme of their own interest in the protection of refugees. A/AC.96/370, App. at 7–8 (1967). See also A/AC.96/386, at 10 (1967).

[15] N.Y. Times, Feb. 9, 1969, §1, at 29, col. 2.

Equally long-standing precedents for intergovernmental agency negotiation exist where the agency is a group rather than a single official. The procedures of the International Labor Organization, according to C. Wilfred Jenks, Deputy Director-General and former Legal Adviser, "which it has taken almost fifty years to bring to their present state of development, have saved some men's lives and secured the release of others, promptly or less promptly, from prison or protective custody . . ." [16] In such procedures negotiation has a prominent place. Negotiation which is technically non-compulsory but nonetheless apparently effective is based on government reports on compliance with ILO Conventions and recommendations.[17] The reports are examined by an ILO Committee of Experts on the Application of Conventions and Recommendations. The Committee sends its comments back to the Government, which then is invited to participate in further examination of its compliance by a Conference Committee composed of government, employers' and workers' representatives. The ILO has observed that "almost all Governments . . . accept this invitation," and that "cooperation by States is also shown by the measures which they take to meet the observations of the Committee of Experts and the Conference Committee and to eliminate discrepancies with ratified Conventions." [18]

Compulsory ILO negotiation takes place when complaints of non-compliance are lodged by other governments or by private groups. Article 27 of the ILO Constitution requires the respondent State to place all its information relevant to a complaint at the disposal of a Commission of Inquiry appointed by the ILO Governing Body. The Government also is required to inform ILO whether it accepts the Commission's recommendations or, if not, whether it

[16] THE INTERNATIONAL PROTECTION OF HUMAN RIGHTS 245 (E. Luard ed. 1967). Four of the ILO's conventions are classified by the UN Office of Public Information in Reference Paper No. 6 (1967) as pertaining to human rights: (1) Abolition of forced Labor, 320 U.N.T.S. 292; (2) Discrimination in respect of Employment and Occupation, 362 U.N.T.S. 32; (3) Equal Remuneration for Men and Women Workers for Work of Equal Value, 165 U.N.T.S. 304; (4) Freedom of Association and Protection of the Right to Organize, 68 U.N.T.S. 18.

[17] See E. LANDY, THE EFFECTIVENESS OF INTERNATIONAL SUPERVISION: THIRTY YEARS OF I.L.O. EXPERIENCE (1966).

[18] E/4144 at 11, 12, (1965). Subsequent reports dealing with ILO procedures include E/CN.4/918/Add.1 (1966), A/6699/Add.1 (1967), and A/7170 (1968).

proposes to refer the matter to the International Court of Justice. The only complaint during ILO's first 40 years was made by an Indian worker's delegate against his own Government, which undertook to remedy the situation without the appointment of a Commission of Inquiry. In the present decade, complaints by Ghana against Portugal and by Portugal against Liberia, both alleging forced labor violations, were settled by acceptance of Commission recommendations.[19]

A special ILO negotiation procedure applies in freedom of association cases. Preliminary examination of such complaints is conducted by a Governing Body Committee on Freedom of Association created in 1951 and composed of three members each from government, employers, and workers. Further examination may be made by a Fact-Finding and Conciliation Commission on Freedom of Association jointly set up in 1950 by ILO and ECOSOC. Of the 450 or more freedom of association cases handled preliminarily by the Governing Body Committee, a notable recent instance examined in late 1965 and early 1966 arose from complaints by two workers' groups against Burundi, a non-member of the relevant Convention. Dissatisfied with Burundi's failure to answer inquiries, ILO asked the UN Human Rights Commission to take jurisdiction. Burundi complained that Commission involvement would intervene improperly in its internal affairs, but agreed to send a mission to ILO Headquarters in Geneva, whereupon the ILO withdrew its request to the Commission. In the resulting consultations Burundi agreed to ratify or apply ILO Conventions, receive an ILO Mission, and keep the ILO informed, adding that "we shall try, subject to the circumstances rendering it possible, to give effect to the promises we have just made." [20]

The secondary examination of freedom of association cases by the Fact-Finding and Conciliation Commission, requiring governmental consent, was employed first in 1964–65, the Government concerned being Japan. In mid-1965 Japan ratified the ILO Freedom of Association and Protection of the Right to Organize Convention of 1948. Later, Government acceptance of the Commission's report was indicated.[21] In the second such case, Greece consented in 1965 to

[19] See Chapter V, at note 26.
[20] E/4237, at 16 (1966).
[21] "On 23 January 1965 the Commission submitted certain proposals for im-

Commission consideration of a complaint which a year later was withdrawn on certain undertakings by the Greek Minister of Labor. The Commission decided to consider the case as terminated.[22]

The possible effectiveness of negotiation in protecting individuals also is shown by the experience of the two regional human rights commissions. Proceedings before the European Commission have seemed to prompt government correction of abuses.[23] An accused Government is required by Rules 44, 45, and 46 of the European Commission's Rules of Procedure to be invited to submit written and possibly oral observations on the admissibility of any complaint against it. Where a State has consented under Article 25 of the Convention to petitions against itself "from any person, non-governmental organization or group of individuals claiming to be the victim of a violation," the Commission is required by Article 28 to "undertake, together with the representatives of the parties, an examination of the [admissible] petition and, if need be, an investigation, for the effective conduct of which the States concerned shall furnish all necessary facilities, after an exchange of views with the Commission," which also "shall place itself at the disposal of the parties concerned with a view to securing a friendly settlement of the matter."

The Inter-American Commission's accomplishments in aiding oppressed Dominicans in mid-1965 relied heavily on negotiation. One of the Inter-American Commission members, Dr. Durward V. Sandifer of the United States, has described in graphic terms the negotiations his group carried on:

> The Commission repeatedly visited all the principal prisons in the Santo Domingo area and most of those in the interior. It kept up a steady pressure for release of prisoners against whom no charges had

---

mediate action. . . . They were accepted promptly and without qualification by the Government. . . . They have now been carried out in full by the Government and Diet, which . . . have shown imagination and courage in adopting a wholly new approach to the problem of labour relations in the public sector in Japan." 49 I.L.O. OFF. BULL., No. 1, Special Supp. at 482 (1966).

[22] 49 I.L.O. OFF. BULL., No. 3, Special Supp. at 87 (1966).

[23] According to Robertson, a "striking result of the Convention is the action taken by various governments to bring their legislation into line with the Convention," including "the amendment of the Austrian Code of Criminal Procedure while a number of cases attacking it were pending before the Commission." THE INTERNATIONAL PROTECTION OF HUMAN RIGHTS 123–24 (E. Luard ed. 1967).

been filed, or for proper hearings and trials, for improved food, sanitary and medical facilities and treatment of the ill. It interviewed prisoners, checked lists, searched for missing persons, and inspected cells and prison facilities.

. . . .

The Commission's effort was to maintain a steady pressure on the authorities of both Governments to maintain normal order to the extent possible under the disturbed and abnormal conditions, and to repress and punish excesses and violations by military, police, and other government personnel. It maintained continuous contact with top officials of each government from the President down, with military and police commanders, with the Procurador General and with prison commandants. It maintained a continuous stream of written representations and information through the Ministers of Foreign Affairs, and where appropriate to other officials, on all violations reported to or discovered by it. It maintained a steady follow-up on these representations.[24]

The Inter-American Commission's use of negotiations was endorsed later in 1965 by the Second Special Inter-American Conference, which resolved "to authorize the Commission to examine communications submitted to it and any other available information, so that it may address to the government of any American state a request for information deemed pertinent by the Commission, and so that it may make recommendations, when it deems this appropriate, with the objective of bringing about more effective observance of fundamental human rights." [25] The success of the two existing regional human rights bodies may have helped to stimulate the 1968 decision of the Council of Ministers of the League of Arab States to recommend to the League's Political Affairs Committee "the establishment of a permanent Arab regional Commission for Human Rights within the framework of the League of Arab States." [26]

[24] THE ASSOCIATION OF THE BAR OF THE CITY OF NEW YORK, THE DOMINICAN REPUBLIC CRISIS 1965, at 131, 132 (J. Carey ed. 1967). See also K. VASAK, LA COMMISSION INTERAMÉRICAINE DES DROITS DE L'HOMME 155–73 (1968); Schreiber & Schreiber, *The Inter-American Commission on Human Rights in the Dominican Crisis,* 22 INT'L ORG. 508 (1968); A. SCHREIBER, INTER-AMERICAN COMMISSION OF HUMAN RIGHTS (1969).

[25] Quoted 60 AM. J. INT'L L. 459 (1966). The Statute and Regulations of the Inter-American Commission appear in 1 HUMAN RIGHTS J. at 144–59 (1968).

[26] Quoted in E/CN.4/975, at 27 (1968).

New intergovernmental groups for human rights negotiation are authorized in recently drafted UN instruments. In October 1968 the first potentially global agency for human rights negotiation came into being with the effective date of the 1962 UNESCO Protocol instituting a Conciliation and Good Offices Commission to be responsible for seeking the settlement of any disputes which may arise between States parties to the Convention against Discrimination in Education.[27] The 1965 Convention on the Elimination of all Forms of Racial Discrimination established an 18-expert Committee to which States Parties must explain or clarify complaints from other States Parties, taking part if desired in the Committee's proceedings, which may be followed by recommendations by an *ad hoc* Conciliation Commission.[28] If a State Party to the Convention on Racial Discrimination has "declare[d] that it recognizes the competence of the Committee to receive and consider communications from individuals or groups of individuals within its jurisdiction claiming to be victims of a violation by that State Party," then the respondent government is required by Article 14 to "submit to the Committee written explanations or statements clarifying the matter and the remedy, if any, that may have been taken by that State."

Besides the above arrangements for negotiation as a feature of inquiry, the Racial Discrimination Convention requires States Parties to submit periodically "for consideration by the Committee, a report on the legislative, judicial, administrative or other measures which they have adopted and which give effect to the provisions of this Convention." The Committee, which may request further information, "may make suggestions and general recommendations." Similarly mild procedures are called for by the 1966 Covenant on Economic, Social and Cultural Rights. The Human Rights Commission may make "general recommendations," on which States Parties and specialized agencies may comment to ECOSOC, and it may submit

[27] E/CN.4/Sub.2/292 (1968).

[28] A/Res/2106 (XX) (1965). See note 5 in Chapter II concerning ratifications. See Newman, *The New International Tribunal on Racial Discrimination*, 56 CALIF. L. REV. 1559 (1968); and Coleman, Pollock and Robinson, *Rules of Procedure for the New Tribunal: A Proposed Draft, id.* at 1569. The provisions of the Convention are analyzed by Natan Lerner of the Institute of Jewish Affairs, World Jewish Congress, in a recently published monograph entitled "The U.N. Convention on the Elimination of All Forms of Racial Discrimination."

to the General Assembly "recommendations of a general nature and a summary of the information received." [29]

Negotiation also is called for on the part of the Human Rights Committee provided for in the 1966 UN Covenant on Civil and Political Rights and its Optional Protocol.[30] Three forms of negotiation are envisaged: (a) "general comments" on reports from Governments, which may reply with "observations"; [31] (b) "good offices" made available by the Committee, where a State Party complains against another State Party which has consented to Committee jurisdiction over such complaints; [32] and (c) compulsory "written explanations or statements clarifying the matter [raised in an individual's complaint against a consenting State Party] and the remedy, if any, that may have been taken by the State," [33] followed by the Committee's forwarding "its view to the State Party concerned and to the individual." [34]

The United States in early 1968 advanced a proposal for using negotiation as a means to aid oppressed persons in South Africa. Morris B. Abram, then US Representative in the UN Human Rights Commission, stated that:

> without detracting from the need for other approaches, we are convinced that much can also be done through this device of negotiation. By negotiation, we refer to the safeguarding of human rights through the good offices of an official operating without formal legal procedures, without the glare of publicity, depending primarily on quiet discussions with government representatives, having always in the

[29] A/Res/2200 (XXI) (1966).

[30] *Id.* See note 4 in Chapter II concerning ratifications of the Covenants and the Protocol.

[31] Covenant art. 40 (4, 5).

[32] Covenant art. 41. The Committee may call on such States "to supply any relevant information," and they "shall have the right to be represented when the matter is being considered in the Committee and to make submissions orally and/or in writing." The Committee must send a report to the States Parties concerned, with whose consent a further stage of negotiation may be conducted through the "good offices" of an *ad hoc* Conciliation Commission with power to call on the same parties for "any other relevant information" and with the duty of sending them a further report. Article 42.

[33] Protocol art. 4.

[34] Protocol art. 5. Negotiation provisions have been proposed for the still uncompleted Draft Convention on Elimination of All Forms of Religious Intolerance. See E/CN.4/920, Ann. II (1965); E/Res/1233 (XLII) (1967); A/6660 (1967).

background the possibility of exposure to public scrutiny of human rights violations as an implied threat resorted to only when absolutely necessary.[35]

Mr. Abram went on to cite the negotiation experience of the International Labor Organization, the UN High Commissioner for Refugees, the International Committee of the Red Cross,[36] the Inter-American Commission on Human Rights, and the Minorities Section of the League of Nations Secretariat. He pointed out the advantages of the device of negotiation being available without respect to ratification of any international agreement and with a minimum basis for objection on the grounds of being intervention in essentially domestic matters under UN Charter Article 2(7).[37]

[35] Press Release USUN–19, at 2 (1968); E/CN.4/SR.953, at 3–6 (1968).

[36] Fully described in Bissell, *The International Committee of the Red Cross and the Protection of Human Rights*, 1 HUMAN RIGHTS J. 255 (1968).

[37] The Secretary-General had attempted consultations with the Government of South Africa in 1960–61. See A/Conf.32/6 at 202–203 (1967). The following UN statement was issued on March 3, 1969, as Note No. 3513:

The Secretary-General has seen a press report to the effect that the South African Foreign Minister is said to have informed his Parliament that South Africa's offer to the Secretary-General to receive a personal representative to discuss South West Africa has still not been taken up.

In 1968, when the Security Council adopted resolution 246 by which it demanded that the Government of South Africa forthwith release and repatriate a number of South West Africans who had been tried in South Africa, the Secretary-General transmitted the resolution to the Minister of Foreign Affairs of South Africa and informed him that he was planning to send to South Africa a personal representative for the purposes laid down in operative paragraph 2 of that resolution.

In a letter dated 27 March 1968 (S/8506) the South African Minister of Foreign Affairs replied, among other things, that in the interest of all the peoples of South West Africa, convicted terrorists could not be released nor could their release be discussed. The communication of the Foreign Minister added that "South Africa has all along been ready and willing to enlighten whoever is objectively interested in the well-being of the inhabitants of South West Africa. In this light we shall be willing to receive your personal representative provided he is mutually acceptable, and provided also we can be assured that factual information made available to him will not, as so often in the past, be ignored."

The matter of sending a personal representative has been under consideration since that time. While it may not be too difficult to find a Secretary-General's personal representative mutually acceptable, the question is not one of enlightening whoever is objectively interested in the well-being of the inhabitants of South West Africa but one of discussing the implementation of the relevant solutions of the General Assembly and of the Security Council relating to Namibia. The Secretary-General ear-

The United States' belief in negotiation as a means of international protection was underlined by Ambassador Arthur J. Goldberg shortly after Mr. Abram's plea. Ambassador Goldberg told the Security Council in February 1968 that "earlier this week it was suggested in the Human Rights Commission that a special representative of the Secretary-General might be dispatched to Southern Africa to undertake all possible humanitarian measures to alleviate the unfortunate conditions now prevailing in the area. This suggestion was well received. Encouraged by the response of several members of the Commission, my delegation would like to offer it for the consideration of the Security Council." [38]

During 1968 and 1969 UN human rights negotiations were proposed or employed on several occasions. On August 23, 1968, eight governments introduced in the Security Council a draft resolution which would have requested the Secretary-General "to appoint and despatch immediately to Prague a Special Representative who shall seek the release and ensure the personal safety of the Czechoslovak leaders and who shall report back urgently." [39] At the same time, primarily for information-gathering purposes, the Secretary-General was seeking unsuccessfully to obtain agreement among the govern-

---

> nestly believes that, at an appropriate stage, discussions should be initiated. However, he has had no indication that at this present time such discussions could have any useful result.

The South African Prime Minister commented on March 21, 1969 that the offer to receive a UN representative who was

> acceptable to both sides . . . was not accepted by the Secretary-General. And in the spirit of the precedent created by the late Dag Hammarskjöld's visit to South Africa in 1960, we are still prepared, without prejudice to South Africa's juridical and other standpoints, to discuss matters of mutual concern. . . . But if that discussion is to be conducted in the spirit that the United Nations has already taken over South West Africa, and that they now want to come here to hear when they can have the Territory, then I am not at home for such discussions.

S/9204, Ann. I, at 15 (1969).

[38] Press Release USUN–21 (68), at 4 (1968). A similar special representative proposal had been advanced by a group of non-governmental organizations at the 1967 UN Seminar in Zambia. See note 10 in Chapter VII. The South African Prime Minister in March 1969 replied "to a friendly suggestion that was put forward by the United States of America . . . that we should receive a representative of the United Nations in South Africa unconditionally. I am sorry but I cannot do that. . . ." S/9204, Ann. I, at 14 (1969).

[39] S/8767 (1968). The apparent need quickly became academic when the leaders managed their own extrication.

ments concerned to send a second "representative to the Middle East, in particular for the purpose of meeting my reporting obligations under Security Council resolution 237 (1967) of 14 June 1967 and General Assembly resolution 2252 (ES–V) of 4 July 1967 concerning humanitarian questions." [40] The Security Council in resolution 259 (1968), described by its authors as "humanitarian," [41] then requested the Secretary-General "urgently to dispatch a special representative to the Arab territories under military occupation by Israel." Jordan had submitted details "on the inhuman and other arbitrary measures taken by the Israeli authorities against innocent people in the occupied territories," [42] but Israel insisted "that the mission should have an equal opportunity to investigate the situation of Jewish communities cruelly persecuted in the Arab countries since the recent conflict." [43] The deadlock remained,[44] and in December 1968 the General Assembly decided to establish "a special committee of three Member States to investigate Israeli practices affecting human rights of the population of the occupied territories." [45]

Towards the end of 1968 a UN official did actually negotiate on behalf of individuals with their own government. The Secretary-General's representative for West Irian consulted with the Indonesian Government regarding the "act of free choice to be made by the inhabitants of the Territory under the 1962 Agreement between Indonesia and The Netherlands. The representative received numer-

[40] A/7149–S/8699, at 1 (1968). Syria in May 1968 expressed its understanding that the Secretary-General "shall not give instructions to the Special Representative to look into the situation of the so-called Jewish communities in the Arab countries." *Id.* at 4. The Secretary-General, in a "brief legal analysis," asserted that Security Council resolution 237 (1967) "applied without question to the area occupied by Israel since 1967. Strictly interpreted it would not, however, apply to Arabs in, for example, Nazareth or Haifa, and of course could not apply to Jewish persons in Arab States since paragraph 1 is addressed solely to Israel." *Id.* at 16–17. Israel expressed "regret that the Secretariat's legal analysis should now seek to disengage itself from your own firm and published opinion of last year." *Id.* at 24.

[41] S/PV.1453, at 11 (1968).

[42] S/8820 (1968).

[43] S/PV.1453, at 42 (1968).

[44] See S/8851 (1968).

[45] A/Res/2443 (XXIII) (1968). As noted in Chapter IX at note 25, the UN Human Rights Commission at its 1969 session also instructed a group to investigate "allegations concerning Israel's violations of the 1949 Geneva Convention" on protection of civilians in occupied territories.

ous petitions and resolutions from individuals and organizations which he sent on to the Government without disclosing the sources. His proposals for release of political prisoners and to allow return of exiles were accepted by the Government.[46] When the Government's proposal for conducting the "act of free choice" by means of *musjawarah* or group discussions between regional councils and Indonesian officials was followed by disturbances, the Secretary General's representative reportedly called unsuccessfully for an amnesty and for expanded basic rights.[47] A UN statement discretely noted that "it is completely beyond the terms of reference of the United Nations Representative to make any investigation regarding matters that fall within the jurisdiction of the administering power." However, said the statement, the Representative was "trying to keep himself informed in order to assess what bearing these events might have on the act of free choice." [48]

A final instance of a UN official seeking to protect individuals who are in difficulty with their own government is the Secretary-General's Representative to Nigeria on Humanitarian Activities. His report for January through April 1969, during which time he was "on no occasion prevented from going where he wanted when he wanted or from speaking privately to anyone he wished," noted a report that "professional Ibos were not permitted by the other side to cross the lines, and those who did so did it at the risk of their lives. Coupled with this was the genuine fear of reprisals in a still fluid military situation." [49]

Although the Nigerian Federal Government, according to the same report, had been aware of the problem and had endeavored to reassure those Ibos who wished to return, the conflict continued, possibly prolonged by fear of reprisals which the Government is powerless to allay. A UN presence capable of affording at least what protection is possible through negotiation might help reassure the apprehensive Ibos. Similarly the South Vietnamese leaders of both

[46] UN Press Release SG/1723 and SG/1727 (1969). In early 1969 a special representative of the Secretary-General assisted in solving a partially human rights problem in Equatorial Guinea, from which Spanish nationals were able to withdraw. See UN Press Release SG/SM/1073 (1969); S/9055; S/9066; S/9101 (1969).

[47] N.Y. Times, May 11, 1969, §1, at 3, col. 4.

[48] Note No. 3530 (1969).

[49] UN Press Release SG/1731 (1969).

sides might be readier to lay down their arms if such an impartial agency would remain to watch over their safety. To the same effect, Bilder has suggested—as to white Rhodesians and South Africans —that "given credible guarantees that their own human rights would be safeguarded, perhaps coupled with international commitments for long term technical and economic assistance to prepare black populations for eventual control, some compromise and progress might be achieved." [50]

The possibility of protecting threatened minorities through a UN official stationed in Nigeria, South Vietnam, Rhodesia, or South Africa recalls a similar proposal advanced in another troubled country and adopted in a certain form. Cyprus declared in 1965 its willingness to accept for a time ". . . by way of international guarantee . . . the presence in Cyprus of a United Nations Commissioner" to protect the Turkish minority.[51] The declaration was reiterated in 1969 and described as a "legally binding document." [52] While not formally accepted by the minority group, Cyprus' commissioner proposal has in a sense been carried out, through the similar device of UNCIVPOL, civilian policemen from several countries who help to keep the peace between the two communities.[53] UNCIVPOL's effectiveness may well depend on the presence as well of UNFICYP, the UN's military force.

The Cyprus experience probably shows that human rights protection through UN negotiation is helpful when coupled with other factors working towards solution of underlying problems. It is doubtful if peace can be found in any of the world's other trouble spots through the presence of international officials alone.

[50] Bilder, *Rethinking International Human Rights: Some Basic Questions,* 1969 WIS. L. REV. 171, 204 (1969).

[51] A/6039 (1965). Cyprus explained the proposal in a General Assembly Committee. A/C.1/PV.1141, at 71 (1965).

[52] S/9241, at 2 (1969); also S/PV.1474, at 62 (1969).

[53] See S/9233, at 15, 17 (1969); S/8914, at 13–14 (1969); S/8446, at 24 (1968); S/8286, at 29–34 (1967); S/7969 (1967); S/7611, at 27 (1966).

Chapter IX

Investigation as a Means
of Protection

"The mere existence of an official and impartial fact-finding body might deter violations of human rights," according to the Montreal Statement of the Assembly for Human Rights.[1] However, the Statement noted "the absence of effective and impartial fact-finding mechanisms," and urged the UN Human Rights Commission to "establish a committee of experts to which the Commission could refer any communication received by it in order to determine whether the evidence presented shows a gross violation of human rights or a consistent pattern of violations of such rights." The Commission responded in March 1969 with a far-reaching proposal which, if approved by ECOSOC and employed according to its terms, will revolutionize the UN's role in protecting human rights. The UN's earlier practice gave little hint of any such development.

During the United Nations' first two decades, it seemed to be firmly established that the UN would take no action with respect to the complaints of persons claiming to be oppressed by their own governments. However, towards the end of these two decades, as described in Chapter XII, a set of practices grew up, applicable only to colonies and to the Republic of South Africa, which took account of individuals' complaints and gave them wide notice. So extensive a set of practices seemed bound in the end to lap over into the broader area of human rights complaints generally.

In the first half of the decade of the 1960's, the Committee on Colonialism of the UN General Assembly, followed shortly thereafter by the Committee on South African Apartheid, began holding hearings for complainants and publishing their written complaints. While some persons felt that this process produced very few results, the mere publication, either in writing or orally, of individuals' complaints was a new field of activity for the UN. As a result of some of the complaints which were brought to the surface by this process in

[1] Chapter II, at note 20.

the Colonialism Committee, the General Assembly in October of 1966 by its landmark resolution 2144 invited the Economic and Social Council and the Commission on Human Rights to give urgent consideration to ways and means of improving the capacity of the UN to put a stop to violations of human rights wherever they might occur. The resolution was, in one view, "in accordance with an entirely new doctrine, namely, that it is the right and duty of the United Nations to consider specific violations of human rights and to recommend appropriate measures to halt such violations wherever they may occur." [2] The new doctrine opened a door which would be difficult to close. Efforts were made to close the door during the February–March 1968 session of the UN Human Rights Commission, but other efforts kept it open.[3]

How far open the door is, and how much effort is necessary to keep it even that far open, can be seen by looking at developments which have occurred since October 1966 when the General Assembly declared the "new doctrine." The UN Human Rights Commission, meeting in early 1967 shortly after Assembly resolution 2144 was adopted, resolved to ask the Sub-Commission on Prevention of Discrimination and Protection of Minorities to bring to the Commission's attention any situation whch the Sub-Commission had reasonable cause to believe revealed a consistent pattern of violations of human rights and fundamental freedoms in any country, including policies of racial discrimination, segregation, and apartheid, with particular reference to colonial and dependent territories.[4] In addition, the Human Rights Commission asked the Sub-Commission to prepare a report containing information on violations of human rights and fundamental freedoms from all available sources.

A little later, in June 1967, the ECOSOC gave its blessing to these arrangements, and in addition took a step of great significance by giving authority to both the Commission and the Sub-Commis-

[2] The Chairman of the General Assembly's Third Committee, Erik Nettel of Austria, speaking at the special meeting of the General Assembly on December 9, 1968, in commemoration of the twentieth anniversary of the Universal Declaration of Human Rights. UN Office of Public Information Newsletter No. 8, Supp. 1, at 31 (1969).

[3] The events at the Human Rights Commission's 1967 and 1968 sessions described herein are officially set forth in its Reports, E/4475–E/CN.4/972, at 58–79 (1968) and E/4621–E/CN.4/1007, at 135–48 (1969).

[4] Commission resolution 8 (XXIII); see Report of the Twenty-Third Session, E/4322–E/CN.4/940, at 131 (1967).

sion to inspect all of the many thousands of written human rights complaints which flow year by year to the UN.[5] This authority was granted for the explicit purpose of complying with the duties assigned to the Commission and Sub-Commission with respect to their annual consideration of the question of violations of fundamental rights throughout the world. Prior to June 1967, the thousands of written complaints coming to the UN each year were handled in accordance with a highly restrictive arrangement contained in ECOSOC resolution 728F of 1959, the latest of a series of similar provisions dating back to the early days of UN.[6] Under these rules, complaints relating to any part of the world other than colonies or South Africa simply were filed at UN Headquarters and a form letter sent to the complainant advising substantially that nothing could be done. A copy was sent without the name of the author to the state complained against for any comments which it might care to make.

The new procedure approved by ECOSOC, allowing the Commission and Sub-Commission to look at these complaints in the original form instead of in the form of summaries prepared by the Secretariat, first was put into effect at the meeting of the Sub-Commission in Geneva in October 1967. The outcome was a resolution, adopted without any contrary vote, which recommended to the Human Rights Commission further investigation concerning not only those parts of Southern Africa which had become traditional targets of UN investigation, but also two countries elsewhere in the world, Greece and Haiti.[7] It was in this manner that the Sub-Commission complied with the Commission's request that situations revealing consistent patterns of violations be brought to the Commission's attention. The Commission's other request, that the Sub-Commission

[5] E/Res/1235 (XLII). The Commission and Sub-Commission were authorized "to examine information relevant to gross violations of human rights and fundamental freedoms . . . contained in the communications listed" under resolution 728F (XVIII).

[6] As early as 1947 the Economic and Social Council in resolution 75(V) had approved a statement that the Human Rights Commission "recognizes that it has no power to take any action in regard to any complaints concerning human rights." A Secretariat history of UN procedures for dealing with human rights complaints was included in A/Conf.32/6, at 142–49 (1968), and is reproduced in Appendix B hereto.

[7] See report of Sub-Commission's Twentieth Session, E/CN.4/947–E/CN.4/Sub.2/286, at 38 (1967).

prepare a report containing information on violations from all available sources, was met by means of a one-page annex to the resoultion.[8] As to Southern Africa, this annex cited various documents already published by the UN and therefore fully available to any member of the public. As to Greece and Haiti, however, a new departure was represented in the annex, which referred to communications received by the Sub-Commission pursuant to ECOSOC resolution 1235 and identified at a meeting of the Sub-Commission held in private by virtue of ECOSOC resolution 728F.[9] In the case of Greece, the government's response was also cited. By this kind of coded reference, the secrecy of the communications was retained, while at the same time making clear that definite documents, two in the case of Greece and one in the case of Haiti, were being specified and could be individually identified through reference to the minutes of the private Sub-Commission meeting, which, though unpublished, were available to all Sub-Commission members.

When the matter came before the Human Rights Commission meeting in February and March 1968, an assortment of currents swirled and surged over a period of several days, buffeting but finally leaving intact the flimsy structure created during the previous months for the examination of communications complaining about governmental oppression anywhere in the world. The Commission declined the Sub-Commission's request for further investigation of Greece and Haiti, but did not scold the lower body for requesting it. Representatives of the Greek and Haitian Governments spoke at length before the Human Rights Commission in an effort to vindicate their governments and to defend them against any accusation of human rights violation. The Greek representative based his defense primarily on the proposition that his government had properly exercised its right of derogation, which he implied precluded all possibility of human rights violations.[10] The Haitian actually discussed

---

[8] *Id.* at 42.

[9] ECOSOC resolution 728F (XXVIII) requested the Secretary-General to distribute "in private meeting" to Commission and Sub-Commission members "a confidential list containing a brief indication of the substance" of complaints alleging specific human rights violations. ECOSOC resolution 1235 (XLII) authorized examination by the Commission and Sub-Commission of "information . . . contained in the communications listed . . . pursuant to . . . resolution 728F."

[10] E/4475–E/CN.4/972, at 66–67 (1968).

at length various of the hitherto confidential communications directed at his government.[11]

Self-defense by the governments accused was therefore one of the currents surging at the Human Rights Commission meeting in early 1968. Political attacks also were heard. The Soviet Union launched an attack against Greece, also assaulting Israel because of its alleged aggression, and the United States in regard to Vietnam.[12] No one else attacked Greece, although the representative of Sweden, which had taken an initiative in the Council of Europe against the Greek régime, spoke of the service rendered by the Sub-Commission in bringing situations to the Commission's attention.[13] No government representative attacked Haiti, nor did any non-governmental organization, although one non-governmental organization did attack Greece,[14] and one attacked Israel.

By launching its three-pronged attack, the Soviet Union was sanctioning a broad interpretation of the proper scope of the UN's concern with the agenda item on violations of human rights. Its assaults against Greece, Israel, and the United States were inconsistent with the narrower view that only racial discrimination like that in Southern Africa is a proper human rights subject for UN concern.

The United Arab Republic advanced a theory which may be considered as in part a separate current from that of mere political attack because of its abstract rather than *ad hoc* approach. The Egyptian principle explicitly proposed was that the Commission should concern itself not only with Southern Africa, but also with human rights violations occurring in war situations.[15] This scope enabled it to bring under its guns both Israel and the United States, a substantial advance beyond the notion that the Sub-Commission, under its existing authority, was confined to apartheid in Southern Africa and other phenomena of equal virulence. The latter position was argued

[11] *Id.* at 69. See also E/CN.4/SR.970 (1968).

[12] E/CN.4/SR.965 (1968).

[13] E/CN.4/SR.964 (1968).

[14] At the Teheran Conference on Human Rights in May 1968 Greece responded to a critical presentation by the International Confederation of Free Trade Unions by asserting that "the ICFTU has already aired the same charges before the Commission on Human Rights which after exhaustive debate 'reached the consensus . . . that no action be taken' (Document E/CN.4/972)." A/Conf. 32/35, at 3 (1968).

[15] E/CN.4/SR.966 (1968).

by some countries, with the suggestion being made that consideration of other types of wrongs than apartheid would jeopardize the
sovereignty of any nation represented in the Commission and open
it to malicious and slanderous attack.

Tanzania introduced a draft resolution which, while not clearly
saying so, was described by its author as having the purpose of cut-
ting down the jurisdiction of the Sub-Commission to limit it in the
future to matters of apartheid and similar practices in southern
Africa.[16] The features of the Tanzanian resolution which were most
objectionable from the US standpoint were eliminated upon withdrawal of a separate US proposal. The watered-down Tanzanian
resolution would have left the record somewhat obscure and given a
basis for argument in the Sub-Commission at its next session in October 1968, over whether the Commission in fact had reduced the
Sub-Commission's area of responsibility. However, Austria and the
Philippines submitted amendments to the Tanzanian proposal to endorse fully and renew the Sub-Commission's previously wide scope,
whereupon Tanzania withdrew its resolution altogether.[17]

This development left no proposal before the Commission under
the pending agenda item except an entirely separate UAR draft
aimed at Israel. The anti-Israel draft was presented as being humanitarian in purpose, and dealt with persons displaced during hos-
tilities and their right to return to their homes. Compromise on the
wording, brought about through lengthy consultations, resulted in
language that all members except Israel were able to support, while
even Israel did not find it necessary to vote against or even abstain,
but simply did not participate in the voting.[18] The significance of
the consultations can be judged by the fact that the original wording included the word "deportation," which, if found as a fact,
would have rendered Israel subject to being charged with "crimes
against humanity," on the theory advanced at other times in the
Commission that the definition in the Nuremberg Charter can be
applied to current situations.[19]

[16] Quoted in the Commission's Report, E/4475–E/CN.4/972, at 59 (1968).
[17] Id. at 62.
[18] Id. at 77–79.
[19] The Commission's Special Rapporteur on apartheid and racial discrimination presented a report asserting that conditions in southern Africa "constitute
a 'crime against humanity' within the language of Article 6(c) of the 1945 London Charter of the International Military Tribunal which sat at Nuremberg."
E/CN.4/949/Add.4, at 496 (1968).

The unanimous adoption of the UAR resolution can be said to have confirmed that the UN's geographic capacity to take specific positions with respect to human rights violations was as broad as the whole world. While it is true that the Middle East situation is an international one, an international war in this respect is not far from a war within the borders of one country. This fact is demonstrated in the Geneva Conventions of 1949, which concern themselves with both types of hostility. Once into the sphere of civil war, it is no great step to be concerned also with civil unrest short of war. The UAR resolution, together with the fact that the Commission left undisturbed the broad scope of the Sub-Commission's authority to concern itself with human rights violations the world over, indicated that international human rights protection procedures were evolving apart from those embodied in treaties. While non-treaty procedures seem essential in view of the reluctance or refusal of certain governments to ratify human rights treaties [20] and the limited scope of their protection for the oppressed,[21] the rate of development of such procedures depends on the ingenuity of their proponents.

Ingenuity was indeed applied at the next following Sub-Commission session, held at Geneva in October 1968. Specific cases such as Greece and Haiti were set aside for the moment and attention given to improving methods. The Greek situation, in any event, was being handled by the Council of Europe with an array of procedures far exceeding anything yet devised by the UN. Besides the coercive measures described in Chapter IV, investigation was being applied in a manner bound to inspire those persons wishing to see the UN more active in the field.

Shortly before the UN Sub-Commission met, a Council of Europe

[20] As noted in Chapter II, the United States has become a party to only two human rights treaties in the past twenty years, the treaty on practices akin to slavery and the protocol on refugees, to which the Senate gave its advice and consent in 1967 and 1968 respectively, while several others dealing with subjects such as genocide, political rights of women, and forced labor have not been approved. The Communist countries, on the other hand, usually seek to avoid compulsory judicial jurisdiction over such treaties. See Carey, *Implementing Human Rights Conventions: The Soviet View*, 53 Ky. L.J. 115 (1964).

[21] Of the non-regional treaties, only the 1965 Convention on the Elimination of All Forms of Racial Discrimination provides for receipt of petitions from individuals, and that at the separate option of States Parties. The 1966 Covenant on Civil and Political Rights contains no such provision, although an Optional Protocol thereto does do so.

Human Rights Sub-Commission in September 1968 began hearing the parties on the merits of the applications brought against the Greek Government by Denmark, Norway, Sweden, and The Netherlands. Further hearings in Strasbourg were held in November and December, 29 witnesses testifying in all. Hearings *in camera* of 51 witnesses in Greece were held in March 1969, but they were terminated when the Sub-Commission felt it was being barred unjustifiably by the Government from hearing other witnesses and visiting certain places of detention other than the Asphalia (security police) stations in Athens and Piraeus.[22] After final submissions by the parties and any further evidence, the plenary Commission must give the Committee of Ministers its opinion on whether the Convention has been violated. Final decision, absent a settlement among the parties, will be by the Committee of Ministers, since Greece has not accepted the jurisdiction of the European Court of Human Rights.

The UN Sub-Commission, under the leadership of Professor John P. Humphrey of Canada, former Director of the UN Division of Human Rights, adopted in October 1968 a far-reaching resolution on procedures for handling complaints.[23] After lengthy debate in the Human Rights Commission in March 1969, in which US Representative Rita Hauser took a strong stand in favor of the Sub-Commission's resolution, the text was passed along with little change to the Economic and Social Council.[24] ECOSOC approval could help eliminate the double standard on treatment of complaints described in Chapter XII. Thereafter complaints relating to any part of the world would be subject to orderly UN inquiry and possible public exposure.

The Humphrey rules, as passed by the Commission, would have a

[22] Council of Europe Press Release C (69) 11 (1969). See also Council of Europe Press Release C (69) 10 (1969), which cited previous visits of Sub-Commissions or delegated members to Cyprus in 1958, Vienna in 1966 and 1967, and Berlin in 1967.

[23] Resolution 2 (XXI), E/CN.4/976–E/CN.4/Sub.2/294, at 34 (1968). The resolution was co-sponsored with Mr. Humphrey by members from Kenya, UAR, and India. The members from Poland and the USSR voted against, and five members abstained.

[24] E/4621–E/CN.4/1007, at 212 (1969). The Commission vote was 15–4–12. Two proposed deletions failed by votes of 12–14–3 and 13–13–5. ECOSOC in June 1969 asked for the comments of UN members on the proposed new procedures, and invited further study by the Commission. E/Res/1422 and Corr. 1 (XLVI) (1969).

Sub-Commission working group meet in separate session to consider all complaints coming to the UN and to refer to the Sub-Commission those complaints revealing a consistent pattern of gross violations of human rights. The full Sub-Commission would then decide whether to refer particular situations to the Commission, which in turn would determine whether any such situation warranted either its own further study or investigation by an *ad hoc* group which it appointed. Investigation would not proceed without consent from the Government accused, a practice followed to good effect by the ILO in freedom of association cases where the great bulk of problems are disposed of by preliminary inquiries for which consent is not required. Secrecy until the Commission's final stages should encourage governments to adjust in private without indignity rather than suffer full exposure.

Another UN Human Rights Commission action at its 1969 session was to launch an investigation by the members of its *Ad Hoc* Working Group of Experts—described in Chapter X—acting as a Special Working Group, into charges of violations in Israeli-held lands of the Geneva Convention of 1949 on Protection of Civilian Persons in Time of War.[25] This step duplicated action already taken the previous fall by the General Assembly in establishing its own group for a similar purpose.[26] The need for an orderly probe of Middle Eastern human rights is made clear by the very severity of the charges exchanged by Israel and her neighbors. All parties would be served by the opportunity to test the allegations through quasi-judicial scrutiny. The UAR asserted to the Human Rights Commission in February, for example, that

> Israeli occupying forces fired on demonstrators after tear gas bombs had failed to disperse them, thus resulting in the killing and wounding of more than a hundred school girls between the ages of fifteen and twenty, several of whom were transported to hospitals as a result of bullet wounds inflicted by occupying forces. . . . Two weeks ago, when women and children carried out peaceful demonstrations in the town of Rafah to protest against the detention of the entire male pop-

[25] Commission resolution 6 (XXV), E/4621–E/CN.4/1007, at 183 (1969). The Special Working Group began a series of meetings on June 30, 1969. Other new tasks assigned to the *Ad Hoc* Group are described in Chapter X.

[26] A/Res/2443 (XXIII) Concerning procedures for the appointment of the three states comprising the group, see A/7495 and Add.1, 2 (1969).

ulation of the town, they were savagely confronted by Israeli occupation forces and many mercilessly fired upon, as a result of which women were killed and wounded.[27]

When the same charges were made to the Secretary-General and circulated publicly,[28] Israel had its answer similarly aired, but no impartial body weighed the two positions and found the facts. Israel said that:

> under Egyptian inspiration, the terrorist organizations do not shrink from exploiting women and children in furtherance of their objectives nor do they show any qualms about wounding peaceful Arab civilians, as indeed occurred again in the course of the demonstration by the schoolgirls in Gaza on 2 February 1969; and as has happened on other occasions when grenades have been thrown at local schools and cinemas, or at Israeli vehicles passing through Gaza's streets when they are full of local inhabitants. For instance, on 3 February 1969 a grenade was thrown at an Israeli vehicle in the main square of Gaza at a time when it was crowded with passers-by. The grenade missed the vehicle, but wounded ten of the local inhabitants, two of whom have since died, one a child aged seven and the other a young man aged nineteen. After the perpetrators had been apprehended, they boasted quite openly to the commander of the Gaza area, Brigadier-General Mota Gur, that it was a matter of utter indifference to them whether civilians were being killed so long as the normal rhythm of life was being disturbed and hostility to the Israeli forces increased.[29]

Israel's consent to UN investigations in the occupied Arab territories has been conditioned on reciprocal inquiry into the plight of Jews in Arab countries. Israel's own accusations are serious enough to engage UN attention, and the respondent governments should welcome the opportunity to rebut charges such as "the nazi-like persecution of the Jews of Iraq." [30]

Investigation is being increasingly used by the UN in human

[27] E/CN.4/1003 (1969).

[28] S/8991 (1969). See also similar accusations in 1969 documents A/7518–S/9028, S/9131, S/9141, and S/9164 (Syria A/7517–S/9029 (Southern Yemen); and A/7531–S/9102, A/7542–S/9162, A/7551–S/9197, and A/7559–S/9225 (Jordan).

[29] A/7506–S/8994 (1969). See also denials in A/7544–S/9174 and A/7554–S/9208 (1969).

[30] A/7102 (1968). See also Israeli complaints in S/8997, S/9031, S/9095, and S/9277 (1969).

rights matters, as appears from this and the succeeding three chapters. The UN General Assembly's "belief that an important contribution to the peaceful settlement of disputes could be made by providing for impartial fact-finding" [31] may come to be matched by an equally valid belief in the efficacy of impartial fact-finding in civil and political rights problems.

[31] A/Res/2182 (XXI) (1966).

Chapter X

The UN's Southern Africa Investigations

INTRODUCTION

During the past several years, the UN has conducted experiments in human rights investigation whose results and techniques can be usefully examined for future guidance. When the Commission on Human Rights early in 1967 established by resolution an *Ad Hoc* Group of Experts to "investigate the charges of torture and ill-treatment of prisoners, detainees or persons in police custody in South Africa," [1] the head of the Secretariat's Human Rights Division described it as "one of the first occasions that an inquiry of this type had been organized under United Nations auspices." He predicted that "the work that the Group did would probably provide a number of examples for future investigations." [2]

The predication of future investigations was quickly and repeatedly borne out. The *Ad Hoc* Group had scarcely begun its work on South African prisoners when, in June 1967, ECOSOC gave it the further area of South African trade union rights to examine. [3] No sooner was the Group's report on this subject adopted in February 1968 [4] than the Human Rights Commission expanded the Group's scope on prisoners to most of southern Africa. [5] ECOSOC in May 1968 asked the Group to look at trade union rights in Southern Rhodesia and Southwest Africa as well as South Africa itself. [6]

[1] Human Rights Commission resolution 2 (XXIII), quoted in Report on the Twenty-Third Session, E/4322–E/CN.4/940, at 76–78 (1967). The vote was 25–0–5, the abstainers being France, Italy, New Zealand, the UK, and the US.

[2] E/CN.4/AC.22/SR.1, at 4 (1967).

[3] E/Res/1216 (XLII) (1967). ECOSOC also approved the Working Group's formation by the Commission, and "condemn[ed] the Government of South Africa for refusing to cooperate with the United Nations in expediting the work of the *Ad Hoc* Group of Experts." E/Res/1236 (XLII) (1967).

[4] E/4459 (1968).

[5] Commission resolution 2 (XXIV), E/4475–E/CN.4/972, at 145–46 (1968). This resolution also endorses the conclusions and recommendations of the *Ad Hoc* Working Group.

[6] E/Res/1302 (XLIV) (1968).

Meantime the UN Sub-Commission on Prevention of Discrimination and Protection of Minorities had urged investigations by similar working groups of conditions not only in southern Africa but also in Greece and Haiti.[7] As described in Chapter IX, the latter two countries have not been further scrutinized, but Israeli-occupied Arab lands are the subject of human rights inquiries launched in 1968 by the General Assembly and in 1969 by the UN Human Rights Commission.

Such an outbreak of human rights investigation is a novel development for the UN. In spite of the Charter's authorization to ECOSOC in Article 62(2) to "make recommendations for the purpose of promoting respect for, and observance of, human rights and fundamental freedoms for all,"[7] ECOSOC as early as 1947 approved a statement that the Human Rights Commission "recognizes that it has no power to take any action in regard to any complaints concerning human rights."[8] While European and Inter-American regional human rights methods were being evolved, the UN lagged behind except as human rights were touched by assaults on colonialism and South African apartheid.[9] The *Ad Hoc* Group was breaking new ground when it undertook a systematic inquiry of the treatment of South African prisoners.

In view of the novelty of the *Ad Hoc* Group's endeavors, its methods are worthy of note as possible precedents for succeeding inquiries. The Group was given, by its basic resolution, wide authority to "(b) Receive communications and hear witnesses and use such modalities of procedure as it may deem appropriate; [and] (c) Recommend action to be taken in concrete cases." Its use of that power will be examined first.

NATURE OF AD HOC GROUP'S PROCEDURES

While the *Ad Hoc* Group had the power under the resolution establishing it to "use such modalities of procedure as it may deem appropriate," it adopted no formal rules and seldom reached explicit

---

[7] Sub-Commission resolution 3 (XX), quoted in Report on the Twentieth Session, E/CN.4/947–E/CN.4/Sub.2/286, at 38 (1967).

[8] E/Res/75(V) (1947). Similar provisions were adopted in later resolutions. See Chapter IX.

[9] See Chapter XII.

procedural decisions. A member of the Group, Professor Felix Ermacora, reported after its first inquiry that

> the working group has not discussed and established specific rules of procedure. . . . The only points which were agreed upon were that the statements of the witnesses and the questions of the Commissioners were to be recorded in full and that every witness was to be asked to take an oath or to give a declaration before his statement . . . taken . . . from Article 55 of the rules of procedure of the European Commission of Human Rights. All the other problems have been solved by tacit consent through the behaviour of the group's members and of the Chairman.[10]

An inquiry which dealt so casually with procedural questions was bound to be followed by calls for more precision. The call came a few months after the Group's report on South African prisoners. The 1968 Teheran International Conference on Human Rights urged ECOSOC to ask the Human Rights Commission to prepare "model rules of procedure for the guidance of the United Nations bodies concerned." [11] The Commission at its 1969 session decided to prepare model rules and asked the Secretariat for a draft.[12] The groundwork for drafting such model rules might be laid by examining the Working Group's *de facto* procedures, as they may be iden-

---

[10] Ermacora, *International Enquiry Commissions in the Field of Human Rights*, 1 HUMAN RIGHTS J. 180, 192 (1968). In contrast, the General Assembly's 1963 inquiry into allegations of religious persecution in South Viet Nam did employ written rules of procedure, however brief. 18 U.N. GAOR, Annexes, Agenda Item No. 77, at 77–78.

[11] A/Conf.32/34, at 42 (1968). The Teheran Conference also may have been influenced by the situation in the General Assembly's "Committee of 24" on decolonization, where no rules existed to guide a Sub-Committee on petitions in deciding which of the many complaints it receives should be published. In a debate the prior fall Uruguay had urged that the full Committee "indicate norms and standards to the Sub-Committee on Petitions," since "we must be the judges . . . as to whether certain documents offered for circulation should be given world publicity through the United Nations." A/AC.109/PV.569, at 26–27 (1967). The Chairman of the "Committee of 24" shared the "view that at some future date the Sub-Committee on Petitions should have some terms of reference. However, in the absence of terms of reference, I suppose we have to operate in the same way as we have operated in the past." *Id.* at 37. The UK argued that "the only defensible criteria which can be applied by the Sub-Committee are whether a communication is relevant and whether it is from someone who has a claim to have his views considered. . . ." *Id.* at 42.

[12] E/4621–E/CN.4/1007, at 185 (1969).

tified from the record and report of its initial investigations. The setting in which the Group arose should first be sketched.

ORIGINS OF THE AD HOC GROUP

Shortly before the UN Human Rights Commission's early-1967 session, the General Assembly's Special Committee on the Policies of Apartheid of the Government of the Republic of South Africa drew its attention "to the continuing ill-treatment of prisoners, detainees and persons in police custody in the Republic of South Africa, particularly the numerous opponents of apartheid who have been imprisoned under arbitrary laws." [13] The Commission was asked in the same document "to secure an international investigation with a view to ameliorating the conditions of these victims." The document referred to the 1964 and 1965 reports of the Apartheid Committee in which it had "suggested the establishment of an international commission composed of eminent jurists and prison officials to investigate the charges of torture and ill-treatment of prisoners in South Africa." The earlier suggestions, the document stated, had not been "pressed in the General Assembly because it was hoped that the expression of international concern might persuade the South African Government to improve conditions so as to conform with civilized standards and the regulations in South Africa itself."

Seven separate Apartheid Committee documents containing allegations of ill-treatment were listed in the same request for Commission action. These documents were considered by the Commission, together with a further complaint, and denials, written and oral, from the South African Government. The Commission in the March 1967 resolution formed the "*Ad Hoc* Working Group of Experts composed of eminent jurists and prison officials to be appointed by the Chairman." The resolution's preamble recited that "the General Assembly by its resolution 2144A (XXI), paragraph 12, invited the Commission to give urgent consideration to ways and means of improving the capacity of the United Nations to put a stop to violations of human rights wherever they may occur." [14] The Commission also reached for authority back to ECOSOC resolution 9 (II) of 1946, which empowered the Commission to "call in *ad hoc* work-

[13] E/CN.4/950, at 9 (1967).
[14] *Id.* at 5.

ing groups of nongovernmental experts in specialized fields or individual experts, without further reference to the Council [ECOSOC], but with the approval of the President of the Council and the Secretary-General." [15]

While establishing a group to "investigate the charges," the Commission in its resolution with little consistency "condemn[ed] the practices described and complained of in the above-cited documents as constituting a double injury against the victims of the inhuman policies of apartheid . . . who are imprisoned or detained for opposing and violating those policies." The Chairman's interpretation of the Commission's action was even less consistent with the notion of investigation. He reported to the UN Secretary-General that "in the course of the Commission's meetings, it was established that persons imprisoned in South Africa were subjected to cruel and inhuman treatment." [16] Continuing, he indicated a possible reason for investigating charges considered to be already proven: "In establishing the *ad hoc* working group of experts, composed of eminent jurists, the Commission was convinced that the group's activities would help to defend the rights of opponents of apartheid who had been seized and imprisoned."

As the Chairman's words disclosed, the resolution's formula of including "prison officials" besides "eminent jurists" was abandoned, along with any notion of recruiting members outside the Commission. The Chairman appointed to the Group Commission members Ibrahima Boye, Procureur général of Senegal, who served as Chairman-Rapporteur; Felix Ermacora, Professor of Public Law at the University of Vienna; Branimir Janković, Rector of the University

---

[15] The United States sought to subject creation of the *Ad Hoc* Group to ECOSOC's approval. E/4322–E/CN.4/940, at 64 (1967). "The Office of Legal Affairs, which had been consulted, doubted whether the Council resolution [9 (II)] of 21 June 1946 was applicable to the establishment of a commission with the powers set forth in the draft resolutions before the Commission, particularly the power of investigation." E/CN.4/SR.914, at 6 (1967). The terms of reference of the Commission, established by ECOSOC resolution 5 (I) of Feb. 16, 1946, and amended by resolution 9 (II), are quoted in E/CN.4/AC.24/L.2, Ann. (1969).

[16] E/CN.4/950, at 11 (1967). The United States differed: "As the Austrian representative had pointed out, the allegations in the documents communicated by the Acting Chairman of the Special Committee were not proved, which was why the Commission was considering the establishment of an international commission of inquiry to verify the alleged facts." E/CN.4/SR.910, at 9 (1967).

of Nis, Yugoslavia; Luis Marchand Stens, Professor of International Law and Deputy Permanent Representative of Peru to the UN Office in Geneva; and Waldo Emerson Waldron-Ramsey, barrister/economist and Counsellor at the Tanzanian Mission to the UN.

Evidence before the Group

The Group searched widely for evidence. All UN Member States were asked for information, particularly the names of witnesses. A communiqué was issued through the UN Office of Public Information inviting contact from "all the persons who believe that they could provide specific and relevant information on this matter, in particular those who have been 'imprisoned or detained for opposing or violating the policies of apartheid.' " [17] The Group met in New York, London, Dar es Salaam, and Geneva, but was denied entry into South Africa. In the course of its 44 meetings, 13 of which were devoted to preparation of the report, the Group heard 25 witnesses and received written statements from 13 of them as well as from three other persons. Testimony was tape-recorded and, except for that of witnesses heard in closed sessions, was published currently. Questions put by Working Group members were summarized, while the witnesses' words were included verbatim. Oral testimony was tested occasionally by means of cross-examination ostensibly designed to probe for flaws in its credibility.[18] First issued as single "provisional" documents, the transcripts were reproduced in the Group's report, with the exception of testimony referred to as being in a "restricted document." [19]

The Group omitted from its report a significant document—a 1964 study of South African prisoners by Dr. Georg Hoffman, Delegate General of the International Committee of the Red Cross.[20] In accordance with ICRC practice, the study had been sent privately to the South African Government, which later distributed it through

[17] E/CN.4/950, at 14 (1967).
[18] See E/CN.4/AC.22/SR.29, at 5, 8, 10, 11 (1967).
[19] E/CN.4/950, at 384 (1967).
[20] Since the ICRC study and letter of transmittal have not been published in full to the author's present knowledge, citation for quotations which follow is not possible. Concerning the ICRC's human rights activities, see Bissell, *The International Committee of the Red Cross and the Protection of Human Rights*, 1 HUMAN RIGHTS J. 255 (1968).

the Secretariat to the Working Group.[21] A 1967 visit to South African prisoners by ICRC representative G. C. Senn also was referred to by the Group, but no report thereon was yet before it.[22] To check the authenticity of the document distributed by South Africa, the *Ad Hoc* Group wrote the ICRC asking "whether or not the report on conditions in South African prisons by Dr. Georg Hoffman . . . corresponds exactly and completely to the report prepared by the International Committee of the Red Cross." The Group further asked about "the circumstances in which the investigation . . . was undertaken and, in particular, as to whether the investigation was initiated by the Committee or by the Government of South Africa." [23]

The ICRC's reply assured the Group that the study as distributed by South Africa was authentic, but declined the Group's request for an interview. The ICRC explained that it had asked the South African Government for permission, which was finally granted, to carry out the visits. The reply explained how the four Geneva Conventions of 1949 govern its activities in case of armed conflict between States and how, by analogy, the same rules are followed in civil wars.

> On the other hand, the Geneva Conventions are not applicable to visits of nationals of a State who are interned by reason of special circumstances prevailing within the State. Visits by the ICRC to such persons may only be carried out with the authorization of the government concerned. Reports we issue for these visits are sent only to the government which authorized the visits. In no case does the ICRC give any publicity to these reports nor does it communicate them to third parties, whoever they may be. There has been no exception to this procedure applied by the ICRC and approved by governments generally. The purpose of ICRC visits to persons deprived of their freedom is solely to give them moral and material support and to ensure that they are humanely treated; in that connection the ICRC may intervene to obtain improvements in detention conditions. Whilst there is no secrecy about this work of the Red Cross, neither is there any publicity.[24]

[21] E/CN.4/950, at 32 (1967).
[22] *Id.* at 33. ICRC stated that this mission was not completed as of June 1967. *Id.* at 36.
[23] *Id.* at 34.
[24] *Id.* at 35–36.

The Working Group seemed to distrust the ICRC study. The report asserted "that they [the Group] are all better qualified, as members of the legal professions [*sic*], than a humanitarian organization to carry out the task entrusted to them," and recalled that "several representatives to the twenty-third session of the Commission on Human Rights considered that it would be completely unacceptable to entrust the inquiry to a single person, even to an official of the Red Cross (E/4322, para. 230), at the same time that Government authorized the ICRC to visit its prisons. . . ."[25] The Group concluded that:

> South Africa is clearly seeking to create confusion by publishing another report by the Red Cross at a time when the Working Group publishes its study and conclusions. The Working Group deeply regrets that the ICRC, a non-governmental organization, should have placed itself in such a position as to appear to lend itself to such manoeuvres. . . .
>
> [T]he Working Group notes that: (i) political prisoners are inclined to be suspicious of officials invited by the Government of the Republic of South Africa; (ii) such persons can inspect only what the authorities care to show them; (iii) living conditions in the prisons have not changed, despite Mr. Hoffman's visit; (iv) it is clear from the testimony that when an inspection is announced, a special effort is made to bring the prisons into conformity with the rules (see para. 1020). After the inspection, however, all such efforts cease. The Working Group believes that Mr. Hoffman's visit took place in the circumstances described above and that his report must be evaluated in that context.[26]

Unfortunately, no basis for outside evaluation of the Hoffman study is provided by the Group, which declined to publish the study. Its inclusion would have added at most 43 pages to the Group's 435-page report, and would have made it even more difficult for the reader to understand the Group's critical attitude. While the

---

[25] *Id.* at 38–39. The UK had raised "the possibility of proposing that the International Committee of the Red Cross should take charge of the inquiry." E/CN.4/SR.910, at 11–12 (1967). France agreed. E/CN.4/SR.916, at 8 (1967). Expressions of dissatisfaction with the ICRC by Group members during the preparation of their report can be found in E/CN.4/AC.22/SR.32, at 4, 7; SR.33, at 6–9; SR.37, at 3 and 6–7 (1967).

[26] E/CN.4/950, at 40 (1967). The summary record of the Group's meeting at which the quoted language was approved does not indicate any discussion of its meaning. E/CN.4/AC.22/SR.37, at 7 (1967).

ICRC's letter of transmittal complimented South Africa on its "desire to facilitate the International Committee's humanitarian action," the letter goes on to review improvements suggested by Mr. Hoffman and subscribed to by ICRC, then turning to "questions of a more fundamental character," such as "separation of common law criminals from political detainees (at least, in respect of the latter category, if they are not guilty of serious criminal offences)."

The Hoffman study contains considerable derogatory material which the Working Group should have found corroborative of its other evidence. For example, at the Robben Island Prison, "three out of the seven prisoners, who had the opportunity to speak to the Delegate without witnesses, complained that they did not get enough food." One of these prisoners "pointed out that he had just received a new outfit on the day of the ICRC visit," while "three of them complained that they are beaten by some warders." The Commanding Officer told Hoffman that "he had already reprimanded two warders who had been named by the prisoners concerned." Also, "the prison authorities informed the Delegate that there are four gangs amongst the hard bitten prisoners, which tend to terrorize their fellow prisoners and might even go so far as to 'sentence' fellow prisoners to death." At Leeuwkop Prison, "the Delegate pointed out to the Commanding Officer that the cell with 37 prisoners was, in his opinion, over-crowded. The Officer replied that the prisoners preferred to stay together in order to keep warm." At Vooruitsig Prison, "five out of the six prisoners interviewed by the Delegate in private conversation complained about the attitude of younger warders (beating, smacking and bad language)." At Pretoria Prison, "the 90-day detainees were in single confinement in cells 12' x 9' x 10' high. . . . The Police stations were obviously only meant to provide for short periods of detention; as 90-day detainees are generally held for months, various inadequacies appear. . . . According to official information there has been one death amongst the 90-day detainees, the suicide of Looksmart Solwandle on the 23rd October, 1963." Correspondence and visits are "not permitted as Detainees are incommunicado. . . . Six of the detainees interviewed said that they were in their second period of detention after being re-arrested."

Why such evidence should have been rejected by the Working Group is not clear, especially in view of the reason given by one

Group member, and apparently agreed to by all, for including most of the other evidence in the report: "no conclusions the Working Group could reach would be convincing unless they were backed up by evidence in the report itself, preferably in the actual words of the witnesses. . . . There was no doubt that the report would be attacked, and the wise course was to forestall attack by producing the full evidence in support of the statements made." [27] The Group's report could only have gained strength from reliance on so impartial a source as the ICRC. The basis of the Group's attitude towards ICRC can be surmised from the summary record of a remark by the Chairman. "He agreed that it was especially disturbing that ICRC should have agreed to send another representative to investigate conditions in South African prisons when it was perfectly aware that a United Nations group had just been established for the same purpose." [28]

SOUTH AFRICA'S REACTION TO THE GROUP

The Government of South Africa resisted the Working Group's inquiries at every turn. At the Human Rights Commission's 1967 session a South African Observer made a statement attacking the Apartheid Committee documents to which the Commission's attention had been called, while denying, because of Article 2(7) of the Charter, any accountability to the UN.[29] A letter from the Minister of Foreign Affairs to the UN noted that "the South African Government has always regarded the International Committee of the Red Cross, by reason of its international status and long tradition of objectivity, as the proper body to establish the true facts in a situation

[27] E/CN.4/AC.22/SR.32, at 5 (1967).

[28] E/CN.4/AC.22/SR.33, at 9 (1967). One member had said that "it was difficult to understand the intentions of ICRC, whether it was attempting to prove that it was the only agency capable of visiting South Africa and investigating prison conditions in that country or whether it was setting itself up in opposition to the United Nations and its bodies, especially since it refused to communicate its findings to the international working group most directly concerned. . . . The South African Government . . . was to be commended for its willingness to provide copies of the ICRC report and, in that respect, appeared to have been more cooperative than ICRC itself." *Id.* at 8–9.

[29] E/CN.4/950, at 31–32 (1967); E/CN.4/SR.904, at 4–5 (1967). See also E/CN.4/SR.906, at 13–14, E/CN.4/SR.910, at 5–6, E/CN.4/SR.516, at 13–15 (1967).

such as this, where a concerted campaign has been built up about the treatment of prisoners in South Africa." [30] The Minister questioned whether the Commission had considered the ICRC report before establishing the *Ad Hoc* Group. The South African Permanent Representative at the UN added a "strong protest at this decision [to create the *Ad Hoc* Group] which constitutes a flagrant interference in the internal affairs of a sovereign State Member of the United Nations," adding that the Commission "decided to establish this group of experts *after* it had already reached certain conclusions and in fact condemned the South African Government for alleged malpractices in South African prisons. The approach of the group of experts to this question can, therefore, hardly be expected to be objective when the judgment has already been made." [31]

After the Group's report had been published and generally accepted by the Human Rights Commission, South Africa issued "comments," including "a few examples of contradictions and inconsistencies in the statements made by the individuals who appeared before the Working Group. They must cast doubt not only on the credibility of the individuals concerned, but also on any of the Group's conclusions and recommendations founded on those statements." [32] South Africa also questioned the qualifications of the Group's members under the resolution's formula calling for "eminent jurists and prison officials" and under the requirement of ECOSOC resolution 9 (II) (1946) that experts be "non-governmental." [33] The Government concluded with "analysis of the 'evidence' cited by the Working Group in support of its comment, conclusion and recommendations," to which certain of the witnesses later responded.[34]

[30] E/CN.4/950, at 25–26 (1967), E/4340 (1967).

[31] E/CN.4/950, at 28 (1967), E/4340/Add.1 (1967).

[32] E/4510, at 7 (1968).

[33] *Id.* at 14: "Firstly, whether or not they can be considered 'eminent jurists,' their number certainly does not include prison officials. Secondly, all of the individuals concerned have represented their Governments in the Commission on Human Rights, if not in other United Nations bodies, and they do not, therefore, fall into the category of 'non-governmental experts in specialized fields or individual experts.' "

[34] E/CN.4/AC.22/RT.14, at 26–31 (1969); E/CN.4/AC.22/19 (1969), to which are annexed extracts from a South African paper on the Group's first report.

CRITERIA APPLIED BY THE GROUP

The Working Group in its report cited provisions of the Universal Declaration of Human Rights, the International Covenant on Civil and Political Rights, and the International Convention on the Elimination of All Forms of Racial Discrimination.[35] These instruments were not represented as binding upon South Africa. However, a fourth set of international criteria, the Standard Minimum Rules for the Treatment of Prisoners, was agreed by South Africa to be binding on it, so that established standards existed against which to measure alleged offenses.

The Standard Minimum Rules were adopted in 1955 by the First United Nations Congress on the Prevention of Crime and the Treatment of Offenders. ECOSOC in 1957 approved the Rules and recommended them for adoption by governments. South Africa told the Human Rights Commission that the Rules "were accepted by the Republic of South Africa, and are also mandatorily incorporated in the relative legislation (Prison Act No. 8 of 1959) and departmental directives. These provisions are strictly applied and no discriminative application of them is tolerated."[36] Two months after the Commission had considered the Group's report, the Government sent the Commission data on its compliance with the Standard Minimum Rules.[37]

The Group also considered the evidence before it in the light of the criteria set forth in the Genocide Convention. One member asserted that no "witnesses had mentioned genocide of their own accord: any reference that they had made to it had been elicited by suggestive questioning."[38] Another member said "that a trend towards genocide existed in South Africa and was implicit in the policy of apartheid, but genocide was a legal term and a distinction

[35] E/CN.4/950, at 17–24 (1967).

[36] *Id.* at 32. Later the Group decided that "these international standards also apply in the case of Southern Rhodesia. In particular, as regards the freedom fighters made prisoners by the illegal authorities of Southern Rhodesia, the Standard Minimum Rules on the Treatment of Prisoners should be applied." E/CN.4/984/Add.5, at 2 (1969). Not only the Standard Minimum Rules but also the Geneva Conventions of 1949 on treatment of war prisoners and civilians were held to apply to Nambia (South West Africa). E/CN.4/984/Add.9, at 2 (1969).

[37] E/4510/Add.1 (1968).

[38] E/CN.4/AC.22/SR.34, at 5 (1967).

should be made between the crime of genocide and the looser political senses in which the word might be used." [39]

DECISIONS OF THE GROUP

The Working Group asserted in its report that "in all their main features, the allegations made in the documents of the Special Committee on Apartheid were supported by the evidence given by the witnesses who appeared before, and were questioned by, the Working Group." [40] Such documents, and the written statements, were not relied on as much as live testimony, said the Group, in matching the evidence against the Standard Minimum Rules. This process took up 23 pages of the report, followed by conclusions, the most sweeping of which found that "the legislation of the Republic of South Africa, or the practice of the South African authorities, or both, in the matter of the treatment of prisoners and detainees, violates many of the Standard Minimum Rules for the Treatment of Prisoners." [41] Of the more detailed findings, the most categorical was that "all political prisoners and opponents of apartheid detained under the '90-day' and '180-day' laws, are tortured under interrogation with the hope of extracting confessions and information." [42] As to genocide, the Group concluded that

> the intention of the Government of South Africa to destroy a racial group, in whole or in part, not being established in law, the evidence nevertheless reveals certain elements which correspond to the acts described in article II (a), (b) and (c) of the United Nations Convention on the Prevention and Punishment of the Crime of Genocide and which may, as such, establish the existence of the crime of genocide.[43]

The Group recommended "that a thorough study be undertaken to ascertain whether the elements of the crime of genocide exist in the system at present prevailing in South Africa." [44]

Among the Group's other recommendations arising from its conclusion that the Standard Minimum Rules are violated in several re-

[39] E/CN.4/AC.22/SR.35, at 5 (1967). See also testimony of Albert Sachs, E/CN.4/950, at 229 (1967).

[40] E/CN.4/950; at 392, 415 (1967).

[41] Id. at 415.

[42] Id. at 417.

[43] Id. at 416.

[44] Id. at 419. The Human Rights Commission directed the Group itself to make such a study. Resolution 2 (XXIV), cited *supra* note 5.

spects, the most novel was that the "Government investigate the violations mentioned in this report and hold responsible the persons listed" by name in the report, being jailers and others accused by witnesses of cruelty to prisoners. The final recommendation of the Group was that "to ensure the efficiency of its action both in the South Africa Republic and elsewhere, it is essential to continue its investigations and inquiries on the system of apartheid in a permanent manner." [45]

While permanency is no more attainable at the UN than elsewhere, despite the practice of styling heads of missions as "Permanent Representatives," the *Ad Hoc* Group has functioned further. Whether it should be made permanent, and if so on what basis, depends on the value of its work.

EVALUATION OF THE GROUP'S FIRST PERFORMANCE

Based upon the Group's degree of fulfillment of the first of its several assignments, its continued existence was justifiable with certain reforms in its methods. It was not enough for the Group to serve as a mere sounding board for anti-apartheid propaganda. That function was being carried out by the UN Apartheid Committee and various private bodies. The *Ad Hoc* Group was established to serve a quasi-judicial function requiring impartial search for the truth, a goal not fully achieved in the South African prisons inquiry.

The usefulness of public investigation was testified to before the Group by several witnesses:

> One feels that if there had been more exposures in the thirties about the treatment in concentration camps by the nazis of Jews and political prisoners, the extermination of whole populations in the forties might possibly have been avoided; and that is one of the reasons why one feels strongly that the more publicity given to the illegalities—by any standard of justice—being committed in South Africa today, the more the hand of the Government there and the authorities will be restrained from effecting yet greater crimes against yet larger sections of the South African population. So even if it is not possible to achieve

[45] E/CN.4/950, at 419 (1967). Human Rights Commission resolution 5 (XXIV), after calling upon the South African Government to comply with the standard minimum rules, especially in certain respects, asked ECOSOC to call on the Government to "initiate investigations . . . with a view to establishing the degree of responsibility of the persons listed. . . ." E/4475–E/CN.4/972, at 150–51, 167 (1968).

what one would like to achieve—namely, the liberation of these prisoners and the ending of these practices—nevertheless, the focusing of
attention on what is going on and the exposures of what has been happening are likely to exercise something of a brake on the authorities.[46]

Another witness said that "a permanent body of the United Nations
to investigate conditions and make reports . . . would be a very
good idea. I don't think that the United Nations in itself can get rid
of exploitation or repression in South Africa. . . . [B]ut I do think
by continually examining what happens, continually exposing bad
conditions, maltreatment, oppression, it is possible to make the Government feel embarrassed. I don't think they are totally insensitive
to criticism." [47]
The effectiveness of the process described by the witnesses depends largely on the investigative group's being invulnerable. The
Government of South Africa is not likely to be embarrassed by the
findings of a group with whose composition it can easily find fault.
The exclusion of prison experts and non-governmental persons from
the Group, in view of the requirements of the applicable ECOSOC
resolution and the Commission's own stipulation, gave the Government an easy and unnecessary basis for complaint.[48] South Africa
was given another ground on which to criticize the Group when the
latter summarily dismissed the testimony of a body with the history
and reputation of the International Committee of the Red Cross.
To be effective in giving pause to an oppressive regime like that
of South Africa, a UN investigative body would need to conduct its
inquiries with the utmost circumspection. Justice would not only
need to be done, but also be *seen* to be done. The body or persons
whose accusations gave rise to the investigation should be strictly
separated from the tribunal finding the facts. Conclusions should
not be announced in advance. Testimony should be probed, if the
respondent government does not do so, through intensive questioning by a *advocatus diaboli* using the techniques of either the Euro-

[46] E/CN.4/950, at 235 (1967).

[47] E/CN.4/AC.22/SR.22, at 10–11 (1967). The *Ad Hoc* Group's Chairman
in mid-1969 expressed satisfaction that South African authorities had begun to
reassess conditions in their prisons, which he called the most direct evidence to
justify the Group's existence. UN Press Release HR/308 (1969).

[48] When the Human Rights Commission in 1968 enlarged the Group by one
member, the person appointed was a government-employed Adviser to a Member State of the Commission. E/4475–E/CN.4/972, at 56 (1968).

pean *juge d'instruction* or the Common Law cross-examiner. Without such simple reforms, an opportunity for greater fulfillment of the UN's human rights responsibility may be lost.

THE SOUTH AFRICAN TRADE UNION RIGHTS INQUIRY

The *Ad Hoc* Group's second assignment came from ECOSOC in June 1967, three months after the Human Rights Commission had created the Group. ECOSOC's instructions to the Group were brief. "Having considered . . . the question of the infringement of trade union rights in . . . South Africa, which has been brought to its attention by the International Labour Office on the basis of a communication [E/4305, annex II] received from the World Federation of Trade Unions," the Council decided to "transmit the communication . . . and the comments thereon, if any received from . . . South Africa to the *Ad Hoc* Working Group of Experts." [49] The resolution authorized the Group "to receive communications and hear witnesses, as necessary, and to consider the comments received from . . . South Africa on the communication received from the [ILO] in its examination of the allegations regarding infringements of trade union rights in South Africa." The Group was further requested in the resolution to report to ECOSOC "at the earliest possible date on its findings and to submit its recommendations for action to be taken in specific cases."

The Working Group concluded that "the international standards relating to trade union freedoms are being seriously and persistently violated by South African legislation and by administrative and penal measures." [50] Seven rules were considered by the Group to "form part of the international principles relating to trade union rights," since such rules are "so general in nature that no State can, without rejecting the common heritage of civilized nations, contend that they are not relevant to its attitude with regard to trade union rights," even if the State were not a party to the instruments in which the principles are embodied.[51] The Group made several recommendations, primarily designed to eliminate discrimination

---

[49] E/Res/1216 (XLII) (1967), quoted in the Group's report, E/4459, at 6–8 (1968).
[50] *Id.* at 87.
[51] *Id.* at 85.

against African workers in respect to trade union rights.[52] Two specific cases were mentioned calling for release of certain trade unionists kept in solitary confinement and review of certain convictions with a view to releasing the persons in question.

Once again the Group failed to adopt formal rules of procedure. The Secretariat's representative made an unsuccessful effort when he

> drew attention to a note communicated by the Director-General of the International Labour Office (E/CN.4/AC.22/11) which would be circulated shortly on the ILO's procedure for examining complaints of allegations of infringement of trade union rights. In view of the ILO's wide experience in the matter, the Working Group might consider adopting a similar procedure.[53]

Later one of the Working Group members, Professor Ermacora of Austria, urged that the Group "derive what benefit it could from the work done by the ILO Committee on Freedom of Association. He therefore proposed that the Working Group should proceed on the lines taken by that Committee in such cases as Nos. 63, 102, 300, 311 and 321." [54] The only reply came from Mr. Waldron-Ramsey of Tanzania, who argued that

> the procedure used by the ILO Committee could not be taken over *in toto* by the Working Group, not only because as Mr. Ermacora had pointed out—it would have the advantage of hearing oral testimony, but also because the ILO employed a procedure different from that of the United Nations. The Group, in its previous work, had evolved a synthesis of the two procedures, reviewing written testimony from affidavits or statements made beforehand and hearing direct testimony from witnesses who were made available for cross-examination.[55]

There was little if any cross-examination of the few witnesses who testified at the *Ad Hoc* Group's second inquiry. One instance occurred when "Mr. Ermacora said that it would therefore [since persons in transit camps can leave and visit friends] not be correct to describe the transit camps as concentration camps because, in the

---

[52] *Id.* at 88.
[53] E/CN.4/AC.22/SR.45, at 4 (1967).
[54] E/CN.4/AC.22/SR.50, at 5 (1967).
[55] *Id.* at 7.

European concentration camps during the Second World War, persons were not allowed out and the camps were surrounded by barbed wire fences." To this statement the witness replied: "I agree that a concentration camp, as I know it, is not the same as that to which we are referring." [56] More systematic cross-examination would have made for a more convincing inquiry.

The number of witnesses was considerably smaller than in the first *Ad Hoc* Group inquiry. Three persons who had testified before were considered to have given evidence relevant to the second investigation: two of them gave further oral evidence, while the third expressed regrets at not being able to appear.[57] In addition to these two and the "cross-examined" witness, the Group heard only Mr. Nicholas Valticos, Chief of the Department of International Labour Standards of the ILO, and a representative of the World Federation of Trade Unions. The shortage was not the fault of the Group, which asked all UN Member States not only for "any information which would be likely to assist the Working Group" but also for the names of witnesses.[58] Thirteen replies yielded no names, although one urged contact with the African Liberation Committee, which in turn provided two names and addresses from which no information was received. Another reply gave several names that did not answer.[59] France's reply was censored from the Group's report for questioning its legal authority, which was considered "irrelevant." [60] Another government reply, that of South Africa, termed the *Ad Hoc* Group's inquiry "unconstitutional." [61] The Group, after considering an even more fiery retort tendered by Mr. Waldron-Ramsey,[62] deplored South Africa's "lack of good sense

---

[56] E/CN.4/AC.22/SR.53, at 22 (1968).

[57] E/4459, at 17 (1968).

[58] *Id.* at 18. The Group had before it as documentary evidence the ILO report, E/4305, and certain statements which it appended to its own report, E/4459 and Add.1.

[59] E/4459, at 19 (1968).

[60] E/CN.4/AC.22/SR.55, at 7 (1968) and SR.56, at 6–7 (1968).

[61] E/4459, at 65 (1968). The ILO Committee on Freedom of Association "had ruled that South Africa was not under a conventional obligation in the matter, but that it was the Committee's duty to examine the allegations made against that country and to report thereon to the Governing Body of ILO." E/CN.4/AC.22/SR.50, at 4 (1967).

[62] E/CN.4/AC.22/SR.60, at 10–11 (1968).

and continuous intention . . . to evade deliberately its obvious humanitarian and international responsibilities." [63]

THE AD HOC GROUP'S THIRD AND FOURTH ASSIGNMENTS

In 1968 the Group undertook concurrently two new tasks.[64] The first was assigned by the Human Rights Commission and dealt with the treatment of political prisoners in Namibia (Southwest Africa), Southern Rhodesia, and the Portuguese territories, as well as in South Africa, the subject of the Group's original inquiry. The second 1968 assignment came from ECOSOC and covered trade union rights in Namibia and Southern Rhodesia, besides South Africa which the Group had studied as its second task.

Still the Group adopted no rules of procedure, instead deciding issues as they arose. Without discussion, the Group heard testimony on mistreatment of prisoners in Portugal itself, as opposed to its African territories,[65] and despite objections evidence sometimes was allowed on destruction and killing by military action at villages in the territories.[66] Although as few as three of the six Group members had attended certain of the 1968 sessions,[67] it was not until April 1, 1969, that the three members then present decided that a quorum

---

[63] E/4459, at 65 (1968). The Group's impartiality was not stimulated by ECOSOC's having already, in the resolution assigning the Group its second task, condemned "the infringement of trade union rights and the unlawful prosecution . . . of trade union workers reflected in the legislation and practices of the Republic of South Africa as a violation of the right of freedom of association, and as a manifestation of the criminal policy of apartheid." *Id.* at 7. One can only guess whether lack of impartiality was reflected in the notation that "the summary records of the second part of the sixty-third and of the sixty-fourth and sixty-fifth meetings are restricted as they were closed meetings." E/CN.4/AC.22/SR. 55–63 and 66 [*sic*], at 1 (1968).

[64] The Chairman drew the Group's attention in January 1969 to General Assembly resolution 2489 (XXIII) of December 1968, according to which no fees or other honoraria shall be paid in addition to travel and subsistence allowances to individuals appointed by UN bodies to make special studies or do other *ad hoc* tasks in their personal capacity. After a brief debate in open meeting on the implications of the resolution for its further work, the Group decided to continue discussing the matter in closed session. E/CN.4/AC.22/SR.123 (1969). Members had previously received a *per diem* honorarium.

[65] E/CN.4/AC.22/RT.25, at 5–15 (1969).

[66] E/CN.4/AC.22/RT.27, at 5–6; RT.28, at 2, 9, 12; RT.35, at 33; RT.36, at 24; RT.39, at 21, 49–50 (1969).

[67] E/CN.4/984, at 5 (1969).

could be less than a majority because they were an expert body, but that each member should be given an opportunity to signify his approval of the report.

The two 1968 tasks took the Group on a lengthy journey. After sessions in New York, London, and Geneva, hearings were held in August in Conakry, Kinshasa, Brazzaville, and Lusaka. Further hearings were held in Dar es Salaam in September and Geneva in December. "Due to unforeseen circumstances, the Group was not able to carry out its decision to go to Prague to hear witnesses on Trade Union rights in South Africa," stated the Group's report.[68]

The Group heard a far larger number of witnesses during its 1968 sessions than previously. Twenty-five testified on trade union violations, one of them in a closed meeting.[69] There were 13 witnesses on South Africa, four on Namibia, and eight on Southern Rhodesia. Seventy-six testified concerning ill-treatment of prisoners and detainees, 14 of them being heard in closed meetings at their request.[70] Besides asking all UN Member States excepting South Africa and Portugal for information and the names of witnesses on this subject, the Group also sought help from the Organization for African Unity and various private organizations, including African liberation movements. The private sources supplied most of the names of the witnesses who were heard.[71] The UN Office of Public Information issued a communiqué in June inviting all persons concerned to furnish information orally or in writing. A number of written statements were received. The Secretariat provided summaries of relevant legislation.[72]

[68] E/4646, at 9 (1969).

[69] *Id.* at 13.

[70] E/CN.4/984, at 7 (1969). There were 19 witnesses who testified on South Africa, 6 on Namibia, 9 on Southern Rhodesia, 24 on Angola, 9 on Mozambique, 9 of Guinea-Bissau, and 1 on Sao Tome and Principe. *Id.* at 8–9. According to the Group's report, "the evidence heard in camera is freshly adduced by deponents who have had the most recent, post-UDI [Rhodesian Unilateral Declaration of Independence] experience of conditions in detention camps and prisons." E/CN.4/984/Add.8, at 2 (1969).

[71] E/CN.4/984, at 7. All UN Members but South Africa were asked for information and the names of witnesses concerning trade union violations. E/4646, at 11 (1969). South Africa was asked for information and permission to visit, but it did not reply. *Id.* at 12.

[72] Legal Provisions of the Republic of South Africa Governing Prisoners, Detainees and Persons in Police Custody, E/CN.4/AC.22/6/Add.1 (1968); Legal Provisions Governing Prisoners, Detainees and Persons in Police Custody

Faith in the Group's effectiveness, based usually on its power of exposure to public opinion, was expressed by many persons who appeared before it. The Guinean Secretary of State for Foreign Affairs expressed the

> deep conviction that the labours of your Working Group will be an effective contribution towards the evolution of the political struggle in the territories which have for decades been illegally occupied by Portugal, and that those labours will also help to enlighten world public opinion with regard to the crimes being committed daily by Portugal, in defiance of the rules of international law.[73]

One witness put the question:

> What can the United Nations do for us? What can this Commission do for us? By listening to us, by amassing all the evidence, as you have been doing, you can accomplish a great deal. We believe that you can inform world public opinion and uphold our fundamental rights within the United Nations.[74]

Another witness hailed the Group as

> an instrument which—had it been fully understood—might have prevented the crimes that the Portuguese troops and colonialists are daily committing against innocent populations. . . . We therefore hope that some sort of "white paper" dealing with the way in which Portugal is trampling on the most elementary human rights may be drawn up and given a wide enough distribution that the conscience of mankind may condemn with even great vigour the fascist Portuguese colonial system.[75]

The precise reason why exposure is helpful was described by some witnesses. In reply to the question whether "anything at all

---

in South West Africa, E/CN.4/AC.22/12 (1968); Legal Provisions of Southern Rhodesia Governing Political Prisoners, Detainees and Persons in Police Custody, E/CN.4/AC.22/13 (1968); Legal Provisions of Portugal Governing Political Prisoners, Detainees or Persons in Police Custody in the Portuguese Territories of Africa, E/CN.4/AC.22/14 (1968); Legislation Relating to Trade Unions Rights in South West Africa, E/CN.4/AC.22/15 (1968).

[73] E/CN.4/AC.22/RT.25, at 2 (1969).

[74] E/CN.4/AC.22/RT.28, at 16 (1968). When in May 1969 South Africa announced it would release Robert Sobukwe, Somalia declared in the Apartheid Committee that world public opinion was responsible. UN Press Release GA/AP/162 (1969).

[75] E/CN.4/AC.22/RT.35, at 16–17 (1969).

would result from enquiries at an international level like this one," a witness pronounced them

> very useful, because we believe that this problem which exists in Rhodesia should be exposed to the international world. The world at large knows very little of what is going on in Rhodesia. When the entire international community is quiet on Rhodeisa, the Smith regime feels that it is now acceptable to the international community and nobody is making a noise about it.[76]

Another witness declared that

> conditions in Namibia are worse than in South Africa. One thing which is not known here is that what is being done in Namibia is being done in an unknown country; things are done, the prison authorities knowing very well that nobody is going to see whatever is being done there. In South Africa you have got the situation that international attention or pressure is being exerted directly on Pretoria, and whatever is being said about Namibia is rather second-hand. Those who are in authority do not bother. They do not expect to be questioned for crimes committed. This is the thing. They do not feel that pressure from outside.[77]

Similarly, a former prisoner described his experience as "one of the most common ways of treating people in South Africa, but the world is kept in permanent ignorance. The South African authorities have strong reason in not allowing foreign bodies to inspect South African prisons." [78] A newspaper man said that victims of police beatings are sometimes

> taken to restriction camps where no one can see them, because all restriction areas are out of bounds; no persons could get into a restriction area except the restrictees themselves, and very few—there are very few like myself who went in and managed to get out and are able to tell this tale.[79]

The limited practical extent of aid through international investigation was highlighted by certain testimony. A South African im-

---

[76] E/CN.4/AC.22/RT.6, at 62 (1969). "The Working Group, impressed by the opinions of witnesses that investigations such as those being carried out by it do have an impact within Southern Rhodesia, recommends that the widest publicity be given to the present report." E/CN.4/984/Add.8, at 29 (1969).

[77] E/CN.4/AC.22/RT.16, at 12 (1969).

[78] E/CN.4/AC.22/RT.42, at 36 (1969).

[79] E/CN.4/AC.22/RT.17, at 12 (1969).

prisoned for Communist membership and activity, when asked why he wished to testify, replied:

> I should very much like this group to make known my views to the world and to the South African Government and for them to alleviate the conditions of political prisoners, to stop discrimination and to make life more bearable for them, if not release them.[80]

A representative of the African National Congress of South Africa asserted that

> a politician is a man of some status in his community. This status is with him wherever he is, in prison or out of prison. . . . The modern approach is the rehabilitation of a prisoner. The central thesis of my argument is that a political prisoner is not involved in any common law or moral crime, he cannot be the subject of any schemes of reformation and rehabilitation.[81]

Another witness, when asked his reason for wishing to testify, said: "It's for the treatment that we received in gaol—the fact that I was mixed with those criminals, and I thought it was wrong. The treatment should have varied for political prisoners and criminals." [82] A representative of the Southwest Africa Peoples Organization stated that "we are appealing to the United Nations to send a team of investigators to investigate prison conditions in Namibian gaols and to see that all freedom-fighters in Namibia are treated as prisoners of war when captured." [83]

Achievement through international investigation of even such limited objectives as better treatment for prisoners was doubted by some witnesses. The representative of the Zimbabwe African People's Union said that

> ZAPU is fully aware of the inadequacy and limitations of the United Nations in the implementation of its decisions, particularly when in direct confrontation with the racist forces of southern Africa. . . . It is not that we are despising this Committee, this august body or commission, not at all. It is not that we feel that we are wasting your

---

[80] E/CN.4/AC.22/RT.12, at 32 (1969).

[81] E/CN.4/AC.22/RT.38, at 38–40 (1969).

[82] E/CN.4/AC.22/RT.20, at 16 (1969). See also RT.44/Add.1, at 13 (1969). The same witness urged a UN demand that prisoners simply be shown the applicable prison rules. *Id.* at 11.

[83] E/CN.4/AC.22/RT.43, at 4 (1969).

time—not a bit. But we are engaged in a war. We have appeared before many commissions, including the Special Committee of Twenty-
four and other commissions of the United Nations. We have seen fail-
ures, as I pointed out, and limitations. We know that there are limitations of commissions of the United Nations. We felt that there was no
need for us to continue year after year giving evidence of torture.
This evidence of torture was even given to the Special Committee of
Twenty-four. It was not a human rights commission. It was the Special Committee of Twenty-four. All of this was given to them. But
then ZAPU felt that we cannot just keep away from the Committee.[84]

One witness was asked

whether or not, since the investigation by this expert group and the
publishing of its report early this year, you get the impression that
anything has been done by the South African authorities to alleviate
the conditions of your compatriots in South West Africa . . . have
any outside agents made any visits to the South African gaols or the
South West African gaols to investigate conditions—whether they
were outside agents, officials from other countries, or from the International Red Cross, for instance, etc.? [85]

The disappointing answer was that, according to recent information,
"even the man who was defending them then is not allowed to go
and see them any more. So nobody is allowed to go and see them."
The effectiveness of a recent Red Cross investigation was attested
to by a witness from the African National Congress:

Our information—and this is as far as I can go—from people who
have been in South African prisons recently—ascribe the changes
which have taken place to the revelations contained in the Hoffman
report which calls on the South African Government to comment on
the findings of the Red Cross experts who made an investigation. So I
would say that they flowed directly from the publication of the Hoffman report and the fact that some of the findings have not been chal-
lenged by the South African Government must have led them to improve the conditions in prisons slightly. But, as I said, this has come
from some people who have been in South African prisons recently.[86]

[84] E/CN.4/AC.22/RT.40, at 3, 18–20 (1969).
[85] E/CN.4/AC.22/RT.5, at 18–20, 21 (1969).
[86] E/CN.4/AC.22/RT.38, at 81 (1968). The witness gave the following personal opinion: "There are aspects of the Hoffman report which we feel are
concessions to the prison authorities, the presentation of the views of General
Steyn. Some acceptance of these explanations tends to blur the actual situation

The witness then gave a contrastingly diffuse answer when asked by a Working Group member: "Have you and your organization noted that our group has also presented a very substantial report to the United Nations at the beginning of this year or do you know nothing about this report?" He replied:

> We are aware of the report which came under some attacks from the South African Government. Are you referring to the one whose Rapporteur was Mr. Ganji? I was asked specifically about the Hoffman report and I have confined my remarks to that. The Amnesty International has written on this subject, the Defence and Aid International has written on the subject. Without prejudice to your report I was replying to the question as it was put to me.[87]

These comments show how little impact the Working Group's first inquiry had, despite the potential newsworthiness of the subject of mistreatment of prisoners and detainees in South Africa. The press in the United States, for example, paid little or no heed, at a time when prison conditions within the United States were being given considerable attention.[88] If the Group's chief weapon is exposure, lack of publicity means failure and raises the question of how to gain attention.

---

which the report, I feel, should have rigorously pointed out. For instance, on Robben Island, when the Hoffman Commission arrived the prisoners were allowed to sleep on beds and to wear pyjamas and the whole impression was given for the purpose of impressing on the Hoffman investigation team that prisoners were allowed to sleep on beds and were allowed to wear pyjamas. That is what is reflected in the report so that my opinion is that it could have done more than what it has in fact exposed. But its main limitation is that it tends to stress very much the official point of view." *Id.*

[87] *Id.* at 81–82. The Group objected in its report to the fact that "in many African countries the United Nations information centres do not even have document E/CN.4/950," its first report. E/CN./984/Add.17, at 16 (1969). A plea in March 1969 for impartial medical inquiry at Robben Island Prison sought the aid of the UN General Assembly's Apartheid Committee, the International Committee of the Red Cross, and the International Commission of Jurists in bringing the inquiry about. A/AC.115/L.242, 243 (1969). The Secretary-General passed the plea along to the UN Human Rights Commission in accordance with a request from the Apartheid Committee Chairman referring to the Commission and the International Committee of the Red Cross, but not to the International Commission of Jurists, whose consultative status was in contention at ECOSOC. E/CN.4/L.1115 (1969).

[88] See, for example, *Ex-Official Tells of Brutalities in Arkansas Prisons*, N.Y. Times, March 5, 1969, §1, at 23, col. 1.

With the United States press, contests are news, especially contests involving suspenseful confrontation. Both features were available to the Group but neither was employed. Assured publicity in the United States was missed, and with it the chance to influence policy in a way much sought after by persons opposing apartheid. A contest could have been produced through cross-examination, and suspenseful confrontation would have ensued if the Group had determined to enter Southwest Africa and Southern Rhodesia with the rightful authority's consent, despite the wrongful *de facto* authority's refusal.

As in the Group's first inquiry,[89] one of the members, Mr. Waldron-Ramsey of Tanzania, recognized the need for cross-examination, and announced that he would pursue the matter as a devil's advocate in the absence of a respondent government representative, but his pursuit was brief. The government in question was the United Kingdom as the "final authority" in Southern Rhodesia in 1960. "It seems to me that at least we should carry out the formality of being consistent with the principles of natural justice in that we allow the accused to be able to be heard to defend itself. . . . Our mandate indeed would seem to insist that the United Kingdom be put in the position where it could defend itself."[90] Mr. Waldron-Ramsey then told a witness from Southern Rhodesia that "my task is to cross-examine. And in cross-examination I shall cross-examine from a certain vantage point, and as such I am not defending the interest of the United Kingdom."[91]

Since the witness had testified against the authorities in Southern Rhodesia, cross-examination would have sought to reduce its impact, which would have been in the United Kingdom's interest to the extent it was responsible. However, Mr. Waldron-Ramsey did not question as if he were representing the United Kingdom: his aim was clearly to implicate, not exculpate, that country. Two days later, when he asked whether another witness tried to "communicate the difficulties under which you were detained to any representative of the British Government, either in Salisbury or elsewhere," the witness told him that "Southern Rhodesia has been responsible for its internal affairs since 1923. This applies to questions of political

[89] See text at note 18 *supra*.
[90] E/CN.4/AC.22/RT.1, at 33 (1969).
[91] *Id.*

detainees and other like questions. So that there was actually no ground, no reason for appealing, since the British Government has always alleged to have no say in the matter." [92] Thus taken aback, Mr. Waldron-Ramsey scolded the witness: "I should not dispute this with you, of course, because you are not competent to deal with these matters. But let us go on to another question."

Other members of the Group questioned witnesses, sometimes leading them on in the direction their previous testimony had taken,[93] sometimes in true cross-examination fashion,[94] but no person present consistently tested each witness' credibility by appropriate probing. Had this procedure been followed, by a Group member or preferably by an experienced cross-examiner appointed from outside the Group, the investigation would have enjoyed both greater precision and the added acclaim that comes with the excitement of adversary proceedings.[95] The precision and excitement would have been greatest if actual representatives of respondent government au-

---

[92] E/CN.4/AC.22/RT.2, at 28 (1969). Other witnesses testified that the United Kingdom did have responsibility in Southern Rhodesia following 1923. E/CN.4/AC.22/RT.6, at 57 and RT.13, at 18–20 (1969). For ILO's view, see E/4610, Ann. at 5 (1969). The Group concluded that the UK was still responsible for Southern Rhodesia. E/CN.4/984/Add.8, at 2 (1969); E/4646, at 49 (1969).

[93] "Mr. JHA.: Would you say from your experience of the camp that, after serving a certain period of time, not only the person's physique and mind but his spirit would be so entirely crushed that he would really be a misfit for a long time in the outside world after he comes out of such a camp?

Mr. GUTU: That is true. . . ."
E/CN.4/AC.22/RT.2, at 21 (1969).

[94] "The CHAIRMAN: Do you know of anyone who was actually shot or hanged? . . . Did you personally, while you were in your country, see anyone shot down by the police or did you see anyone hanged?" E/CN.4/AC.22/RT.3, at 26 (1969). See also for example, RT.32, at 7; RT.34, at 8, 10–12, 27; RT.44/Add.1, at 23; RT.46, at 10–11; RT.50, at 28, 31 (1969).

[95] Cross-examination would have been less useful, of course, in testing the hearsay evidence that was admitted, no doubt necessarily. For example, one witness was asked if he was certain human flesh had been given to prisoners as food. He answered: "I am absolutely certain that it was human flesh, because the prisoners told me so; they swore it was true." E/CN.4/AC.22/RT.35, at 6 (1969). The Group's report explicitly characterized this question as "cross-examination." E/CN.4/984/Add.17, at 10 (1969). See also RT.35, at 27 and RT.5, at 13; RT.41, at 24; RT.42, at 14–15 (1969). In certain cases witnesses declined to name their sources. E/CN.4/AC.22/RT.41, at 21; RT.43, at 18 (1969). One witness refused to answer on the ground that the information sought was "classified." E/CN.4/AC.22/RT.40, at 23–25 (1969).

thorities had participated. In their absence the devil's advocate technique could have been used to advantage.

Confrontation certain to have attracted wide notice would have ensued had the Group determined to visit Southwest Africa and Southern Rhodesia. These places, unlike South Africa and the Portuguese colonies, possessed *de jure* authorities which might have furnished the Group with technically valid leave to enter. Whether or not the British Crown would have done so as to Southern Rhodesia, the UN Council for Namibia surely would have given consent, having itself sought to enter there.[96] It is not clear whether leave was sought from either the *de jure* or *de facto* authorities in Namibia or Rhodesia.[97] Mr. Waldron-Ramsey stated that "the South African authorities, who are illegally occupying Namibia, refused to facilitate our entry and comfortable stay; therefore, we are not able to go." [98] This conclusion does not necessarily follow.

The suffering for a cause described by the witnesses calls for corresponding devotion by the Group charged with succoring the sufferers. If an airborne approach to Namibia, by parachute if landing were forbidden, was considered too hazardous (or too expensive, because of the need to insure a chartered plane), as concluded by the Council for Namibia, then perhaps its boundaries could have been approached by sea, or through Zambia and the Caprivi Strip. If barred at the frontier or territorial seas, the Group at least would have come to the excited notice of all the world. Its findings then

[96] With little consistency, the Group noted that the General Assembly had created the UN Council and Commissioner "to administer Namibia" and then pronounced itself "unable to visit the territory because of lack of co-operation by the Pretoria authorities." E/CN.4/984/Add.9, at 2 (1969). The Group did recommend that competent UN bodies declare international trade union rights to be applicable to Namibia and replace an existing group of workers with freely constituted trade unions. E/4646, at 49 (1969).

[97] The Group's report stated that no reply was received to its request to enter South Africa and the Portuguese colonies, E/CN.4/984, at 7 (1969), and that the Group was "unable to visit [Namibia] because of lack of co-operation by the Pretoria authorities," E/CN.4/984/Add.9, at 2 (1969). The Human Rights Commission's Special Rapporteur on apartheid and racial discrimination in southern Africa in 1967 inconsistently requested permission to visit from the *de facto* authority, South Africa, as to South West Africa, but from the *de jure* authority, Sir Humphrey V. Gibbs, the British Crown's appointed Governor of Southern Rhodesia. He had no response from either. E/CN.4/949, at 5 (1967). See his similar requests in 1968. E/CN.4/979/Add.6, Ann. III (1969).

[98] E/CN.4/AC.22/RT.5, at 18–20 (1969).

would have had an audience outside diplomatic circles. If apprehended, the Group—at little risk—would have caused a surge of anti-Pretoria resentment.

Resentment against governmental authorities undoubtedly was sought through the Group's assignment of exploring whether alleged atrocities constituted the crime of genocide, an inquiry on which the Group concluded that it could not, "in the present state of South African legislation, . . . say that the South African Government has expressed an intention to commit genocide." [99] Several witnesses were led into essentially legal speculations. One former prisoner said that "indifference to one's health and genocide immediately are the same thing in that one is meant to go slow and another one is done systematically." [100] Another witness believed that "what is happening there [in South Africa] is genocide by neglect and indifference." [101] The uprooting and moving of communities were regarded by one witness as "another manifestation of the genocidal social practices that grow with the intensification of *apartheid* in South Africa, . . . a process calculated to reduce them, to destroy them; . . . irrespective of what the intention is, the implementation of *apartheid* laws results in what I consider to be genocide." [102]

Different witnesses displayed different degrees of caution in their approach to the genocide issue. One said, "I would not like to say positively that the crime of genocide is committed in South Africa according to the strict definition of it here. But certainly there are elements of genocide in the policies of the South African Government, especially in so far as they affect the masses of the African oppressed, especially in the rural areas." [103] Another witness declared the belief "that the criminal acts committed against our people by the Portuguese, especially in the countryside, are acts of genocide. . . . The Portuguese, through massive bombing raids . . .

[99] E/CN.4/984/Add.18, at 22 (1969).
[100] E/CN.4/AC.22/RT.3, at 31 (1969).
[101] E/CN.4/AC.22/RT.12, at 51 (1969).
[102] E/CN.4/AC.22/RT.38, at 51, 56, 61 (1969).
[103] E/CN.4/AC.22/RT.42, at 21 (1969). See also RT. 44/Add.1, at 15–17 and RT.50, at 46 (1969). The Group in its report "noted that many of the witnesses did not unhesitantly draw the conclusion that the acts described by them constituted genocide," E/CN.4/984/Add.18, at 4 (1969), and added that "it would be useful, as in the case of South Africa, for the Group to study the question whether elements of the crime of genocide exist in the African territories under Portuguese domination." E/CN.4/984/Add.17, at 15 (1969).

committed acts that were, in our opinion, clearly aimed at destroying the population. . . . Consequently, in our opinion, there has been intentional genocide." [104]

The former of these statements is likely to appear the more credible, just as is evidence from witnesses who have not themselves suffered the wrongs alleged, such as that of a former Rhodesian public prosecutor [105] and of a witness who told of observing Portuguese mistreatment of prisoners while working as a driver before voluntarily joining the nationalist forces.[106] Particularly telling was the latter's evidence implicating named individuals of acts of brutality. Identification of wrongdoers was encouraged by the Group, as in its first inquiry, for the deterrent effect it might have.[107] One witness made very clear his intentions:

> The captain's name was Luis Soares Dos Reis Gonçalves. I am giving his full name so that one day he may be called to account for his actions before a war crimes tribunal. The soldiers said to him: "Captain, we came upon this old woman in the hut, what shall we do with her?" The captain's curt reply was: "Kill her." And that is what they did. The poor woman was killed by a burst from a G-3 machine-gun aimed at her head.[108]

FUTURE INVESTIGATIONS

The UN's Southern Africa investigations are likely to continue several years at least, making tighter methods essential to credibility and consequent effectiveness. The Human Rights Commission in 1969 gave the *Ad Hoc* Group, with ECOSOC's approval, new assignments on top of continuing with treatment of political prisoners in South Africa, Namibia, Southern Rhodesia, and Portuguese-ad-

---

[104] E/CN.4/AC.22/RT.28, at 19–20 (1969).

[105] E/CN.4/AC.22/RT.13, at 30 (1969).

[106] E/CN.4/AC.22/RT.26, at 8–13 (1969). One witness enhanced his credibility by the remark that "what I am going to say is not very flattering to myself." E/CN.4/AC.22/RT.48, at 41 (1969).

[107] See also E/CN.4/AC.22/RT.26, at 2, 6, and E/CN.4/AC.22/RT.1, at 7; RT.2, at 18–20; RT.3, at 7, 28; RT.14, at 6; RT.17, at 26; RT.20, at 3; RT.25, at 8, 10, 16; RT.27, at 2–3; RT.28, at 10; RT.33, at 5; RT.34, at 28; RT.36, at 26; RT.39, at 18–19; RT.40, at 16; RT.42, at 22 (1969). Names are listed in the Group's report, E/CN.4/984/Add.4, at 5, 8 (1969). See also E/CN.4/AC.22/19 Ann. V (1969).

[108] E/CN.4/AC.22/RT.28, at 11 (1969).

ministered territories: capital punishment in southern Africa, treatment of captured freedom fighters in southern Africa, transit camps and "Native Reserves," grave manifestations of apartheid in South Africa, and grave manifestations of colonialism and racial discrimination in Namibia, Southern Rhodesia, Angola, Mozambique, and Guinea-Bissau.[109] Besides these new tasks, ECOSOC authorized the *Ad Hoc* Group "to continue its investigations into the infringements of trade union rights" in South Africa, Namibia, and Southern Rhodesia and "to follow the procedure it has adopted in the past, as well as any other established procedure necessary, in order to carry out its tasks with maximum dispatch." [110] The *Ad Hoc* Group embarked on its new tasks at the end of June 1969.

The significance of the *Ad Hoc* Group's work was well described in the course of its 1968 hearings by its acting chairman, Professor Branimir Janković of Yugoslavia:

> Twenty years ago the question of human rights was considered as a matter falling exclusively within the national competence of each State. . . . Today, with the establishment of this investigating group and certain other bodies, I believe it can be said that the United Nations is placing the accent no longer upon the proclamation of norms and the adoption of general resolutions, but also upon the necessity for gathering and evaluating concrete facts and detailed testimony concerning charges of serious, continual and systematic violations of human rights, violations involving the torture and ill-treatment of political prisoners and violation of trade-rights in southern Africa.[111]

What remains to be seen is whether the Group, by improving its methods, can make good Mr. Janković' conclusion, which to date can only be called understandable exaggeration:

[109] Commission resolution 21 (XXV), E/4621–E/CN.4/1007, at 196 (1969); E/Res/1423 (XLVI) (1969); E/Res/1424 (XLVI) (1969).

[110] E/Res/1412 (XLVI) (1969). The Group's attention, like that of ECOSOC, had been drawn by the Secretary-General to new allegations of trade union infringements in South Africa. E/4613 (1969). ECOSOC also had been put on notice by ILO of new allegations of trade union rights violations in Southern Rhodesia. E/4610 (1969). The Group received documents entitled Recent Information Concerning the Treatment of Political Prisoners and Freedom Fighters in South Africa, E/CN.4/AC.22/16 (1969), and Information Concerning the Condition of Africans in the So-Called "Native Reserves" in Namibia, E/CN.4/AC.22/18 (1969).

[111] E/CN.4/AC.22/RT.37, at 3 (1969).

Our experience during the last year has shown us that the concrete conclusions and recommendations of our Group, based on the substantial and consistent testimony of witnesses and widely publicized throughout the world, have made a significant contribution towards convincing world public opinion of the reality of the terrible evils which the peoples of southern Africa are suffering.[112]

[112] *Id.*

Chapter XI

Sources of Information on Violations

International organizations have used a number of sources for obtaining human rights information, chiefly government reports, non-governmental reports, individuals' petitions, hearings, and observation on the scene. These sources are described below.

GOVERNMENT REPORTS

As long ago as the League of Nations, government reports were used in human rights matters for mandated territories and protection of minorities.[1] Reports on trust territories, the UN version of mandates, and non-self-governing territories generally are required by the UN Charter.[2] Certain specialized human rights agreements call for government reporting,[3] among them the Convention on Elimination of all Forms of Racial Discrimination, which became effective in January 1969, and the not yet effective 1966 Covenants on Civil and Political Rights, and on Economic, Social and Cultural Rights.

Government reporting may be required even without the governmental consent given by ratifying a treaty. The Convention on the Political Rights of Women [4] calls for reports not only from States

---

[1] See F. WALTERS, A HISTORY OF THE LEAGUE OF NATIONS chs. 9, 16, 17, 34, 38 (1952); Macartney, *League of Nations Protection of Minority Rights,* in THE INTERNATIONAL PROTECTION OF HUMAN RIGHTS 22 (E. Luard ed. 1967).

[2] Article 88 and Article 73(e) respectively. Both trust and non-self-governing territories were the subject of a 1962 questionnaire issued by the Special Committee on Decolonization. A/AC.109/6 (1962). For a description of Government reporting procedures established under the UN Charter, see A/Conf.32/6, at 124–34 (1968).

[3] For example, the 1951 Convention Relating to the Status of Refugees, 189 U.N.T.S. 150; the Convention Relating to the Status of Stateless Persons, 360 U.N.T.S. 130; the 1926 Slavery Convention, as amended by the 1953 Protocol, 212 U.N.T.S. 18; the 1956 Supplementary Convention on the Abolition of Slavery, the Slave Trade and Institutions and Practices Similar to Slavery, 266 U.N.T.S. 40.

[4] 193 U.N.T.S. 136. The Secretary-General publishes an annual report con-

Parties but also from UN Members not parties to the Convention. Government reporting regardless of consent has been requested in a number of human rights areas by the General Assembly.[5]

A periodic reporting system on human rights matters was begun in 1956 by ECOSOC and made annual in 1965.[6] Reports are received from specialized agencies and non-governmental organizations as well as governments. A three-year cycle is used: the subject in one year being civil and political rights; the next year economic, social, and cultural rights; and the third year freedom of information. After the system had been tested through one full cycle and the second round of reports on civil and political rights had been examined, the Human Rights Commission's *Ad Hoc* Committee on Periodic Reports concluded that

> the relative scarcity of reports made a thorough assessment of the situation with regard to civil and political rights, which required a world-wide survey, impossible. However, they recognized that the system of periodic reports on human rights, besides serving as a source of information, also furnished a valuable incentive to Governments to promote and protect those rights.[7]

UN requests for human rights information from governments are numerous enough to have drawn criticism from some governments. Requests are issued to supply the Yearbook on Human Rights with materials.[8] Special studies rely on governments for information, such as the one on forced labor made by an *ad hoc* UN–ILO committee,[9] the reports on slavery,[10] and those studies made by the

---

taining data both on laws relating to women's rights and on implementation of the Convention. See A/7197 (1968).

[5] Resolution on Manifestations of Racial Prejudice and National and Religious Intolerance, A/Res/1779 (XVII) (1962), A/6397 and Addenda (1966); Declaration on Elimination of All Forms of Racial Discrimination, A/Res/1904 (XVIII) (1963), E/4174 and Add.1–4 (1966), E/4306 and Add.1–4 (1967), A/6691 and Add.1, 2 (1967); Recommendation on Consent to Marriage, Minimum Age for Marriage and Registration of Marriages, E/CN.6/510 and Add.1 (1968); see also A/Res/2144A (XXI), A/6830 and Add.1–3 (1967).

[6] E/Res/1074C (XXXIX) (1965). The system was amended in minor respects by E/Res/1230 (XLII) (1967).

[7] E/CN.4/AC.20/L.19, at 17 (1969). See analytical summary of reports and other material on civil and political rights for 1965–68. E/CN.4/980/Rev.1 (1969).

[8] See for example the 1965 Yearbook, Sales No.: 68.XIV.1.

[9] E/2431 (1951).

[10] E/4168 and Add.1–5 (1966).

Sub-Commission on Prevention of Discrimination and Protection of Minorities.[11] As a consequence, a survey of the UN's work program concluded that "questionnaires addressed to Governments as a source of information for the drafting of studies in the field of human rights are too numerous and too detailed and that the information so requested is very often available through other sources." [12]

Among the UN specialized agencies, both ILO and UNESCO request States Members to report on implementation of Recommendations as well as Conventions. The use which the International Labor Organization makes of government reporting is illustrated in its 1968 submission under ECOSOC's periodic reporting system, which stated that

> the ILO Committee of Experts on the Application of Conventions and Recommendations, at its session in March 1968, made a survey of the situation regarding the implementation of the Forced Labour Convention, 1930 (No. 29) and the Abolition of Forced Labour Convention, 1957 (No. 105). This survey was based on reports due, under the ILO's regular reporting procedures, from ratifying States and on reports which had been specially requested by the Governing Body of the International Labour Office, on the occasion of the International Year for Human Rights from States which had not ratified these Conventions.[13]

The other UN specialized agency using government reporting is the Educational, Scientific and Cultural Organization. UNESCO's General Conference in 1960 adopted a Convention and Recommendation against Discrimination in Education.[14] Reports on implementation of the Convention or Recommendation had been submitted by late 1968 from 70 UNESCO Member States, of which only 27 were Parties to the Convention.[15] The reports were examined by a Special Committee of the UNESCO Executive Board, which sent

[11] Listed in E/CN.4/Sub.2/276, at 134 (1967).

[12] E/4383–E/AC.51/12, at 33 (1967).

[13] E/CN.4/974, at 14–15 (1968). See generally E/4144 (1965), a summary by ILO of its human rights procedures.

[14] The Convention has been in effect since 1962. A 1962 Protocol, instituting a conciliation and good offices Commission to be responsible for seeking the settlement of any disputes between States Parties to the Convention, came into force in 1968. E/CN.4/Sub.2/292/Add.1, at 3 (1968). The Convention and Protocol have been published by the UN with other human rights instruments, A/Conf.32/4, at 30, 33 (1968).

[15] E/CN.4/Sub.2/292/Add.1, at 2–3; E/CN.6/520, at 7–8 (1969).

its conclusions with the Board's own comments to the General Conference.

The two presently operating regional human rights organizations also use government reporting on human rights matters. The 1950 European Convention for the Protection of Human Rights and Fundamental Freedoms requires States Parties to explain on request how they have implemented its terms. Complaints of specific instances of non-compliance set in motion procedures involving government response.[16] The 1961 European Social Charter also calls for various official reports. The 1965 Second Special Inter-American Conference resolved "to authorize the Commission to examine communications submitted to it and any other available information so that it may address to the government of any American state a request for information deemed pertinent by the Commission." [17]

NON-GOVERNMENTAL ORGANIZATION REPORTS

The insufficiency of government reports alone for providing balanced information is widely recognized. The Soviet Union in September 1967 asserted "that the Secretariat should not confine itself in preparing the documents which are placed before the Committee of Twenty-Four to the information given by the colonial Powers. . . . It is imperative to include information from other sources which would be useful to the Committee." [18] In making the same point two years earlier, the USSR had referred to "other sources of information such as the statements of petitioners, written petitions, economic and social studies, surveys and similar material." [19]

Non-governmental organizations have a long history as sources of human rights information. As early as 1815, the Congress of Vienna considered certain communications from private groups. Later use of information from such sources is said to have been made by the Congress of Berlin in 1878 and by the Hague Peace Conferences of

[16] See Articles 24 and 57, Commission Rules 40 *et seq.* As described in Chapter IX, allegations made by Denmark, Norway, Sweden, and The Netherlands against Greece are in process.

[17] Resolution XXII, Final Act of the Second Special Inter-American Conference, Doc. 150 OEA/Ser.E/XIII.1 (1965). See also Report of the Inter-American Commission of Women, "the only *official regional organization* that is empowered to speak, on behalf of the women of the Americas, directly to the heads of government." E/CN.6/525, at 3 (1969).

[18] A/AC.109/PV.557, at 63–65 (1967).

[19] A/6000/Add.7, at 190 (1965).

1899 and 1907.[20] At the League of Nations, NGO representatives at times played a significant role in activities which included the informal furnishing of information. Explicit recognition was given NGOs in the UN Charter. Article 71 required ECOSOC to make "arrangements for consultation with non-governmental organizations which are concerned with matters within its competence." [21] ECOSOC resolution 288 B(X) of 1950 established qualifications, previously existing on a temporary basis, for admission to three classes of consultative status, "A," "B," and "register." All three alike could submit "objective" periodic reports on human rights under the system described above in relation to government reporting, but other information-supplying rights varied by class.[22]

In 1968 ECOSOC approved new arrangements concerning consultation with NGOs, including revised criteria for consultative status.[23] Three new classes were established, general and consultative status (category I), special consultative status (category II), and the non-consultative status of listing on the Roster.[24] The process of awarding the new categories was the occasion for searching

[20] See Secretariat study on the right of petition, E/CN.4/419 §§ 13–18 (1950).

[21] René Cassin has said that the inclusion of human rights provisions of the UN Charter "was due in large part to the 'consultants' from the big international, or specifically American citizens' associations. . . ." Human Rights, Final Report of the International NGO Conference 20 (1968). The Secretariat has issued a "brief history of the consultative relationship of non-governmental organizations with the Economic and Social Council," E/C.2/661 (1969), and a report on such relationships with other UN bodies, E/C.2/662 (1968). NGOs also are used by the UN outside the confines of Article 71. See for example complaints published by the General Assembly's Special Committee on Apartheid in A/AC.115/L.229 and L.231 (1968). The Committee on Apartheid, having contacted sympathetic NGOs in January 1968, published their responses to the Committee's requests for information on activities and for "continued and close co-operation." A/AC.115/L.219 (1968). See also review of communications received relating to General Assembly matters, A/INF/122/Add.6 (1968); list of communications received from private individuals and non-governmental bodies relating to matters of which the Security Council is seized, S/NC/190 (1969).

[22] A list of NGOs in consultative status with ECOSOC appeared in ST/CS/SER.F/203 and Corr. 1 (1966).

[23] E/Res/1296 (XLIV) (1968), which was amended by E/Res/1391 (XLVI) (1969). The changes had been recommended by a Council Committee on NGOs in E/4485 (1968).

[24] Id., Ann. at 5. Also, in May 1968 ECOSOC adopted E/Res/1297 (XLIV) concerning procedures of associating NGOs with the UN Office of Public Information, existing arrangements for which had been described in a Secretariat report listing NGOs so associated. E/4476 and Corr. 1 (1968).

inquiry by an ECOSOC committee into the activities and financing of many of the groups already in consultative status. Strong forces sought to limit the role of NGOs, especially in ventilating individuals' complaints. One view, on the other hand, favored "a sharing of representation on regional and international organs, by governments with their private human rights associations," comparable to the sharing of representation in ILO organs.[25] Any serious curtailment of NGO activity would detract from a generally progressive influence in UN protection of basic rights, as illustrated by René Cassin when he said that "it is well known . . . that but for the counsel given by the competent non-governmental organizations to the governmental delegations to the Assembly, the protocol [to the Civil and Political Rights Covenant, allowing individuals to petition], inadequate though it is, would never have been adopted." [26]

Further use by ECOSOC of NGO information on human rights also should be noted. The *Ad Hoc* Committee on Forced Labour, jointly established by ECOSOC and ILO in 1951, having been authorized to study the problem not only by examining the laws and their application but also "if the committee thinks fit, by taking additional evidence into consideration," [27] "sought to enlist the cooperation of non-governmental organizations, since it felt that they might be in possession of documentary material and information." [28] Other human rights communications arriving at the UN from NGOs, like those from individuals, are treated in accordance with the double standard described in Chapter XII.

Two UN specialized agencies rely on NGOs. The International Labor Organization by its Constitution admits complaints of infringements both from other governments and from non-governmental organizations. The ILO elevates non-governmental employers' and workers' organizations to a status practically equal to that of governments. Constitution Articles 24 and 25 allow such NGOs to represent that "any of the members has failed to secure in any respect

[25] From statement of Sir Egerton Richardson, Jamaican Ambassador to the United States, Human Rights, Final Report of the International NGO Conference, 27 (1968).

[26] *Id.* at 21.

[27] E/Res/350 (XII) (1951).

[28] E/2431, at 11–13 (1953). One NGO used by the *Ad Hoc* Committee, The Anti-Slavery Society, was relied on heavily in the ECOSOC-sponsored slavery studies. See E/4168 and Add.1–5 (1966); A/6228, at 10 (1966).

the effective observance within its jurisdiction of any Convention to which it is a party." ILO rejects complaints from international NGOs with no affiliates in the country concerned and from national NGOs in other countries "having no direct interest in the matters raised in the allegations." [29] Complaints of non-observance, available to member states, also may be lodged by delegates to the International Labour Conference. A special procedure relating to freedom of association uses complaints from governments or from employers' or workers' organizations directed against governments whether or not they have ratified the pertinent conventions. In the official view of ILO, "the participation of non-governmental elements (organizations of employers and workers), which may file complaints, comment on the information and reports supplied by Governments and participate in the discussions of the Conference, unquestionably contributes to the dynamic character of the system." [30]

Another UN specialized agency, UNESCO, also utilizes NGO information, although in the cautious manner typical of international organizations understandably anxious to avoid offending their government constituents. As described by UNESCO itself,

> the Special Committee of the Executive Board charged with examining the first periodic reports by Member States on implementation of the Convention and Recommendation [against Discrimination in Education] . . . did not consider that it could officially invite the international non-governmental organizations to take part in its work or to examine and comment upon the reports of Member States. It would, however, be prepared to receive in accordance with normal procedures, any objective information that international non-governmental organizations having consultative relations with UNESCO might wish to submit concerning the problems of discrimination in education that the Committee is called upon to study.[31]

At the regional level, the Inter-American and European procedures both permit use of NGO human rights reports. The Inter-

[29] 50 I.L.O. OFF. BULL., No. 3, Supp. II, at 27 (1967).

[30] E/4144, at 24 (1965). U Thant told ILO at its fiftieth anniversary that "your unique composition gives you relative immunity from some of the political inhibitions which have tended to weaken effective action for the international protection of human rights." UN Press Release SG/SM/1118–ILO/1618, at 6 (1969).

[31] E/CN.4/Sub.2/283, at 2 (1967).

American Commission has received NGO information in much the same manner as that from individuals.[32] The 1965 Second Special Inter-American Conference resolved "to authorize the Commission to examine communications submitted to it and any other available information . . . with the objective of bringing about more effective observance of fundamental human rights." [33]

The European Commission may receive petitions against consenting States "from any person, non-governmental organization or group of individuals claiming to be the victim of a violation" by such State.[34] The Council of Europe employs NGO consultative status before both its Consultative Assembly and its Committee of Ministers; the Council-sponsored European Social Charter, in force since February 26, 1965, provides in Article 23 for comment by non-governmental organizations on governmental reports relating to both binding and non-binding Charter provisions, and in Article 27 for participation by non-governmental organizations in the review of such reports by a Council Sub-Committee.

Another regional body concerned with human rights, the Organization for African Unity, has granted recognition to certain "Liberation Movements," suggesting the extent to which the UN's human rights activity might be projected through recognition of militant NGOs. Six such Liberation Movements were recognized, as well as eight other NGOs including an American militant group, the Student Non-Violent Coordinating Committee (SNCC), at the 1967 UN International Seminar on Apartheid, Racial Discrimination and Colonialism in Southern Africa.[35] In 1967 James Forman, of SNCC, told the General Assembly's Fourth (Trust and Non-Self-Governing Territories) Committee that "we are confident that the day is not too far off when the desperate plight of the people of African de-

---

[32] See "Report on the Situation Regarding Human Rights in the Dominican Republic" OEA/Ser.L./V/II. 4, at 11–14 (1962).

[33] *Supra* note 17.

[34] Convention, art. 25; see Commission Rules 40 *et seq.*

[35] A/6818, at 11–12 (1967). Six liberation movements participated in a conference in 1969 at Khartoum where a Declaration was adopted which "requests all governments of the world to recognize as the sole official and legitimate authorities of the respective countries the following fighting movements: MPLA (Angola), PAIGC (Guinea-Bissau), FRELIMO (Mozambique), ANC (South Africa), SWAPO (South West Africa), and ZAPU (Zimbabwe)." A/AC.115/L.240, at 5 (1969). The Apartheid Committee in 1969 heard testimony from Students for a Democratic Society (SDS). AC/AC.115/SR.109, at 10 (1969) and A/AC.115/SR.111, at 11 (1969).

scent who were wrenched from the shores of Africa . . . will be fully debated in the United Nations as a human rights problem." [36] In 1964 the late American Black Nationalist, Malcolm X, had declared his intention of "internationalizing" American racial problems on the theory that

> if South African racism is not a domestic issue, then American racism also is not a domestic issue. . . . If United States Supreme Court Justice Arthur Goldberg a few weeks ago could find legal grounds to threaten to bring Russia before the United Nations and charge her with violating the human rights of less than three million Russian Jews—what makes our African brothers hesitate to bring the United States Government before the United Nations and charge her with violating the human rights of 22 million African-Americans? [37]

In 1969 SNCC expressed the "hope that the United Nations will see fit to expose racism . . . in the United States. . . ." [38] Such a development clearly is possible, but it is not likely to occur because of the greater effectiveness of domestic protests and the possible reluctance of many Africans to expand the UN's role in domestic inquiry, even on the appealing issue of racial discrimination.

INDIVIDUALS' PETITIONS

It has been persuasively argued that the most relevant sources of human rights information are neither governments nor NGOs but actual alleged victims or persons close to them. [39] "L'Assemblée Consultative [Européenne] avait, dès le début, insisté sur le fait qu'il incombait à l'individu d'être le gardien des ses propres libertés. . . . Aux yeux de l'Assemblée, l'intervention d'un gouvernement en faveur d'un individu aurait pour conséquence de transformer 'une réclamation individuelle en litige interétatique,' tandis que le recours individuel dépolitiserait les litiges." [40]

The Anti-Slavery Society has suggested that the reason why no

---

[36] UN Press Release GA/T/1688, at 3 (1967).

[37] N.Y. Times, Aug. 13, 1964, §1, at 22, col. 2.

[38] A/AC.115/L.251, at 4 (1969); A/AC.115/SR.112, at 7 (1969).

[39] See for example arguments in the 1965 General Assembly Third Committee debates on implementation provisions for the Convention on the Elimination of All Forms of Racial Discrimination at the 1344th, 1347th, 1349th, 1355th, 1357th, and 1364th meetings.

[40] P. Modinos, *Coexistence de la Convention Européenne des Droits de l'Homme et du Pacte des Droits Civils et Politiques des Nations Unies*, 1 HUMAN RIGHTS J. 41, 51 (1968).

Member State had called for machinery to implement the Supplementary Slavery Convention was explained by the attitude revealed in a Human Rights Commission delegate's remark that "we have no slavery in my country, but we have neighbors who do have it and we have no intention of embarrassing them." [41] This attitude also may suggest why states are not always reliable sources of human rights information and why one must often look to injured individuals. A. K. Brohi of Pakistan in his paper at the Teheran Conference said that

> the main weakness of the system of confining the "complaint-making" initiative with States as has been done in the provisions of the Covenant on Civil and Political Rights is that States are unlikely to complain about the conduct of other States towards individuals unless they have, what in ordinary parlance is called a "political reason" for doing so. Experience has shown that a similar procedure which is available in the constitution of the ILO has been involved only twice during the forty-nine years of its existence. The Optional Protocol is an attempt to repair this defect. [42]

Individuals' complaints are used systematically at the regional level. The Inter-American Commission's blanket authority on sources of information, clearly broad enough to include the individual, is quoted above in connection with NGOs. Furthermore, by September 1968, the European Commission had registered 7 cases brought by one Member State against another Member State under Article 24 of the Convention, and 3,700 cases brought against States by individuals or groups of individuals under Article 25. [43] This number of individuals' complaints, according to the Council of Europe itself, "is not excessive and has not posed an undue strain either on national Governments or on the international body and its secretariat." [44] Therefore it has been fairly stated that "the individual's right of petition is undoubtedly the cornerstone of the structure devised in Rome in 1950. It is also the most original feature of the whole procedure under the Convention; for the first time indi-

---

[41] E/C.2/664 (1968).

[42] A/Conf.32/L.4, at 21 (1968).

[43] McNulty, Remarks at World Law Day Human Rights 1968, World Peace Through Law Center, Pamphlet Series No. 12, at 20 (1969).

[44] E/CN.4/975, at 23–24 (1968).

viduals may have direct recourse to an international judicial organ concerned with human rights." [45]

The European belief in petitions is not shared by all at the UN:

> Sur la base des statistiques, nous pouvons affirmer qu'au Conseil de l'Europe la querelle d'écoles est déjà dépassée. Tel n'est assurément pas le cas aux Nations Unies, devant lesquelles les deux doctrines s'affrontent: celle qui accepte qu'un individu puisse, par une action directe, saisir l'instance international et celle qui refuse à l'individu la faculté de faire valoir directement, sur le plan international, ses droits personnels.[46]

The lack of consistent UN treatment of individuals' petitions is detailed in Chapter XII. A step toward consistency was the inclusion in the 1965 Racial Discrimination Convention of provisions, though optional for States Parties, allowing individuals' complaints against their own governments to be considered.[47] A year later similar provisions were annexed in the Optional Protocol to the Covenant on Civil and Political Rights.[48] The wider use of petitions by the UN Human Rights Commission has been described in Chapter IX.

Among the issues bound to arise in connection with individuals' petitions is that of standing. In one formula on standing, the Optional Protocol to the International Covenant on Civil and Political Rights refers to "communications from individuals subject to its jurisdiction who claim to be victims of a violation by that State Party." [49] The International Labor Organization accepts no complaints from individuals, only from organizations of workers or employers, and then only if the organization is situated in the country

---

[45] K. Vasak, *The European Convention on Human Rights: A Useful Complement to the Geneva Conventions,* INT'L REV. RED CROSS (August 1965).

[46] P. Modinos, *supra* note 40, at 52. See also Parson, *The Individual Right of Petition: A Study of Methods Used by International Organizations to Utilize the Individual as a Source of Information on the Violations of Human Rights,* 13 WAYNE L. REV. 678 (1967). Lists of communications received relating to General Assembly matters are published occasionally, *e.g.,* A/INF./122 and Add.1–6 (1967–68).

[47] A/Res/2106 (XX) (1965). The 1961 Convention on the Reduction of Statelessness, not yet in force, requires in Article 11 that Contracting States promote establishment of a body to which individuals could make claims. The Convention has been published in the compilation cited *supra* note 14, at 53.

[48] A/Res/2200 (XXI) (1966). ECOSOC's new procedures for handling complaints are described in Chapter IX.

[49] A/Res/2200 (XXI) (1966).

to which the complaint relates.[50] The European Commission's requirements that a petition emanate from a "victim of violation" may be read, in one view, to include "indirect victims" or "potential victims." [51] The problem is to allow some category broader than only victims, who may be prevented from petitioning, and narrower than all parties desiring to petition, of whom there may be too many. The considerations are not unlike those controlling standing for taxpayers' suits in US usage.

Another issue in practice is whether anonymous petitions will be admitted. A petition signed "A True Micronesian" and expressing a desire "to remain anonymous until such appropriate time in the future when I shall stand up publicly against the United States" was circulated by the Trusteeship Council in 1968.[52] Article 3 of the Optional Protocol to the Civil and Political Rights Covenant would require the Human Rights Committee established by the Covenant to consider "inadmissible any communication under the present Protocol which is anonymous, or which it considers to be an abuse of the right of submission of such communications or to be incompatible with the provisions of the Covenant." The Sub-Committee on Petitions of the General Assembly's Special "Committee of 24" on decolonization prepared proposals on admissibility of unsigned communications, but the full Committee asked it to reconsider them.[53] The Sub-Committee determined that a number of communications had been circulated over the years "from public or private organizations or groups which had not borne the name of any person representing the organization or group." [54]

---

[50] 52 I.L.O. OFF. BULL., No. 1, Supp. at 19 (1969). The USSR similarly argued, in resisting consultative status for the International Commission of Jurists in 1969, that the Commission had no right to criticize governments of countries where it had no branches or whose nationals were not among its membership. The Commission reportedly pointed out that such a rule would prevent organizations from criticizing the regimes in South Africa, Southern Rhodesia or the Portuguese African Territories. A/AC.115/SR.111, at 7 (1969).

[51] A-M NAY-CADOUX, ESSAIS SUR LES DROITS DE L'HOMME EN EUROPE 63, 66 (1966), reviewed in 9 HARV. INT'L L.J. 346, 349 (1968). See Inter-American Commission's Regulations on admissibility of communications. Regulations of the Inter-American Commission on Human Rights, OEA/Ser.L/V/II. 17 (Doc. 26) (1967).

[52] T/PET.10/L.12 (1968). For description of the Trusteeship Council's procedures on petitions and hearings, see A/Conf.32/6, at 72–75 (1967).

[53] A/AC.109/SC.1/SR.103, at 3 (1967).

[54] A/AC.109/SC.1/SR.118, at 4 (1967).

An awkward admissibility problem concerns the petitioner's attitude. Decision was postponed in 1967, by the same Sub-Committee, on a communication to which two representatives objected because, by favoring South African presence in South West Africa, it "ran counter to the decision taken by the General Assembly at its twenty-first session."[55] Later that year a 15–5–1 majority of the full Special Committee approved a Sub-Committee report[56] reciting how seven communications on Gibraltar apparently had been ruled inadmissible by the Sub-Committee as being critical of Spain, a State other than the Administering Power, although the United Kingdom cited prior circulation of petitions critical of non-administering States: "The Sub-Committee on Petitions is not a board of censors. Its function is not to decide what we should read and what should be suppressed. It is the duty of our Committee, and indeed its right, to study all points of view."[57] The Special Committee's Chairman advanced "the view that at some future date the Sub-Committee on Petitions should have some terms of reference. However, in the absence of terms of reference, I suppose we have to operate in the same way as we have operated in the past."[58] The United Kingdom replied that "the only defensible criteria which can be applied by the Sub-Committee are whether a communication is relevant and whether it is from someone who has a claim to have his views considered. . . ."[59] In March 1968 the Sub-Committee Chairman expressed the hope that the Sub-Committee would be able to adopt its rules at an early date, including a definition of "petition" that would distinguish it from a mere expression of opinion.[60]

HEARINGS AND OBSERVATION

Evidence from alleged victims can be obtained even more directly by hearings than through written petitions. Hearings have been used

[55] A/AC.109/SC.1/SR.103, at 7 (1967).
[56] A/AC.109/L.435 (1967).
[57] A/AC.109/PV.569, at 7 (1967).
[58] *Id.* at 37.
[59] *Id.* at 42.
[60] A/AC.109/SC.1/SR.122–27, at 9–10 (1968). In October 1968 the Sub-Committee decided not to circulate a communication on Gibraltar, A/AC.109/L.522, A/AC.109/SC.1/SR.136, at 2–3 (1969), which action the UK attributed to the petitioner's opposition to Spanish acquisition of Gibraltar. UN Press Release GA/COL/846 (1968).

by the UN and ILO,[61] and by the regional human rights organizations.[62] In 1967, UN use of oral hearings reached a new level of
development, as described in Chapter X, when the *Ad Hoc* Working Group of Experts, besides receiving 23 written statements,
heard 25 witnesses. South African refusal, however, prevented the
Group from using on-the-scene observation, a source of information
well established in international organization usage and enlarged
upon at Teheran by A. K. Brohi's imaginative suggestion for "duly
trained United Nations correspondents accredited to important capi-
tols of the world, charged with the duty of reporting from their stations the actual state of affairs observable in various Member States
in regard to the way in which they are fulfilling the high ideals of
human dignity and fundamental freedoms that have been proclaimed by them so ostentatiously in the Universal Declaration." [63]

Perhaps the most notable UN human rights mission was the one
sent by the General Assembly to South Viet Nam in 1963.[64] More

[61] For historical background, see E/CN.4/419 (1950); the ICJ's advisory
opinion on the hearing of petitioners by a UN Committee on South West
Africa, [1956] I.C.J. 23, 51–52; concerning use of hearings by the UN's Fourth
and two Special Committees, see Chapter XIII; concerning oral statements by
NGOs in consultative status with ECOSOC, see E/Res/288B(X) §24 (1950),
E/4485 Ann. at 7, 10 (1968), and E/Res/1296 (XLIV) (1968); concerning
the ILO's use of hearings in human rights matters, see E/4144, at 11, 16, 20
(1965); see also Report of the *Ad Hoc* Committee on Forced Labor, E/2431,
App. III (1953); regarding UN measures relating to forced labor, see A/
Conf.32/5, at 157–60 (1967) and A/Conf.32/6, at 152 (1967).

[62] The European system provides for oral testimony both before the Commission, Rules, 46, 47, 53–57, and the Court of Human Rights, Rules 38–45.
The Inter-American Commission, with less formality, has heard hundreds of
witnesses. See Chapter VIII at note 24.

[63] A/Conf.32/L.4, at 77–78 (1968). For a description of the Trusteeship
Council's use of visiting missions, see A/Conf.32/6, at 75–77 (1967). A recent
illustration of the use of visiting missions by the Trusteeship Council was its
1967 mission to the Trust Territory of the Pacific Islands. T/1658 and Corr.
1 and Add.1 (1967); S/8020 (1967). A 1962 visit to South West Africa by
the Chairman and Vice-Chairman of the General Assembly's Special Committee
for South West Africa is described in Reference Paper No. 5, at 17–19 (1966).
As described in Chapter VI, South Africa invited the ICJ to visit South West
Africa, but the Applicants Ethiopia and Liberia objected and the Court declined.

[64] Volio-Jimenez. *International Protection of Human Rights: Balance
Sheet of a Promising Action*, 1 U.N. MONTHLY CHRONICLE No. 7, at 75 (Dec.
1964); A/5630 (1963). The "Committee of 24" on decolonization in 1969 held
its fifth series of meetings away from UN headquarters. UN Press Release GA/
COL/904, at 3 (1969).

recently the Secretary-General sent a Representative on Humanitarian Activities to Nigeria, who said in October 1968, after visiting the southern and western fronts, that there were no confirmed reports of wanton destruction of civilian life, maltreatment or cruelty to civilians.[65] Elsewhere, as in southern Africa and Israeli-held Arab territories, visitation efforts have been barred, although Israel has said it would agree if Jews in Arab lands also could be visited.[66]

Visitation is used by one specialized agency and both operating regional human rights organizations. The ILO in 1967 accepted a Spanish invitation to send a study group to examine the trade union situation there.[67] A three-man group visited Spain in 1969, interviewing officials and meeting privately with over 100 persons including detainees.[68] European Commission Rule 58 and European Court Rule 38 contemplate observation on the spot and, as described in Chapter IX, Greek detention places were visited by a Sub-Commission in 1969. A Rapporteur of the Council of Europe Assembly had gone to Greece in April 1968 to inform himself about the human rights situation there.[69] The Inter-American Commission visited the Dominican Republic in 1961, 1963, and 1965. Commission member Sandifer has stated about the 1965 visit that "in the midst of the approbrium heaped indiscriminately on the representatives of the OAS, the Inter-American Peace Force, and the United States, it has not been unusual to hear the Commission's representatives popularly called 'los buenos'—'the good ones.' " [70] Indications of the success of the Commission's mission are the Dominican Institutional Act of August 31, 1965 providing for the Commission to be present during the electoral process, and the remarkable appeal to the Commission from the Chief of the Domini-

[65] UN Press Release WS/370, at 6 (1968). A non-UN team of military observers from the United Kingdom, Canada, Poland, and Sweden concluded that Nigeria was not committing genocide in Biafra. N.Y. Times, Dec. 7, 1968, §1, at 56, col. 1. See also Chapter VIII.

[66] See Chapter IX.

[67] 50 I.L.O. OFF. BULL., No. 3, Supp. II, at 90–92 (1967). ILO's visitation practice is described in E/4144, at 16, 18, 20 (1965).

[68] The group conveyed certain conclusions to the Government. UN Press Release ILO/1603 (1969).

[69] Council of Europe Press Release C (68) 9 (1968).

[70] THE ASSOCIATION OF THE BAR OF THE CITY OF NEW YORK, THE DOMINICAN REPUBLIC CRISIS 1965 120 (J. Carey ed. 1967).

can National Police to "take due note of . . . and redouble its efforts to prevent any recurrence" of armed assaults during February 1966 by mobs against policemen.[71]

In some instances, international organizations are given carte blanche as to what sources of human rights information they may consult. Sometimes repositories of information of unspecified origin may be consulted, such as UN specialized agencies, the Secretary-General, and the writings of scholars.[72] Elsewhere the lack of limit is articulated even more clearly. The European Court's Rule 38(2) allows it to "obtain information in any other manner." The Inter-American Commission's post-Dominican crisis mandate from the Second Special Inter-American Conference allows it to examine "any other available information." [73]

It seems clear that all possible sources of human rights information should be employed by the UN. It is particularly important that private sources—both individuals and groups—be fully used, since government reports are almost sure to be incomplete.

[71] S/7163, at 7 (1966).
[72] A/6228, at 7–8 (1966).
[73] *Supra* note 17. Assorted sources were consulted by the UN-ILO *Ad Hoc* Committee on Forced Labor as explained in its 1953 Report, *supra* note 61, at 4, 10–11, 15.

Chapter XII

The UN's Double Standard on Treatment of Complaints

There was a risk that a double standard might be introduced and that procedures might be applied in some cases and not in others. On a number of occasions ICFTU had submitted petitions on behalf of workers in South West Africa, the Portuguese colonies, Aden, and Southern Rhodesia but had been unable to refer to violations of human rights in other countries.[1]

This 1967 complaint to ECOSOC's Social Committee by an International Confederation of Free Trade Unions representative was echoed by the UK in the General Assembly's Third Committee:

If the United Nations were to apply a double standard in dealing with human rights matters, its reputation would inevitably be impaired and the whole purpose of United Nations human rights activities would be put in question.[2]

Unfortunately, such a double standard has developed. As noted in Chapter IX, however, recent events in the UN Human Rights Commission and its Sub-Commission have shown that, if ECOSOC approves, procedures can be put into effect shortly to inquire into human rights complaints anywhere in the world. Previously, only complaints on colonies and South Africa could be publicly aired at the UN. Other independent nations were protected by a veil of UN secrecy, while the ILO and the regional arrangements in Europe and the Americas allowed public investigation. Without reform in ECO-SOC's procedures, the double standard would have persisted in an altered form, as will be shown, even after both the Racial Discrimination Convention and the Covenant on Civil and Political Rights were effective.

---

[1] E/AC.7/SR.566, at 13 (1967).
[2] A/C.3/SR.1626, at 12 (1968).

143

THE DEVELOPING PARADOX

In the early years of the United Nations a paradox was noticed in the relative standing of individual human rights complainants depending on their nationality. It was stated that persons under Trusteeship "had the right to petition the Trusteeship Council, whereas the citizens of the administering countries did not possess that right."[3] Standing to petition the Trusteeship Council arose from Article 87 of the UN Charter, which allows "the General Assembly and, under its authority, the Trusteeship Council, in carrying out their functions [to] . . . b. accept petitions and examine them in consultation with the administering authority."

The jurisdictional limits imposed by the language of the Charter have been outgrown in recent years. The acceptance by UN bodies of petitions as well as the hearing of petitioners on various subjects, including the denial of human rights, has expanded from the trust territories contemplated by Article 87(b) to non-self-governing territories and even to one independent state, South Africa.[4]

Subject to the completion of reforms described in Chapter IX, there still remains a paradox. Persons complaining about South Africa may petition the United Nations in writing, charging that government with denials of human rights, receive a hearing and have both their written and oral testimony mimeographed and circulated to 127 Member States and nearly 200 libraries in various countries. All other persons complaining of human rights violations by their own government rather than by a foreign or colonial government are told the United Nations cannot help them. The difference in treatment reflects a double standard, which was noted at the eighteenth (January 1966) session of the Sub-Commission on Prevention of Discrimination and Protection of Minorities, when

> one member contrasted the frequent publication by United Nations bodies of human rights complaints regarding dependent areas and

[3] A/C.3/SR.158, at 2 (1948). The French representative was credited by the Belgian with having "clearly stated the paradox."

[4] General Assembly action respecting apartheid and the human rights aspect of colonialism have been noted in R. GARDNER, IN PURSUIT OF WORLD ORDER 243 (1965), and Buergenthal, *The United Nations and the Development of Rules Relating to Human Rights,* 59 PROCEEDINGS OF THE AMERICAN SOCIETY OF INTERNATIONAL LAW 132 (1965).

South Africa with the private treatment of complaints regarding other areas.[5]

THE PREVAILING STANDARD

Most of the hundreds of communications arriving each year at the United Nations in which the writers complain of human rights violations by their own governments are given scant attention. In spite of the fact that Article 62, paragraph 2, of the Charter authorizes the Economic and Social Council to "make recommendations for the purpose of promoting respect for, and observance of, human rights and fundamental freedoms for all," ECOSOC in 1947 ruled that its relevant subordinate body, the Commission on Human Rights, had no power to take action on individual human rights complaints. Accordingly the Secretariat, at ECOSOC's request, followed a procedure whereby it simply prepared for the Commission a non-confidential summary of communications dealing with human rights "principles" and a confidential summary of "other communications concerning human rights." [6] The latter category included individual complaints. In either case the author's name was not given without his consent, and he was told that "the Commission has no power to take any action in regard to any complaint concerning human rights." Member States named in communications were given copies which did not identify the sender, and could send comments to the Commission, but the Commission might not see an actual communication if it contained a complaint instead of a discussion of "principles."

This treatment of communications was described by Bilder as not providing "any generally applicable and systematic international procedures or institutional machinery for actually receiving and investigating complaints of specific violations of human rights and

[5] E/CN.4/903–E/CN.4/Sub.2/263, at 61 (1966). The present author is the member mentioned.

[6] The procedures are now embodied in ECOSOC Res. 728F (XXVIII) of 1959. For an example of the non-confidential summary see E/CN.4/CR.38 (1968). The Commission on the Status of Women also receives a "Non-Confidential List of Communications," e.g., E/CN.6/CR.21 (1969), as does the Sub-Commission on Prevention of Discrimination and Protection of Minorities, e.g., E/CN.4/Sub.2/CR.13 (1968). The General Assembly and Security Council publish their own lists of communications received. See respectively A/INF/122 and Add.1–5 (1967–68), and S/NC/192 (1969).

taking appropriate steps to remedy them." [7] He also called attention to the absence of "even the minimal function of exposing the facts of such situations before the international community, thus helping to bring the weight of world public opinion to bear on the governments concerned."

Objections to such restrictive treatment of individual human rights complaints bore no fruit for many years. Secretary General Trygve Lie suggested in 1949 that the Human Rights Commission be allowed by ECOSOC "to make recommendations to it on matters which have been brought to the Commission's notice in the course of its examination of communications concerning human rights." [8] While a right of petition in human rights cases was later held by Professor Lauterpacht to be "implied in the Charter as the very minimum" means of safeguarding human rights,[9] and Professors McDougal and Bebr urged that the General Assembly reverse ECOSOC's restrictive rule,[10] another view cautioned that

> an international authority, empowered to deal with complaints of individuals and groups of individuals against their own government, must be built on stronger promises [sic] than on a contested interpretation of a provision of the Charter, which tends to be ambiguous.[11]

This was the situation as to most human rights complaints received at the UN until the recent events described in Chapter IX.

THE EXCEPTIONAL STANDARD

As noted, specific human rights complaints against a non-colonial government are—in the single instance of South Africa—given wide

[7] Bilder, *The International Promotion of Human Rights: A Current Assessment*, 58 AM. J. INT'L L. 728, 731 (1964).

[8] E/CN.4/165, at 7 (1949). At the 18th (January 1966), session of the Sub-Commission on Prevention of Discrimination and Protection of Minorities, to which the Secretary-General presented confidential and non-confidential lists of communications, "various members expressed deep uneasiness about the existing practice in relation to those communications. These members considered that they were placed in an impossible position when they were made aware of the existence of complaints in fields within their expert province but were denied a sight of the text of the complaints or an opportunity to discuss them." *Supra* note 5.

[9] H. LAUTERPACHT, INTERNATIONAL LAW AND HUMAN RIGHTS 244 (1950).

[10] *Human Rights in the United Nations*, 58 AM. J. INT'L L. 603, 640 (1964).

[11] Breugel, *The Right to Petition an International Authority*, 2 INT'L & COMP. L.Q. 542, 547 (1953).

publicity, if not more full investigation or relief. The technique employed, the use of a General Assembly Special Committee rather than the Human Rights Commission or any "executive" body like the proposed UN High Commissioner for Human Rights, had its origins in the process inherited from the League of Nations and developed in the United Nations, particularly since 1960.

Prior to 1960 the Trusteeship Council was using well-established methods for handling petitions. Besides accepting and examining them as explicitly authorized by Article 87(b) of the Charter, the Council that year granted oral hearings in several cases,[12] as did the Fourth Committee of the General Assembly.[13] The latter body took the step in 1961 of granting hearings to petitioners not only from Trust Territories but also from Portuguese Guinea, concerning which Portugal had refused to supply information as called for by Article 73, because it considered this area to be part of Portugal rather than a separate and "non-self-governing" territory. The argument in the Fourth Committee preceding this decision stressed that Article 73, unlike Article 87, does not even mention petitions, let alone hearings.[14]

The extension in 1961 of the petition-and-hearing process to other than Trust Territories breached the dike. The following year the Fourth Committee swept aside legal objections by Britain and Spain to hearing petitioners from areas agreed by their rulers to be "non-self-governing" but on which those Powers had not refused reports. By 1963, when Captain Galvão, whom Portugal was seeking for the seizure of the vessel *Santa Maria,* sought to testify before the Fourth Committee, the only objection to hearing petitioners from other than Trust Territories was made by Spain, which declined to press the point.[15] Other members made it clear they considered any such distinction to have vanished. The United Arab Republic, in the language of the summary record, referred to "the

[12] A/4404 (1960). Recent examples of human rights petitions to the Trusteeship Council include T/PET.10/46 (1969) and T/PET.10/53 (1969).

[13] A/4737, at 32 (1961) and A/4738, at 45–46 (1961).

[14] A/C.4/SR.1208 (1961).

[15] A/C.4/SR.1481, at 10 (1963). However, South Africa stated two years later, in respect to South West Africa, that it did not recognize the right of the Committee to hear petitioners except in the case of Trust Territories. A/C.4/SR.1568, at 12 (1965).

right of petition in relation to Trust and Non-Self-Governing Territories, as provided for in the Charter and developed by the General
Assembly and the Trusteeship Council. . . ." [16] Ceylon conceded
that "invitations to petitioners did not fall under any of the provi-
sons of the Charter [but] in order to carry out [their] functions,
the Assembly, the Fourth Committee and the Special Committees
had recognized the right to hear petitioners." [17]

The Special Committees referred to by Ceylon must have been
those on Colonialism and on Apartheid in South Africa. The former
was hearing complaints against foreign colonial governments, while
the latter heard petitioners attack a government which, however
much hated, was locally selected rather than foreign. Thus the
Apartheid Committee was doing as to one state what ECOSOC had
prevented the Human Rights Commission from even approaching as
to states in general. From the victim's viewpoint it might be said
that a South African possessed a unique if still ineffectual procedural advantage in relation to his own government.

The first of the Special Committees doubtless referred to by Ceylon, that on Colonialism, was established in 1961 with 17 members
to check on implementation of General Assembly Resolution 1514
(XV) of 1960, calling for "immediate steps . . . to transfer all
powers"   to   colonial   peoples,   and   asserting   "the   need
for . . . universal respect for, and observance of, human rights."
The Committee pursued its investigative function, submitting a
questionnaire for governments to answer, and hearing individual
petitioners.[18] These methods were approved by the Assembly in
1962, when it enlarged the Committee to 24 members and trans-
ferred to its jurisdiction supervisory functions with respect to South

[16] A/C.4/SR.1479, at 2 (1963). See also USSR, *id.* at 4; Ghana, *id.* at 9;
Yugoslavia, A/C.4/SR.1481, at 3 (1963).

[17] A/C.4/SR.1480, at 13 (1963). The Fourth Committee was praised by its
Chairman in September 1965 for having "been able to bring about a gradual
and almost imperceptible readjustment of certain provisions of the Charter so
that it might remain, as far as possible, a reflection of the progress and the
major currents of our day. A significant illustration of this continuous process
of empirical adaptation of the Charter to a rapidly and constantly changing
world lies in the way in which it was possible gradually to change the centre
of gravity of United Nations anti-colonial action from the Trusteeship Council
to the Committee of Twenty-Four known as the Decolonization Committee."
A/C.4/640, paras. 12–13 (1965).

[18] A/5238, at 18–19 (1962).

West Africa. The transfer lent further support to the Committee's petition-and-hearing practice, since the General Assembly asked the Committee to carry on the work of earlier special committees in examining petitions "as far as possible in accordance with the Mandates procedure of the League of Nations." [19] South Africa had acquired authority over South West Africa by a League Mandate.

The Committee of 24 lost no time in taking on its new task of investigating conditions in South West Africa. By November 1963, it had examined 94 petitions on that area and had granted hearings to 14 petitioners.[20] The next month the Assembly "endorse[d] its methods and procedures" without dissent.[21] Then the Committee's jurisdiction was further enlarged in such a way as to encourage its petition-and-hearing procedures. To it were given the duties of the long-standing Committee on Information from Non-Self-Governing Territories. Recalling its approval of the Special Committee's methods and procedures, the Assembly requested it "to undertake any special study and prepare any special report it may consider necessary. . . ." [22]

Many of the petitions received and circulated by the Committee of 24 have charged basic rights violations, frequently naming the victims. For example, a complaint addressed to U Thant by the World Federation of Trade Unions in 1965 charged various "brutal acts of repression" and attached a list of eighteen Southern Rhodesian trade union leaders who were stated to have been arrested in

[19] A/Res/1804 (XVII) (1962). The Committee of 24 was thereby given functions previously assigned to the Special Committee for South West Africa, formed in 1961 to take over from the Committee on South West Africa, which in 1953 had replaced an *ad hoc* petition-examining Committee dating back to 1950, the year of the International Court of Justice advisory opinion affirming South Africa's duty to report annually on South West Africa and transmit petitions to the UN, [1950] I.C.J. 128. The Court gave two later advisory opinions on the procedures established by the UN, one on voting, [1955] I.C.J. 67, and the other upholding the Assembly's authorization to the Committee on South West Africa to grant hearings to petitioners, [1956] I.C.J. 23.

[20] A/Res/1900 (XVIII) (1963); Report of Special Committee, A/5446 and Add.1–4 (1963).

[21] A/Res/1958 (XVIII) (1963). France, South Africa, Spain, the United Kingdom, Belgium, and the United States abstained.

[22] A/Res/1970 (XVIII) (1963). Two years later the General Assembly *"Notes with appreciation* the work accomplished by the Special Committee . . . , [and] Requests the Special Committee to continue to perform its task. . . ." A/Res/2105 (XX) (1965).

1964.[23] Like hundreds of other petitions, this one was mimeo-graphed and circulated as an official UN document, in marked con-trast to the restrictive treatment it would have received had it not fallen within the Special Committee's geographical jurisdiction or dealt with apartheid.

Although some persons have suggested that the very nature of apartheid makes it a colonial manifestation,[24] human rights com-plaints by South Africans against their government in essence re-semble human rights complaints by residents of any state against the government of that state. Yet the latters' complaints, as de-scribed above, are kept private, while the former are publicized through the same procedures employed by the Colonialism Commit-tee.

The Special Committee on the Policies of Apartheid of the Gov-ernment of the Republic of South Africa began receiving and circu-lating petitions soon after it was organized in 1962. Details were set forth on political trials, detentions without trial, banning orders, house arrests, and torture of prisoners.[25] Publicity has been an avowed purpose. Costa Rica in March 1965 "associated itself with

[23] A/AC.109/PET.374 (1963).

[24] Mr. A. B. Ngcobo of the Pan-Africanist Congress of South Africa told the Colonialism Committee on June 8, 1965, at Dar-es-Salaam, Tanzania, that South Africa is "ruled by a foreign minority. . . . He therefore could not agree with the Special Committee that it was not competent to hear the na-tionalist leaders of South Africa." A/AC.109/SR.358, at 14–15 (1965). On the other hand, the National Unity Democratic Organization has stated that South African Prime Minister "Verwoerd is not Salazar, who can retire to Portugal, or Smith [of Southern Rhodesia] who can retreat to England." A/AC.109/PET.371/Add.4, at 4 (1965). The Government of The Netherlands, from which came Verwoerd and the ancestors of many of his white fellow-countrymen, in June 1965, pledged Dfl. 100,000 "for the relief and assistance to persons persecuted for their opposition to the policies of apartheid." A/AC.115/L.134 (1965). South Africa lodged an official protest at this action. A/AC.115/SR.64, at 7 (1965). A Netherlands representative in December 1965, told the UN Special Political Committee that "it was distressing for his country to realize that apartheid was practised by a people who traced their origin in part to the Netherlands, where that line of thinking was re-jected as being contrary to the innermost convictions of its people and more important than any ties of kinship." A/SPC/SR.480, at 7 (1965). Costa Rica has stated the view that, "although the fight against apartheid had some po-litical aspects, it primarily reflected a desire to ensure respect for fundamental human rights." E/CN.4/AC.19/SR.2, at 3 (1965).

[25] See for example A/5825/Add.1–S/6073/Add.1 (1964).

the Committee's further effort to arouse world public opinion and to bring its message home to the South African Government." [26] This view, expressed by the original proposer of the UN High Commissioner plan discussed in Chapter VIII, may have shown what is envisaged as one function of that official. His bringing public opinion to bear on all the world's human rights complaints would help to cure the present double standard.

THE RACIAL DISCRIMINATION CONVENTION— STILL A DOUBLE STANDARD

Until December 1965, the UN's double standard on human rights complaints meant simply that individuals' complaints could be lodged publicly with a United Nations body only when directed against colonial governments or against the South African Government, and not when directed by persons generally against their own domestic governments.[27] The double standard was extended at the end of 1965 in the racial discrimination field. A new body was provided for in the UN draft convention, with power to receive in confidence complaints against colonial governments without their consent, but against complainants' own governments only with such governments' prior consent. While Guinea surmised in the Third Committee debate that even South Africa would feel free to ratify the new

[26] A/AC.115/SR.55, at 7 (1965). The Apartheid Committee Chairman later urged that foreign activities "which encouraged the apartheid regime should be given the greatest publicity and mercilessly denounced." A/AC.115/SR.62, at 7 (1965). General Assembly Resolution 2054 (XX), which increased the Committee's membership by six, *"Requests* the Secretary-General, in consultation with the Special Committee, to take appropriate measures for the widest possible dissemination of information on the policies of *apartheid* of the Government of South Africa and on United Nations efforts to deal with the situation. . . ." In March 1966, the Special Committee published a 10-page "Review of Recent Political Trials in South Africa," A/AC.115/L.164, updating its earlier report of August 1965.

[27] When Iraq objected in January 1966, on the floor of the Sub-Commission on Prevention of Discrimination and Protection of Minorities, to the Secretariat's descriptions in a published document (E/CN.4/Sub.2/259) of allegations made in 1963 of genocide by Iraq against the Kurdish People, the descriptions were deleted. E/CN.4/Sub.2/259/Rev.1 (1966). ILO's March 1966 request (E/CN.4/909 and Add.1) that the Commission on Human Rights investigate alleged mass executions in Burundi was withdrawn by ILO after Burundi agreed to cooperate in an ILO investigation. E/4184–E/CN.4/916, at 6–8 (1966).

measure,[28] the United Kingdom found the new double standard objectionable, as described below.

The Convention provides for an 18-expert Committee on the Elimination of Racial Discrimination, to consider reports from States Parties, to hear and conciliate state-to-state complaints with the help of *ad hoc* commissions, and to consider certain complaints of individuals.[29] A compromise on the complaints of individuals resulted in the rule in Article 14 that "no communication shall be received by the Committee if it concerns a State Party which has not made . . . a declaration" so authorizing the Committee. The double standard resulted from the direction in Article 15 that the Committee, without requiring any such declaration,

> receive copies of the petitions from, and submit expressions of opinion and recommendations on these petitions to, the bodies of the United Nations which deal with matters directly related to the principles and objectives of this Convention in their consideration of petitions from the inhabitants of Trust and Non-Self-Governing Territories, and all other territories to which General Assembly resolution 1514 (XV) applies, relating to matters covered by this Convention which are before these bodies.

Besides the Convention, the Assembly, on the recommendation of the Third Committee, adopted a resolution requesting the Secretary-General to make available to the new Committee "all information in his possession relevant to Article 15" and requesting the Colonialism Committee to send to it "copies of petitions . . . relevant to the Convention." [30]

Lady Gaitskell of the United Kingdom described the new double standard as discriminatory in that a higher standard of human rights was created in colonial territories than in the territories of states recognized as fully independent.[31] Her view that the Committee's scrutiny of petitions from dependent territories imposed ob-

---

[28] A/C.3/SR.1374, at 13 (1965). The Convention was opened for signature on March 7, 1966, and became effective on January 4, 1969. See note 5, Chapter II, at note 5.

[29] Much discussion was devoted in the Third Committee to the relative meanings of "complaints," "petitions," and "communications." A/C.3/SR.1353, at 5–11; SR.1362, at 5 (1965).

[30] No mention was made of the Special Committee on South African Apartheid, which could also supply many petitions relevant to racial discrimination.

[31] A/C.3/SR.1373, at 19 and SR.1363, at 11 (1965).

ligations on states without their consent in violation of the law of treaties [32] was disputed by Italy, which agreed that the arrangements discriminated in favor of states with no dependent territories, but denied that scrutiny by the Committee imposed obligations on the state scrutinized.[33]

CURING THE DOUBLE STANDARD

Even with the Convention in effect, there remains a double standard on treatment of complaints to the extent that less than all independent states have both ratified the Convention and consented to complaints, and in that complaints on racial discrimination alone among all human rights are provided for. A more complete remedy is available in the form described in Chapter IX. New Zealand suggested how this cure could be achieved during the 1965 debates in the Third Committee:

> If it was desired to establish a committee having competence in relation to all States Members of the United Nations, that must be done by other appropriate means within the context of the United Nations, i.e., by establishing a subsidiary organ of the United Nations and giving it powers consistent with the Charter, as interpreted by the practice of the United Nations.[34]

The need to cure the double standard was made plain by the Dutch observation that "the right of individual petition [is] the most effective means of giving effect to human rights in general and the present [Racial Discrimination] Convention in particular." [35]

[32] A/C.3/SR.1368, at 11 (1965).
[33] A/C.3/SR.1364, at 7 and SR.1368, at 19 (1965). An additional legal problem raised by New Zealand, The Netherlands, and the United States concerned what Ambassador Goldberg described as "the attempt made in this article [15] to extend the provisions of this convention to territories of States not parties to [the Convention]." A/C.3/SR.1364, at 9; SR.1368, at 12 (1965); USUN Press Release 4752.
[34] A/C.3/SR.1364, at 10 (1965).
[35] A/C.3/SR.1355, at 11 (1965).

Chapter XIII

The Protective Power of Publicity

In the view of the UN Secretary-General, "a purposeful and universal programme of public information is, in fact, a programme of implementation—an essential counterpart of the substantive activities of the Organization." [1] The power of publicity to aid the oppressed has been fervently urged in UN proceedings. As noted in Chapter X, a former South African prisoner has testified that:

> [T]he more publicity given to the illegalities—by any standard of justice—being committed in South Africa today, the more the hand of the Government there and the authorities will be restrained from effecting yet greater crimes against yet larger sections of the South African population. . . . [T]he focusing of attention on what is going on and the exposures of what has been happening are likely to exercise something of a brake on the authorities. [2]

This testimony was given by one of the 25 witnesses heard in 1967 by the UN Human Rights Commission's *Ad Hoc* Group of Experts

[1] A/6301/Add.1, at 5 (1966). See reports on activities of UN Office of Public Information (OPI) in E/4306, at 50–52 (1967), and A/6595 (1966). See also UN pamphlet "United Nations Work for Human Rights," (Sales No. 65.I.19). Concerning distribution of information on the UN in Trust Territories, see T/1665 (1967). The UN Institute for Training and Research is preparing "a pioneer effort to examine in a systematic way, the handling of information about the United Nations by the major mass media throughout the world." UNITAR/EX/8 Ann. 5, at 1 (1967). The Secretary-General has issued a "Review of Public Information Activities," E/4394 (1967).

[2] E/CN.4/950, at 235 (1967). Compare the comment of US Assistant Secretary of State Harlan Cleveland that "sharp beams of international light can . . . burn out the malignancy of man's inhumanity to man," quoted in R. Gardner, In Pursuit of World Order 259 (1964). Compare also the statement of Dr. Durward V. Sandifer, US member of the Inter-American Commission of Human Rights, made even before its work during the 1965 Dominican crisis, that "with no other sanction than publicity, the Commission has effectively established its role as guardian and critic. . . ." Sandifer, *Human Rights in the Inter-American System*, 11 How. L.J. 508, 521–22 (1965). Regarding publicity methods used by the UN, see A/Conf.32/6, at 135, 184–88 (1968).

concerning prisoners, detainees, and others in South African police custody. He was one of several persons who argued that exposure could alleviate prisoners' conditions.[3] Said another witness: "the South African Government does respond to exposure and, therefore, it is worthwhile making this exposure."[4] Said another: "we have found that a continual struggle, continual protests, continual indignation, do eventually begin to bring results in a small way."[5] Still another told what he thought could be accomplished

> since I have said that protests can have some effect, would it be a good idea to set up a permanent body of the United Nations to investigate conditions and make reports? I think it would be a very good idea. I don't think that the United Nations in itself can get rid of exploitation or repression in South Africa. . . . [B]ut I do think that by continually examining what happens, continually exposing bad conditions, maltreatment, oppression, it is possible to make the Government feel embarrassed. I don't think that they are totally insensitive to criticism.[6]

The UN Human Rights Commission, when forming the *Ad Hoc* Group, at the same time "request[ed] the Secretary-General to give the widest possible publicity, as soon as possible, to the documents received from the Acting Chairman of the Special Committee containing the testimony of political prisoners, victims of torture and ill-treatment in the prisons of South Africa, as well as the statements of Nelson Mandela and Abram Fischer in their recent court trials in South Africa. . . ." The Commission even "call[ed] upon all Member States of the United Nations to give the widest national publicity, through all available information media, to the substance of the contents of these documents."[7]

Such publicizing of one side's evidence at the start of an investigation was bound to cause objections. When South Africa complained about two articles in the May 1967 issue of the *UN Monthly Chronicle*[8]—one entitled "The Commission on Human

---

[3] E/CN.4/AC.22/SR.18, at 13 (1967).

[4] *Id.* at 25; SR.19, at 12 (1967).

[5] *Id.* at 17.

[6] E/CN.4/AC.22/SR.20, at 10–11 (1967). See also E/CN.4/AC.22/SR.24, at 20; SR.25, at 22; SR.27, at 18, 20, 24; SR.28, at 4, 7, 9, 27, 28, 31, 32; SR.29, at 12–14, 16.

[7] Resolution 2 (XXIII), quoted in E/4322–E/CN.4/940, at 76 (1967).

[8] A/6688 (1967).

Rights Strongly Condemns the Policies of Apartheid and Repressive Measures in South Africa"—the author of the article, Professor Petr E. Nedbailo of the Ukrainian S.S.R., then Chairman of the UN Human Rights Commission, responded by citing Commission resolution 2 (XXIII) as the basis for writing and publishing the article.[9] South Africa later objected to a UN Office of Public Information pamphlet, "The United Nations and the Human Person: Questions and Answers on Human Rights," questioning the Secretariat's impartiality and urging "a clear distinction . . . between the real problems in the field of human rights and contentious political questions which have no connexion with human rights." [10] South Africa in 1968 objected to "serious weaknesses of fact and argument" in a UN Economic Survey of Africa, stating among other claims that "implementation of the policy of separate development is opening up tremendous employment opportunities for the non-whites in South Africa ranging from the lower unskilled positions to professional as well as entrepreneurial status." [11]

The Human Rights Commission's declaration of a publicity war on South Africa reflected similar action in other UN bodies. At the urging of the Brasilia Seminar on Apartheid for steps "to counteract the propaganda efforts of the South African Government," [12] the General Assembly in 1966 had "request[ed] the Secretary General to establish a unit within the Secretariat . . . to deal exclusively with the policies of apartheid in consultation with the Special Committee on the Policies of Apartheid . . . in order that maximum publicity may be given to the evils of those policies." [13] The Unit on Apartheid has issued releases such as a 15-page list of persons subjected to South African "banning orders" and a paper on opposition to apartheid by students in South Africa and repression against the students.[14] Such publicity already was being issued by the General Assembly's Special Committee on Apartheid, e.g., "Review of Developments in the Republic of South Africa since the Report of 21 October 1966," [15] and a memorandum from the Anti-Apartheid

[9] A/6688/Add.1 (1967).

[10] A/6688/Add.2 (1968).

[11] E/4588, at 7 (1968).

[12] ST/TAO/HR/27, at 37 (1966).

[13] A/Res/2144 (XXI) (1966).

[14] Unit on Apartheid, Notes and Documents No. 3/69 (1969) and No. 7/69 (1969).

[15] A/6864/Add.1 (1967).

Movement, London, entitled "The nature and techniques of South Africa propaganda."[16]

The General Assembly in 1967 "invite[d] all States to encourage the establishment of national organizations for the purpose of further enlightening public opinion on the evils of apartheid," and requested the Special Committee on Apartheid to report in 1968 "on measures which might appropriately be taken to ensure the widest dissemination of information on the evils of apartheid and the efforts of the international community to secure its elimination. . . ." The Assembly added a request to the Secretary-General "to intensify the dissemination of information on the evils of apartheid and to publish periodically information on economic and financial relations between South Africa and other States."[17]

The use of publicity by UN human rights bodies is not confined to the anti-apartheid struggle. ECOSOC's request[18] for wide circulation of the report of the Special Rapporteur on Slavery[19] has been met with a number of newspaper stories.[20] The Anti-Slavery Society

> for twenty years from 1946 . . . deliberately refused to publicize slavery in the hope of securing governmental and international co-operation to end slavery. In doing so it had to sacrifice its public support. The Society has been bitterly disappointed and has no option now but to publicize those reports on slavery which it is convinced are true and where more should be done to end it.[21]

---

[16] A/AC.115/L.226/Add.1/Rev.1 (1968). Skillful South African propaganda appears in the monthly "South African Panorama," e.g., an article on self-determination in the January 1969 issue.

[17] A/Res/2307 (XXII) (1967).

[18] E/Res/1126 (XLI) (1966).

[19] The report has been published in printed form, Sales No.: 67.XIV.2. The Special Rapporteur has recommended "a visible symbol of the permanent and living interest" of the UN in slavery, in the form of a committee of experts which would "examine all information on these institutions and practices available to the United Nations, and prepare recommendations for further action by the United Nations to eradicate them." E/4168/Add.3, at 12, 14 (1966).

[20] N.Y. Times, April 17, 1966, §1, at 2, col. 3; Dec. 4, 1966, §1, at 166, col. 3; March 1, 1967, §1, at 42, col. 3; March 20, 1967, §1, at 11, col. 3; March 28, 1967, §1, at 16, col. 2; The Observer (London), Feb. 26, 1967, §1, at 12, col. 1.

[21] E/C.2/664, at 4 (1968). The Annual Report of the Anti-Slavery Society for the year ended March 31, 1968, lists nine pages of press notices of the Society since early 1966. Regarding UN measures on slavery, see A/Conf.32/5, at 154–57 (1968). Another non-governmental organization often successful in

Brandeis University President Morris B. Abram, basing his position on his experience as U.S. Representative in the UN Human Rights Commission, is convinced of "the effect and force of publicity on the international level. I have seen this work." [22] He related how the delegate of a nation charged in the Commission with labor violations, "though he felt very truculent, he changed his tune as the cameras were turned on him and said, 'We will now submit to the jurisdiction of the International Labour Organization.' " Abram added that he was "sure that in Rhodesia some of the prisoners facing execution had their sentences commuted as a result of the kind of uproar that happened in the U.N." [23]

The actual effectiveness of publicity in protecting basic rights, of course, cannot be determined. Only the opinions of those experts with UN experience can be called on as evidence. In the absence of other assuredly productive procedures, publicity at least is worth trying for whatever results it achieves. The mere satisfaction of those aggrieved, on seeing their oppressions widely broadcast,[24] would suffice for justification even if it could be proved that the experienced persons cited are wrong when they say that sovereigns do care about public opinion.

---

obtaining newspaper publicity for its cause is Amnesty International, described at length in Christian Science Monitor, Jan. 30, 1969, §1, at 9, col. 1.

[22] American Bar Association, Section of Individual Rights and Responsibilities, Monograph No. 2, at 24 (1968).

[23] *Id.* Arthur Larson has referred to the "ground swell of protest against these trials in the United Nations, in the New York Times, in the International Commission of Jurists, in a petition of several hundred lawyers and law professors, in a number of governments, and in various church organizations." *Id.* at 34.

[24] Fawcett, who classified global human rights implementation methods into publicity, judicial process, and international supervision, believes that "publicity for human rights consists in making known to every person at least those minimum standards of treatment to which he or she is entitled; in making known violations of human rights, wherever they may occur; and in continual public debate, serving to rationalize and broaden those standards." HUMAN RIGHTS IN NATIONAL AND INTERNATIONAL LAW 289–90 (A. Robertson ed. 1968).

Chapter XIV

Aid and Comfort for the Oppressed

Even where the international community is powerless to prevent oppression, it may be able to extend protection to the oppressed through aid of various kinds. Aid can be more readily given to victims who have fled the country which oppressed them. Those victims who remain may be kept from contact with any inter-governmental body, so that only private agencies can reach them. Their plight would be improved if established UN machinery for helping refugees were extended or duplicated to include the oppressed who cannot flee.

Once outside their own country, victims may qualify for aid from the UN High Commissioner for Refugees, who as a rule declines to help non-escapees.[1] When the General Assembly asked for "all possible assistance to the people who are suffering as a result of the military operations" in Aden, the High Commissioner pointed out that such persons did not "come within the purview of UNHCR action as defined in the Statute of my office and in various resolutions of the General Assembly."[2] The Aden victims were looked after instead by the International Committee of the Red Cross which, "acting with the consent of the authorities of the Federation and the United Kingdom High Commissioner, was authorized to visit politi-

[1] Aid to certain refugees is provided by the UN Relief and Works Agency for Palestine Refugees in the Near East (UNRWA), whose Commissioner General told the International Conference on Human Rights at Teheran that General Assembly resolution 302 (IV) (1949), the basis of the assistance program, "did not specifically use the phrase 'human rights' or overtly express any connexion between this mandate and the basic concepts of human rights adopted by the Assembly in the Universal Declaration of Human Rights; but the connexion between the two resolutions, both in the period for which they have endured and in their humanitarian aims, is nevertheless clear." A/C.3/L.1636, at 2 (1968), quoting A/Conf.32/22 (1968).

[2] A/AC.109/195, at 2 (1966). But see Chapter VIII at note 12 concerning UNHCR negotiations with the Government of the Federal Republic of Germany on indemnification of persons persecuted by Nazis. Regarding such Assembly resolutions, see A/Conf.32/5, at 171–72 (1967).

cal prisoners and other persons prosecuted because of recent events who are being held in Aden prisons." [3]

The High Commissioner has denied his competence to provide assistance within Southern Rhodesia and the African territories under Portuguese administration, although he has aided refugees from the latter.[4] His position has been similar in regard to Nigeria, where massive suffering from civil war has lain beyond the reach of his assistance. He told his Executive Committee in 1968 that:

> in Nigeria, UNHCR has not been competent, as you know, for the relief operations within the borders of that country. The victims of this tragic war have been referred to as refugees by the press and by public opinion, but they are not refugees who come within the terms of reference of UNHCR. The uprooted peoples inside Nigeria have been assisted, sometimes, in very trying circumstances, by the International Committee of the Red Cross, by UNICEF and by a great many nongovernmental organizations, who have been doing a splendid and extremely difficult job in trying to bring relief to the innocent victims of this tragic conflict. We have maintained the closest cooperation with the ICRC here in Geneva. This has been greatly facilitated by the fact that the Commissioner General of the Red Cross in Nigeria is one of my distinguished predecessors, Ambassador Lindt. Further, the representative of the Secretary-General in Nigeria, Mr. Nils Gussing, is a UNHCR staff member. I seconded him to U Thant at his request to carry out his present mission. We know what the situation is inside the country, and to a large extent we have been able to foresee what problems might arise for UNHCR outside the country. Here UNHCR has been giving a great deal of attention to the problems of refugees, who total a number of approximately 2,500 people.[5]

This pitifully small group of 2,500 able to qualify as "refugees" by leaving Nigeria compared tragically with the masses starving within its borders. Their relief was assigned to the Red Cross. U Thant noted in his 1967–68 annual report that

[3] A/AC.109/195, at 2 (1966).

[4] E/CN.4/979/Add.2, at 28 (1969), noting also at 27 the aid furnished by the UN Food and Agriculture Organization. Aid by UNHCR to refugees from Portuguese Territories is described in A/AC.109/L.570 (1969). "Persons from Southern Rhodesia, however, do not come under the competence of the High Commissioner," he had said. A/AC.109/304, at 20 (1968).

[5] A/AC.96/403, Ann. I, at 2 (1968).

for the purpose of coordinating efforts and thus undertaking the most effective action, it was agreed by a number of organizations, both governmental and private, that all the humanitarian aid to the victims of the Nigerian conflict would be channeled through the International Committee of the Red Cross. This arrangement, which includes the relief activities of the United Nations, mainly those of the United Nations Children's Fund, still stands.[6]

With such heavy burdens, the ICRC has found itself "compelled to consider in the first place those victims of armed conflicts or political disturbances who can only be reached by a strictly neutral body, particularly the prisoners and detainees."[7] One observer has called the Red Cross "probably the best example of a non-governmental organization which, once established, has enjoyed the effective support of state governments."[8] For example, South Africa considers that "by virtue of its international status and long tradition of objectivity, the Red Cross was the most appropriate body to investigate unjustified criticisms of a State's treatment of its prisoners, which were made for political reasons."[9]

Is an official like the UN High Commissioner for Refugees, despite his being an inter-governmental agent, able to sustain the same reputation for impartiality as the Red Cross? His office is not without experience in dealing with alleged oppressor governments. While not providing material assistance to persons still under their own government's jurisdiction, the High Commissioner, with an eye

[6] A/7201/Add.1, at 68 (1968). When a UNICEF official was invited to Hanoi in June 1969, the New York Times noted that:

> because of its reputation as a nonpolitical aid agency, UNICEF has been able on past occasions to gain entry where the United Nations itself failed. In 1956, in the wake of the Soviet occupation of Hungary, Secretary General Dag Hammarskjöld was refused admission as head of the United Nations. However, the late Maurice Pate, executive director of UNICEF, was able to enter and talk about assistance even while the debates over Mr. Hammarskjöld were continuing in the Assembly.

June 4, 1969, §1, at 13, col. 1.

[7] A/AC.109/194, at 12 (1966). The significance of Red Cross visits to South African prisons was debated in the context of the Ad Hoc Group's investigations. E/CN.4/AC.22/SR.8, at 3–9 (1967); SR.18, at 12, 16, 25, 26. See Chapter X.

[8] Archer, *Action by Unofficial Organizations on Human Rights*, in THE INTERNATIONAL PROTECTION OF HUMAN RIGHTS 166 (E. Luard ed. 1967).

[9] E/AC.7/SR.566, at 16 (1967).

to arranging repatriation (one of his main functions), may deal with that government once the victim escapes.[10] Thus UNHCR affords protection of one kind to people in their relations with their own governments as well as with the governments of their country of refuge and of third countries. The significance of this function appears from the terms used to extend UNHCR's office five years from January 1, 1968; the General Assembly requested him "to pursue his activities of protection and assistance and to continue to make every effort to facilitate the repatriation, local integration or resettlement on a voluntary basis of the refugees who are his concern." [11]

Once a refugee is repatriated, UN protection ceases. As the High Commissioner pointed out at Teheran, voluntary return home is the most satisfactory solution for refugees, but there are no international rules to guarantee the security of a returned refugee.[12] The rule on which the Commissioner relies in promoting repatriation has a scope which ends at the border; it is Article 13, paragraph 2, of the Universal Declaration of Human Rights, under which "everyone has the right to leave any country including his own, and to return to his country." Accordingly the Commissioner merely "seeks, in consultation with the Governments concerned, to overcome any difficulties which may exist with regard to the voluntary repatriation of refugees, such as the obtaining of the necessary travel documents, visas and permits." [13] Only by obtaining at that moment a government commitment for fair treatment of the returning refugee could the Commissioner, without a change in his statute by the General Assembly, effectively broaden his reach.

The precedents for aid to escaped victims through UNHCR protection vis-à-vis the Government escaped from, together with the precedents for Red Cross aid to non-escapee victims, suggest the possibility that officials despatched by inter-governmental authority might be just as able as those privately sponsored to contact the op-

[10] "The main functions of UNHCR are to provide international protection for refugees who are its concern and to seek permanent solutions to their problems by facilitating their voluntary repatriation or their assimilation within new national communities, either through local integration or through resettlement in another country." E/CN.14/383, Ann. I, at 4 (1967).

[11] A/Res/2294 (XXII) (1967).

[12] UN Press Release HR/143 (1968).

[13] A/Conf.32/12/Rev.1, at 25 (1968).

pressed on the scene. South Africa's admission of Red Cross visitors to its prisons while turning away the *Ad Hoc* Group as described in Chapter X was justified by insistence on impartiality.[14] This quality the High Commissioner for Refugees stresses, using the graphic assertion that "we are like doctors, who hasten to help the injured without seeking to know who caused the injury." [15] The Commissioner would not seem to have exaggerated when he told his Executive Committee in 1968 that "the purely humanitarian and constructive nature of our actions brings about, I am convinced, a reconciliation and a better understanding between governments on the one hand and individuals on the other." [16]

Were the Refugee Commissioner's mandate geographically broad

[14] South Africa has said that "it would be most helpful . . . if the Commission on Human Rights were to extend the scope of its inquiries to cover all countries through the agency of an authority or authorities, such as the International Committee of the Red Cross, about whose *bona fides* and dedication to the humanitarian ideal there can be no doubt." E/4340/Add.1–E/CN.4/942/ Add.1 (1967). "[I]t was stated in a letter of 5 July 1967 that the International Committee of the Red Cross had been assisting political detainees in Rhodesia for several years past. At that moment a delegate of the International Committee, Mr. G. C. Senn, was carrying out a series of visits to detention camps and prisons in that country. In keeping with established practice, his observations and any proposals he might make would be communicated to the detaining Power." A/AC.109/276, at 10 (1967).

[15] World Health, Oct. 1966, at 19. Other examples of this emphasis: the introduction to UNHCR's 1966–67 Annual Report stated that "the role of UNHCR, as an intermediary of good-will, has been further developed as a result of the purely humanitarian character of his work." E/4390, at 8 (1967); "The UNHCR representative . . . stressed the fact that UNHCR was a completely non-political body acting on behalf of the international community." A/AC.115/L.206, at 6 (1967). For a time the High Commissioner, in the name of impartiality, even resisted association with the anti-apartheid drive. During consultations with the Secretary-General concerning the question of consolidation and integration of the special training program for territories under Portuguese administration and the educational and training program for South Africans, he indicated that "the political motivation underlying the establishment of the South African programme, in particular, precludes UNHCR under its terms of reference from close association with the United Nations training and educational programme." A/6890, at 16 (1967). However, his 1968 report to the General Assembly stated that UNHCR "co-operates in the administration of the United Nations Trust Fund for South Africa, which deals with relief to South African refugees." A/7211, at 6 (1968) "The High Commissioner has also pursued his co-operation with administration of the United Nations Special Education and Training Programmes for refugees from Portuguese territories, South Africa and South West Africa." *Id.* at 20.

[16] A/AC.96/403, Ann. I, at 12 (1968).

enough, it would be at least awkward for any country to refuse his request to visit it. The possibilities were made clear by an African diplomat active in UN human rights matters when he said in late 1967 that the proposed UN High Commissioner for Human Rights

> is to do what now the High Commissioner for Refugees is doing but to a wider and greater political degree. It would be his duty to try personally to intercede on behalf of individuals in their own countries, and intercede between the individual and his government.[17]

Noting "the close link between human rights, in general, and the international protection of refugees," UNHCR has observed that, "as persons often become refugees through the violation of human rights in one form or another, it is all the more important to ensure that, once they are refugees, their human rights are safeguarded."[18] Protection before they acquire the technical status of refugees would seem equally important.

Aid from UN agencies to victims of oppression takes various forms. One form is legal assistance, which the UNHCR Programme for 1967 referred to "as a necessary corollary to the protection function of the Office."[19] The main types of legal assistance provided include "facilitation of naturalization, enforcement of legal provision in the field of social security and pension rights, regularization of refugee status (e.g. legal counselling of refugee seamen) and defense in courts."[20] The legal assistance is furnished through either "a network of legally qualified fulltime counsellors acting under the auspices of voluntary agencies" or by a method tried in Austria using "a number of practicing lawyers in various cities to counsel refugees on legal matters."[21] Similarly the UN Trust Fund

---

[17] A. A. Mohammed of Nigeria, at Hammarskjöld Forum, THE ASSOCIATION OF THE BAR OF THE CITY OF NEW YORK, THE INTERNATIONAL PROTECTION OF HUMAN RIGHTS 65 (J. Carey ed. 1968).

[18] A/7211, at 5, 13 (1968).

[19] A/AC.96/342, at 8 (1966).

[20] A/AC.96/364, at 9 (1967). See A/7211, at 16 (1968).

[21] A/AC.96/342, at 8 (1966). Legal aid for people of insufficient means wishing to press complaints against their own governments is sometimes provided under the Rules of Procedure of the European Commission on Human Rights. The UN General Assembly "1. Recommends Members States: (a) To guarantee the progressive development of comprehensive systems of legal aid to those who need it in order to protect their human rights and fundamental freedoms; (b) To devise standards for granting, in appropriate cases, legal or professional

for South Africa is authorized to give "legal assistance to persons persecuted under the repressive and discriminatory legislation of South Africa." [22]

Another form of aid to victims is education, which is furnished by the UN High Commissioner for Refugees, whose Executive Committee in 1968 "recognized that education for refugees, a fundamental human right, is the concern of the international community." [23] Educational aid projects for victims in southern Africa had proliferated to such an extent by 1967 that the General Assembly decided to integrate the special educational and training programs for South West Africa and for Territories under Portuguese administration and the educational and training program for South Africans; to include assistance to persons from Southern Rhodesia; and to finance the integrated program from a trust fund made up of voluntary contributions.[24]

---

assistance; (c) To consider ways and means of defraying the expenses involved in providing such comprehensive legal aid systems; (d) To consider taking all possible steps to simplify legal procedures so as to reduce the burdens on the financial and other resources of individuals who seek legal redress; (e) To encourage co-operation among appropriate bodies making available competent legal assistance to those who need it; 2. Requests the Secretary-General, in consultation with the appropriate United Nations organs, specialized agencies and other intergovernmental organs concerned, to provide the necessary resources, within the limits of the programme of advisory services in the field of human rights, to facilitate expert and other technical assistance to Member States seeking to extend the availability of competent legal aid." A/Res/2449 (XXIII) (1968).

[22] Established under A/Res/2054B (XX). "Grants are made only to voluntary organizations, host Governments of refugees and other appropriate bodies, and not directly to individuals or families in need." Astrom, *The United Nations Trust Fund for South Africa*, 6 UN MONTHLY CHRONICLE No. 2, at 43, 45 (1969).

[23] A/AC.96/403, at 31 (1968). The Committee "further recognized that the active support of the international community is essential in helping host countries to provide adequate educational facilities for refugees, particularly at the post-primary level." *Id.* A Memorandum of Understanding was signed between UNHCR and UNESCO in 1967 calling for various forms of cooperation. A/AC.96/394, at 5 (1968).

[24] A/Res/2349 (XXII) (1967). A report on the special educational and training programmes for South West Africa is contained in A/6899 and Add.1 (1967), while a report on the special training programme for territories under Portuguese administration appeared in A/6900 and Add.1 (1967). Criteria for determining compensation to the victims of war crimes and crimes against humanity were part of a Secretariat study, E/CN.4/983, at 115 (1969), requested by the Human Rights Commission in its resolution 13 (XXIV).

Financial support for the UN's educational and material aid efforts in southern Africa is widely solicited. Over one-half of the contributions to the Trust Fund as of June 1968 had come from the four Scandinavian countries.[25] The General Assembly later that year appealed to "all States, organizations and individuals" for contributions to the Educational and Training Programme,[26] and to the Trust Fund.[27] By the end of 1968 the Fund had received contributions from 43 UN Member States and other donors, including organizations and individuals, totaling $637,367.[28] In early 1969 the Secretary-General, acting on a Human Rights Commission suggestion calling for "registers for the receipt of contributions from all sources, private and public, for the victims of the policies of apartheid and racism in South Africa in each country," opened registers at UN Headquarters and at two UN Information Centers to receive contributions for both the Programme and the Fund.[29]

As noted in Chapter IV, the suggestion has been made that a UN body exert pressure on private US companies to curtail their activities in South Africa. A less objectionable and possibly more effective procedure would be a call for contributions to the Programme or the Fund. This would afford foreign interests that have profited from

[25] A/AC.115/L.236 (1968).

[26] A/Res/2431 (XXIII) (1968).

[27] A/Res/2397 (XXIII) (1968).

[28] UN Press Release GA/3905–HR/256 (1969).

[29] *Id.* Material aid is sometimes appealed for in a context suggesting a military aspect, as when the Assembly in 1967 asked "all States and organizations to provide appropriate moral, political and material assistance to the people of South Africa in their legitimate struggle for the rights recognized in the Charter." A/Res/2307 (XXII) (1967). Similarly, the Assembly in June 1968, after renaming South West Africa as "Namibia," called upon "all States to provide the necessary moral and material assistance to the Namibian people in their legitimate struggle for independence. . . ." A/Res/2372 (XXII) (1968). A group of non-governmental organizations were asked in March 1969, at a meeting of the General Assembly's Apartheid Committee, "whether their organizations were prepared to lend moral and material support to the freedom fighters, as requested by the General Assembly, should peaceful efforts prove fruitless." A/AC.115/SR.109, at 16 (1969). The American Friends Service Committee replied that it "would not under any circumstances consent to the use of force, even for the purpose of achieving liberation [and] would not supply arms to the liberation movements, but was prepared to come to their assistance in humanitarian, social or educational matters." A/AC.115/SR.110, at 8 (1969). The United Church of Christ said it "was openly supporting liberation movements, particularly in the Portuguese Territories, and that it would continue to do so." *Id.* at 10.

apartheid an opportunity to restore to its victims a measure of what might have been theirs under a less oppressive system. If demands can be made for "reparations" from American churches to compensate victims of the US slave system and its aftermath, how much more clearly can demands be directed towards business corporations profiting currently from a system which, if not slavery, produces a double standard of living whose non-white victims qualify for all the aid and comfort that the UN can obtain for them. As stated by the Chairman of the Trustees of the UN Trust Fund for South Africa, "such humanitarian assistance for the victims of apartheid should help to counteract the growth of racial animosity and to promote the feeling of human solidarity." [30]

[30] A/AC.115/SR.113, at 4 (1969).

Chapter XV

Summary and Conclusion

WHAT THE UN CAN DO, TODAY AND TOMORROW

"Perhaps the boldest innovation of the Charter," according to UN Secretary-General U Thant, was "the unconditional and universal obligation in regard to human rights and fundamental freedoms."[1] The obligation is stated in Article 56, under which "all Members pledge themselves to take joint and separate action in cooperation with the Organization for the achievement of the purposes set forth in Article 55," which in turn provides that "the United Nations shall promote: . . . universal respect for, and observance of, human rights and fundamental freedoms for all without distinction as to race, sex, language, or religion."

Three years after the Charter's adoption, the rights it mentioned were enumerated in the Universal Declaration of Human Rights. The twentieth anniversary of the Declaration's adoption in 1948 was marked in 1968 by the UN's International Year for Human Rights. The final stage in enumerating an international "bill of rights" already had been reached in 1966, when work was completed on treaties putting in legally binding form most of the rights set forth in the Universal Declaration.

The use of declarations or treaties for international "legislation" is one technique for human rights enhancement and protection, since merely setting standards to some extent promotes their fulfillment. Voluntary compliance also is encouraged by the educational process which the UN carries on through seminars and fellowships. Where, however, enforcement is needed, various international legal tools have been employed, ranging in coerciveness from force of arms to mere public exposure. Where none of these methods succeeds, aiding the victims of oppression is the international community's last resort in providing protection.

[1] From statement at opening of forth-fifth session of ECOSOC, Geneva, July 8, 1968. UN Press Release SG/SM/971–ECOSOC/2474 (1968).

Coercion short of force, depriving the offending government of normal benefits, is an enforcement tool now in use against Rhodesia under binding Security Council directions. Another tool is adjudication, employed by the International Court of Justice and European Court of Human Rights, and used at Nuremberg in criminal proceedings of a type now sometimes urged to combat South African apartheid. Non-judicial investigations by international bodies can be effective, and offer a variety of techniques for information-gathering and evaluation. Quiet negotiation to persuade officials not to oppress is a tool whose effect is enhanced by the threat of exposure to world opinion. Such are the tools developed for the international protection of civil and political rights. A brief evaluation of the tools follows.

Legislation and Education [2]

Legislative measures to the number of thirty-seven are at present actual or potential parts of world-wide or regional human rights law.[3] While not by its terms purporting to create legal rights or duties, the 1948 Universal Declaration of Human Rights is said by some authorities to have acquired the status of law. The less-than-universal but explicitly binding European Convention on Human Rights and Fundamental Freedoms is the first such legislation at the regional level. The 1948 American Declaration of the Rights of Man may be succeeded by an Inter-American Convention on Human Rights under discussion among Western Hemisphere Governments.

The effectiveness of standards alone without enforcement measures can be enhanced through educational steps like the UN's program of seminars and fellowships. Government officials and future leaders are thereby exposed to ideas and methods employed in other lands. But where government desire to promote human rights falls short, enforcement is needed. Therefore with UN adoption of the 1966 Human Rights Covenants, the drafting of standards seemed for the moment substantially finished, and attention was focussed on enforcement tools.

[2] See Chapters II and III for detailed descriptions.
[3] *Situation des conventions internationales relatives aux droits de l'homme*, 1 HUMAN RIGHTS J. 315 (1968).

Use of Force [4]

Scholars once believed, and some still do, that a single nation or a group of nations could validly use their might to protect foreigners from their own governments' excesses. With the UN Charter, force was made illegal except in self-defense or when ordered by the Security Council. In theory the Council, after a reasonable finding that South Africa's oppression of non-whites threatens international peace, could send troops to compel apartheid's abolition. The impracticability of such an undertaking is demonstrated both by the problems of reaching UN consensus for far less drastic steps, and by the obvious difficulties of occupying a hostile land—even where the occupier is stronger than the local forces.

Coercion [5]

The UN and its specialized agencies, for human rights purposes, have deprived offending states of a variety of benefits. Southern Rhodesia has been the target of three compulsory Security Council trade prohibitions, but the objective of toppling the Smith regime has not succeeded. South African relations with other countries have been attacked in frequent UN resolutions falling short of legal prohibition. UN specialized agencies like the World Bank and International Monetary Fund have been urged by the General Assembly to withhold their benefits from both South Africa and Portugal, but neither country seems to be affected. Steps by UNESCO and WHO to exclude such states from their activities have had no apparent result. Efforts in 1968 to oust South Africa from the UN Conference on Trade and Development failed to pass in the face of arguments questioning both the legality and the efficacy of such a step. The tool of coercion appears to offer little hope at present of enhancing or protecting human rights.

Adjudication [6]

Disillusionment with judicial process on human rights matters was so widespread after the World Court's 1966 South West Africa cases that the Court was not mentioned in the Human Rights Cove-

[4] See Chapter IV.
[5] *Id.*
[6] See Chapters V, VI, and VII.

nants adopted later that year, in contrast with its prominent place in the 1965 Convention on Elimination of All Forms of Racial Discrimination. Numerous States Parties to the Race Convention have reserved against the Court's jurisdiction.

With the anti-World Court reaction and mounting anti-apartheid frustration, criminal process of the Nuremberg type became increasingly attractive in some quarters. The possibility of using the accusation phase of criminal procedure, with or without the trial stage, began to be studied. Indictment of brutal government officials by UN bodies was discussed as a deterrent, possibly useful even if the accused were at present beyond the UN's physical reach. While deterrence of individuals through merely *prima facie* findings of guilt is speculative, such procedures might do more to relieve the oppressed than protracted interstate litigation.

Investigation [7]

For several decades the International Labor Organization has shown how "supervision," its process of reviewing government compliance with standards, can produce results in human rights affairs. The UN too inquires about human rights, but governments alone are often thought not to suffice as sources of information on cases to which they are parties. Both private groups and individuals are therefore turned to as further sources.

Private groups have standing in the UN Charter for consultative purposes. Some of them which have played an active role in particular human rights cases have encountered government hostility. Individuals are gaining stature in UN usage through the chance to lodge complaints, a possibility previously open to certain Europeans and Americans with access to regional commissions but limited at the UN to petitions concerning colonies or South Africa. Individuals will, where their governments consent, also have standing to complain to international bodies under the 1965 Convention on Elimination of All Forms of Racial Discrimination and, whenever it becomes effective, under the Optional Protocol to the 1966 Covenant on Civil and Political Rights.

Investigation has been seized upon as a human rights tool by the UN Human Rights Commission and ECOSOC since 1967. An *Ad Hoc* Group of Experts was assigned the task at first of looking into

[7] See Chapters IX, X, XI, and XII.

the treatment of prisoners and detainees in South Africa. Later the Group's mandate was expanded geographically to cover other parts of southern Africa, and substantively to include alleged violations of trade union rights. The members of the Group were asked at the Commission's 1969 session to investigate charges that the 1949 Geneva Convention on the treatment of civilians was being violated in Israeli-held Arab lands.

The effectiveness of investigation for protecting human rights depends partly on the respondent government's cooperation and partly on the skill with which the further tools of negotiation and publicity are used.

Negotiation [8]

Quiet persuasion of governments by international agencies is of proven usefulness in relieving victims of oppression. Examples of such agencies are the UN High Commissioner for Refugees and the semi-official International Committee of the Red Cross. UNHCR seeks to protect and aid those who have fled their countries, including arranging for their repatriation. ICRC tries without publicity to succor those who cannot flee. The success of UNHCR and ICRC in being allowed by governments to intercede for their own citizens may be attributed largely to the impartiality for which both agencies are known. The proposed UN High Commissioner for Human Rights, to be allowed a similar role, would need the same reputation.

Publicity [9]

Will governments which have not responded to investigation or negotiation pay heed to outside criticism which follows disclosure of their human rights transgressions? More impressive affirmative testimony scarcely could be found than that of former prisoners of South Africa, presented during a recent UN inquiry. They felt that even that regime was not oblivious to friendly Powers' opinions. In the similar view of the Secretary-General, "a purposeful and universal programme of public information is, in fact, a programme of implementation." [10]

[8] See Chapter VIII.
[9] See Chapter XIII.
[10] A/6301/Add.1, at 5 (1966).

THE MOST EFFECTIVE METHODS

The most effective methods for enhancing and protecting human rights, employing tools already used as well as those which might soon be accepted, would include investigation and negotiation, followed where necessary by publicity, and in extreme cases by impartial judicial procedures including criminal charges under established law. The non-coercive tools of aid to victims of oppression and education of national leaders should be continued.

Investigation is evolving in UN Human Rights Commission usage. Negotiation to aid the oppressed, with publicity where needed, should be added to the functions of the UN High Commissioner for Refugees or assigned to the proposed UN High Commissioner for Human Rights. Judicial *prima facie* findings could be issued usefully even where final judgments were impeded by lack of government consent. Where effective regional machinery exists, its use should be required before resort to world-wide procedures.

THE UN HUMAN RIGHTS AGENDA

While some now feel that the drafting of substantive standards is mostly done and that more attention can be paid to measures of enforcement, the standard-writing process should continue. Instruments in two fields, freedom of association and religious intolerance, remain unfinished. The threats which science and technology pose to human rights should be confronted and suitable limits drawn to protect the individual. Study is overdue on solutions to the inevitable clash between the need for population control and the right to procreate, and on regulation of the newer ways of tempering with the human body and personality. The whole range of human rights could be embodied, as some have urged, in a collection patterned after ILO's International Labor Code.

Intenser interest has been shown in standards touching fields of hot contention. Charges of oppression against inhabitants of Vietnam, Biafra, and Israeli-held Arab territories have brought a call for revision and up-dating of the 1949 Geneva Conventions on treatment of certain persons in wartime. Frustration at inability to combat racial policies in militarily superior South Africa and Rhodesia have led to substitution for whole governments of oppressive individuals as the objects of international legislation, and criminal standards have been set, not only in the 1968 UN Convention on Non-Applicability of Statutory Limitation to War Crimes and Crimes Against Humanity but also in frequent General Assembly resolutions having in theory no binding effect. Interest in branding racial wrongs as crimes may flag, however, for lack of practicability, unless some hijacked airplane yields a practitioner of apartheid, who at such a time would find little solace in his government's assertion that its racial policies are solely of domestic concern.

The UN human rights agenda for enforcement includes much that is urgent. The Sub-Commission's 1968 proposals for considering complaints outside the colonial and South African areas were sent on with little change by the Human Rights Commission but were not acted on by ECOSOC in 1969. If adopted without serious deletion, they will turn a new page in UN human rights history. Their defeat could well close the chapter begun with the General Assembly's 1966 demand for UN action to "put a stop" to violations wherever they may occur.

The two 1966 Covenants, on Civil and Political Rights and on Economic, Social and Cultural Rights, with the former's Optional Protocol allowing individuals' complaints, have far short of sufficient States Parties for effectiveness. This makes even more important the Sub-Commission's rules, to fill the gaps in human rights enforcement left by tardiness or straight refusal of nations to join these pacts. Even when both Covenants and the Protocol have sufficient Parties for effectiveness, these rules will still be needed so that all men everywhere may have some chance of being heard when their governments oppress.

Rules are needed also on the details of procedure. Samples for the use of the Racial Discrimination Committee have been privately prepared and promulgated,[11] but further work is needed for use by other tribunals such as the Human Rights Committee visualized by the two 1966 Covenants. The Human Rights Commission's *Ad Hoc* Group of Experts, after operating for two years without benefit of the most basic rules, approached thus unprepared the inflammatory subject of alleged Israeli oppression in occupied Arab lands. Without rules to buttress its impartiality, the Group could have little hope of influencing disinterested observers of its work.

[11] Coleman, Pollock and Robinson, *Rules of Procedure for the New Tribunal: A Proposed Draft*, 56 CALIF. L. REV. 1569 (1968).

Even more essential will be rules to guide the criminal process in human rights matters. "The possibility of establishing a grand jury of legal experts for Namibia for the protection of life, personal safety and rights of the inhabitants of that territory" [12] is one of several current proposals for international criminal process requiring the greatest care in their development. The pains taken at Nuremberg earned the respect of mankind. Without similar pains, the gathering of evidence and *prima facie* findings of criminal guilt will accomplish nothing. Drastic charges without restraint would only dissipate the sympathy that might be earned by tight procedures guardedly applied.

Structural changes are on the agenda for international organizations, both regional and global. The draft Inter-American Convention on Human Rights currently under discussion provides for "organs of protection," a commission, and a court.[13] The Arab League projects regional human rights institutions whose shape has not yet become apparent. Coordination problems may arise as regional measures evolve and tend to compete with UN procedures.

New UN machinery has been urged, including an Organization for the Promotion of Human Rights (UNOPHR) with status like UNCTAD and UNIDO, gathering in all the now scattered functions and having a Human Rights Council as its main organ.[14] Most pressing at the global level is the question of the proposed UN High Commissioner for Human Rights. After slowly clearing the lower bodies, the matter came to rest in the General Assembly, where its proponents are reluctant to force it to the test in an atmosphere of Soviet hostility and Afro-Asian coolness born of various apprehensions. The type of informational and negotiating function sought might better be achieved at this time by grafting further powers into the role of an existing and trusted official, the UN High Commissioner for Refugees. The tragedy of his statutory inability to aid the sufferers in Biafra because officially they had not fled their country illustrates the need to permit UNHCR to enter countries where his protection is required and permitted.

[12] From document prepared by a special rapporteur for the UN Human Rights Commission. E/CN.4/979/Add.3 (1969).

[13] OEA/Ser.G/V (1968).

[14] Sohn, *United Nations Machinery for Implementing Human Rights,* 62 AM. J. INT'L L. 909 (1968).

It is often said that the basic need for human rights protection is not at the international level but in each state, where government oppression must be curbed. Ambassador Richardson of Jamaica has expressed the belief that "the coercive powers we are attempting to give to international institutions will be of little effectiveness for a very long time to come." [15] This view accepts the proposition that truly adamant regimes cannot now be moved by the world community, and leads inevitably to revolution as the only remedy. Where neighbors are aroused, such revolution threatens the peace. But even accepting this bleak view, the UN is not without its means. Education, not revolution, is its final expedient. The Italian proposal adopted by the General Assembly in 1968 took this line, asking for "regular study of the United Nations and the specialized agencies and of the principles proclaimed in the Universal Declaration of Human Rights and in other declarations on human rights, in the training of teaching staff for primary and secondary schools." [16] Today's restless youth, impatient with injustice, will soon have their turn at nudging the world towards the goals for which their forebears too have yearned. As the Assembly added, "all means of education should be employed so that youth may grow up and develop in a spirit of respect for human dignity and equal rights of man without distinction as to race, colour, language, sex or faith." [17]

[15] Report on Annual Conference of the Non-Governmental Organizations in Co-operation with the United Nations Office of Public Information, Annex III, at 7 (1967).

[16] A/Res/2445 (XXIII) (1968).

[17] A/Res/2447 (XXIII) (1968). Sohn believes that "all scientific and engineering courses should pay more than a minimal attention to the social implications of science and technology. A new scientific ethos must be developed, no longer 'neutral' but strongly humanitarian." L. Sohn, Science, Technology and Human Rights 3 (Policy Paper Series No. 2, Center for International Studies, New York University 1969).

Appendix A

Excerpt from U.N. Secretariat study entitled "Measures taken Within the United Nations in the Field of Human Rights," A/CONF.32/5, at 20–30 (1967).

C. AUTHORITY AND IMPACT OF THE UNIVERSAL DECLARATION OF HUMAN RIGHTS

25. The Universal Declaration of Human Rights, in the nineteen years which have elapsed since it was adopted, has exercised an extremely powerful influence throughout the world both internationally and nationally. Its provisions have been used as a basis for various types of action taken by the United Nations; they have inspired a number of international conventions both within and outside the United Nations; they have exercised a significant influence on national constitutions and on municipal legislation and, in several cases, on court decisions. In some instances the text of provisions of the Declaration was actually used in international instruments or national legislation. There are also very many instances of the use of the Declaration as a code of conduct and as a yardstick to measure the degree of respect for and of compliance with the international standards of human rights.

26. In the paragraphs that follow an attempt is made to indicate some of the most significant actions of the United Nations and its organs and of individual Governments which were inspired by or based upon the Universal Declaration. By and large, one can trace three main areas in which the impact of the Universal Declaration has been felt: (*a*) decisions taken by the United Nations, its organs, the specialized agencies and other intergovernmental organizations; (*b*) international treaties and conventions; and (*c*) national constitutions, municipal legislation and court decisions.

D. IMPACT OF THE UNIVERSAL DECLARATION ON DECISIONS TAKEN BY THE UNITED NATIONS AND ITS ORGANS

27. On several occasions the General Assembly has used the Declaration as a code or standard of conduct and as a basis for appeals in urging and recommending Governments to take measures to promote respect for and observance of human rights and fundamental freedoms.[14] In its res-

[14] General Assembly resolutions 540 (VI) of 4 February 1952; 1041 (XI) of

olution entitled "Essentials of Peace",[15] the Assembly called upon every nation: *"To promote,* in recognition of the paramount importance of preserving the dignity and worth of the human person, full freedom for the peaceful expression of political opposition, full opportunity for the exercise of religious freedom and full respect for all the other fundamental rights expressed in the Universal Declaration of Human Rights . . .". In 1965, the Assembly, in a resolution entitled "Measures to accelerate the promotion of respect for human rights and fundamental freedoms",[16] urged all Governments to make special efforts during the United Nations Development Decade to promote respect for and observance of human rights and fundamental freedoms and invited them to include in their plans for economic and social development measures directed towards the achievement of further progress in the implementation of the human rights and fundamental freedoms proclaimed in the Universal Declaration of Human Rights and in subsequent declarations and instruments in the field of human rights.

28. At its twenty-first session, in 1966, the General Assembly, convinced that "gross violations of the rights and fundamental freedoms set forth in the Universal Declaration of Human Rights continue to occur in certain countries", called, *inter alia,* upon all States "to strengthen their efforts to promote the full observance of human rights and the right to self-determination in accordance with the Charter of the United Nations, and to attain the standards established by the Universal Declaration of Human Rights".[17]

29. At the fourth session in 1949, the General Assembly resolved: "To declare formally that discrimination on racial grounds as regards educational facilities available to the different communities in the Trust Territories is not in accordance with the principles of the Charter, the Trusteeship Agreements and the Universal Declaration of Human Rights".[18]

30. With regard to the question of human rights in Non-Self-Governing Territories, the General Assembly, in 1950, adopted a resolution dealing with information on this subject which noted the provision contained in article 2 of the Universal Declaration of Human Rights that no distinction shall be made on the basis of the political, jurisdictional or international status of the country or territory to which a person belongs, whether it be independent, trust, non-self-governing or under any other

---

20 February 1957; 1775 (XVII) of 7 December 1962; 1776 (XVII) of 7 December 1962.

[15] General Assembly resolution 290 (IV) of 1 December 1949.

[16] General Assembly resolution 2027 (XX) of 18 December 1965.

[17] General Assembly resolution 2144 (XXI) of 26 October 1966.

[18] General Assembly resolution 324 (IV) of 15 November 1949.

limitation of sovereignty. The resolution then invited the Members responsible for the administration of Non-Self-Governing Territories to include, in the information to be transmitted to the Secretary-General under Article 73 e of the Charter, a summary of the extent to which the Universal Declaration of Human Rights was implemented in the Non-Self-Governing Territories under their administration; and requested the Special Committee dealing with this subject to include in its report to the General Assembly such recommendations as it might deem desirable relating to the application in Non-Self-Governing Territories of the principles contained in the Universal Declaration of Human Rights.[19] In the following year, the General Assembly requested that the Administering Members describe "the manner in which human rights, in accordance with the principles set forth in the Universal Declaration of Human Rights, are protected by law, particularly in respect of (a) legal principles and procedures; (b) basic legislation and its application; (c) anti-discrimination legislation".[20] In 1952, the Assembly further recommended to the Members responsible for the administration of such territories "the abolition in those Territories of discriminatory laws and practices contrary to the principles of the Charter and of the Universal Declaration of Human Rights".[21]

31. The General Assembly has had recourse to the Declaration in various decisions concerning the Territory of South West Africa. In 1957, in examining the report of the Committee on South West Africa, it noted with concern that "existing conditions in the Territory of South West Africa and the trend of the administration represent a situation contrary to the Mandates System, the Charter of the United Nations, the Universal Declaration of Human Rights, the advisory opinions of the International Court of Justice and the resolutions of the General Assembly".[22] Similar concern was expressed by the General Assembly in 1959 and 1960 when it noted that the administration of the Territory had been conducted increasingly in a manner contrary to the Mandate, the Charter of the United Nations, the Universal Declaration of Human Rights and the advisory opinions of the International Court of Justice.[23] The Assembly further, in a resolution adopted in 1960 on the same subject, considered that the apartheid policy applied in South West Africa was contrary to the terms of the Mandate, the provisions of the

[19] General Assembly resolution 446 (V) of 12 December 1950.
[20] See annex to General Assembly resolution 551 (VI) of 7 December 1951.
[21] General Assembly resolution 644 (VII) of 10 December 1952.
[22] General Assembly resolution 1142 B (XII) of 25 October 1957.
[23] General Assembly resolutions 1360 (XIV) of 17 November 1959 and 1568 (XV) of 18 December 1960.

Charter of the United Nations and the Universal Declaration of Human Rights.[24] At its twenty-first session in 1966 the General Assembly, convinced that the administration of the Mandated Territory by South Africa had been conducted "in a manner contrary to the Mandate, the Charter of the United Nations and the Universal Declaration of Human Rights", decided that the Mandate was terminated and that South Africa had no other right to administer the Territory.[25]

32. The Universal Declaration has also been invoked in several decisions of the General Assembly concerning the general problem of discrimination. In 1952 the General Assembly emphasized "that the full application and implementation of the principle of non-discrimination recommended in the United Nations Charter and the Universal Declaration of Human Rights are matters of supreme importance, and should constitute the primary objective in the work of all United Nations organs and institutions".[26] At its fifteenth session in 1960, it resolutely condemned "all manifestations and practices of racial, religious and national hatred in the political, economic, social, educational and cultural spheres of the life of society as violations of the Charter of the United Nations and the Universal Declaration of Human Rights".[27] The Universal Declaration of Human Rights has also been recalled and cited in the General Assembly resolution proclaiming and adopting the United Nations Declaration on the Elimination of All Forms of Racial Discrimination.[28]

33. The Declaration was also invoked in several decisions of the General Assembly concerning the treatment of people of Indian and Indo-Pakistan origin in South Africa. In repeated resolutions the Assembly called upon the parties to solve the dispute "in accordance with the purposes and principles of the United Nations Charter and the Universal Declaration of Human Rights".[29]

34. With regard to the problem of racial prejudice and religious intolerance, the General Assembly, in 1962, reiterated "its condemnation of all manifestations of racial prejudice and of national and religious intoler-

---

[24] General Assembly resolution 1567 of 18 December 1960.
[25] General Assembly resolution 2145 (XXI) of 27 October 1966.
[26] General Assembly resolution 532 B (VI) of 4 February 1952.
[27] General Assembly resolution 1510 (XV) of 12 December 1960.
[28] General Assembly resolution 1904 (XVIII) of 20 December 1963.
[29] General Assembly resolutions 265 (III) of 14 May 1949; 395 (V) of 2 December 1950; 511 (VI) of 12 January 1952; 615 (VII) of 5 December 1952; 719 (VIII) of 11 November 1953; 1179 (XII) of 26 November 1957; 1302 (XIII) of 10 December 1958; 1597 (XV) of 13 April 1961; 1662 (XVI) of 28 November 1961.

ance as violations of the Charter of the United Nations and of the Universal Declaration of Human Rights".[30]

35. The Universal Declaration provided the basis of a decision of the General Assembly of 1949, when it took action on the question of discrimination practised by certain States against immigrating labour: "In view of the importance of the principle of non-discrimination embodied in the Universal Declaration of Human Rights" the General Assembly decided that there should be no offensive distinctions with regard to the enjoyment of all facilities for accommodation, food, education, recreation and medical assistance against such workers and their families.[31]

36. In considering the question of interference with radio signals, the fifth session of the General Assembly invoked article 19 of the Universal Declaration of Human Rights and invited the Governments of all Member States to refrain from such interference.[32]

37. In 1952 the Assembly, dealing with the problem of information facilities in under-developed regions of the world, *inter alia,* invited the Economic and Social Council "to recommend to the organizations participating in the technical assistance and other programmes providing aid or assistance at the request of Member States" that they give sympathetic consideration to such requests as "one means of implementing the right of freedom of information as enunciated in article 19 of the Universal Declaration of Human Rights".[33]

38. On the question of the status of women, the General Assembly, at its ninth session in 1954, in recalling "the principles set forth in the United Nations Charter and in the Universal Declaration of Human Rights" and in considering that "in certain areas of the world women are subjected to customs, ancient laws and practices relating to marriage and the family which are inconsistent with these principles", recommended that special efforts be made to inform public opinion in those areas concerning the Universal Declaration of Human Rights and existing decrees and legislation affecting the status of women.[34]

39. The General Assembly and the Security Council repeatedly invoked the Universal Declaration or referred to its principles in their endeavour to put an end to the policy of apartheid practised in South Africa. This question is dealt with in detail in another part of this study.[35] Suffice it

---

[30] General Assembly resolution 1779 (XVII) of 7 December 1962.
[31] General Assembly resolution 315 (IV) of 17 November 1949.
[32] General Assembly resolution 424 (V) of 14 December 1950.
[33] General Assembly resolution 633 (VII) of 16 December 1952.
[34] General Assembly resolution 843 (IX) of 17 December 1954.
[35] See below chap. VI.

here to recall Security Council resolution 182 of 4 December 1963,[36] in which the Council urgently requested "the Government of the Republic of South Africa to cease forthwith its continued imposition of discriminatory and repressive measures which are contrary to the principles and purposes of the Charter and which are in violation of its obligations as a Member of the United Nations and of the provisions of the Universal Declaration of Human Rights". The General Assembly, in previous decisions,[37] had also considered that the racial policies practised in South Africa were "contrary to the United Nations Charter and the Universal Declaration of Human Rights".

40. In resolution 285 (III) of 25 April 1949, the Assembly recommended that one State Member withdraw the measures which prevented its nationals, wives of citizens of other nationalities, from leaving their country of origin with their husbands or in order to join them abroad. In this connexion the Assembly invoked articles 13 and 16 of the Universal Declaration, which provide that everyone has the right to leave any country, including his own, and that men and women of full age have the right to marry without any limitation due to race, nationality or religion. In opposition to this some delegations stated that the matter was exclusively within the domestic jurisdiction of the country concerned.

41. At its fourteenth session the General Assembly adopted a resolution concerning the question of Tibet, in which it recalled the principles regarding fundamental human rights and freedoms set out in the Charter and in the Universal Declaration of Human Rights and called for respect for the fundamental human rights of the Tibetan people.[38] Delegations opposed to the resolution pointed out that it was contrary to Article 2, paragraph 7, of the Charter. At its sixteenth and twentieth sessions the General Assembly adopted resolutions on the question of Tibet in which it reaffirmed its conviction that respect for the principles of the Charter and for the Universal Declaration of Human Rights was essential for the evolution of a peaceful world order based on the rule of law.[39]

42. The Universal Declaration also provided the basis for action in several decisions and recommendations of the Economic and Social Council. In 1955, the Council noted article 23, paragraph 2, of the Universal

[36] S/5471.

[37] General Assembly resolutions 721 (VIII) of 8 December 1953 and 820 (IX) of 14 December 1954.

[38] General Assembly resolution 1353 (XIV) of 21 October 1959.

[39] General Assembly resolutions 1723 (XVI) of 20 December 1961 and 2079 (XX) of 18 December 1965.

Declaration of Human Rights, which, referring to all men and women workers, stated that "Everyone, without any discrimination, has the right to equal pay for equal work", and recommended that Governments give practical effect to the principle of equal pay for equal work.[40] In another resolution, the Council recommended to Governments that they take the necessary steps to remove legal and other obstacles impeding the access of married women to public services and functions and the exercise by them of such functions. In doing so, the Council invoked article 21 of the Universal Declaration of Human Rights, which provides that everyone has the right to take part in the government of his country and the right to equal access to public service in his country.[41]

E. INFLUENCE OF THE UNIVERSAL DECLARATION ON INTERNATIONAL TREATIES AND CONVENTIONS

43. In the International Covenants which the General Assembly adopted on 16 December 1966 the provisions of the Universal Declaration of Human Rights were—with some exceptions—transformed into international conventional law. However, independently from the Covenants, the drafting of which occupied the United Nations organs for many years, a considerable number of international conventions were prepared and put into effect after 1948, the purpose of which was to implement rights proclaimed in the Declaration. The text of the Preambles of the Conventions often specifically refer to the Declaration or reproduce the relevant provisions thereof.

44. These Conventions are, in part, of a world-wide character and, in part, of territorially limited application, i.e., of a regional or bilateral character. The Conventions of world-wide application were prepared and adopted by the United Nations, by conferences convened by the General Assembly or by the Economic and Social Council or by specialized agencies (International Labour Organisation and UNESCO). In chronological order these instruments are the following: the Convention relating to the Status of Refugees (1951), the Equal Remuneration Convention (1951) (ILO), the Convention on the Political Rights of Women (1952), the Convention on the Status of Stateless Persons (1954), the Supplementary Convention on the Abolition of Slavery, the Slave Trade and Institutions and Practices Similar to Slavery (1956), the Convention on the Nationality of Married Women (1957), the Convention on the Abolition of Forced Labour (1957) (ILO), the Discrimination (Employment and Occupation) Convention (1958) (ILO), the Convention against Discrimination in Education (1960) (UNESCO), with the Pro-

[40] Economic and Social Council resolution 587 (XX) of 3 August 1955.
[41] Economic and Social Council resolution 771 (XXX) of 25 July 1960.

tocol of 1962; the Convention on the Reduction of Statelessness (1961), the Convention on Consent to Marriage, Minimum Age for Marriage and Registration of Marriages (1962), the Employment Policy Convention (1964) (ILO) and the International Convention on the Elimination of All Forms of Racial Discrimination (1965).

45. The European Convention for the Protection of Human Rights and Fundamental Freedoms, signed at Rome on 4 November 1950, proclaims in its Preamble that it was agreed to by the States Parties in order "to take the first steps for the collective enforcement of certain of the rights stated in the Universal Declaration". The Universal Declaration is listed as the first of the considerations which led the signatory Governments to conclude the Convention. As far as substance is concerned, the European Convention contains detailed provisions on most of the civil and political rights set forth in the Universal Declaration of Human Rights. Protocols to the Convention agreed to in 1952 and in 1963 give effect to a number of additional rights proclaimed in the Declaration.

46. The following instruments applying to specific countries or territories or to a whole region refer to the Universal Declaration of Human Rights: the Trusteeship Agreement with Italy concerning Somaliland under Italian Administration (1950), the Peace Treaty with Japan (1951), the Special Statute concerning Trieste (1954), the Charter of the Organization of African Unity (1963).

F. INFLUENCE OF THE UNIVERSAL DECLARATION ON NATIONAL CONSTITUTIONS, MUNICIPAL LAWS AND COURT DECISIONS

47. Evidence of the impact of the Universal Declaration may be found in texts of various national constitutions which were enacted after the adoption of the Universal Declaration.[42] Several of these constitutions expressly refer, either in their preambles or in their operative provisions, to the Universal Declaration. In addition, many other constitutions contain detailed provisions on a number of human rights, most of which are inspired by, or often modelled on, the text of the articles of the Declaration. Several constitutions drafted with the assistance of United Nations experts, such as those of Libya (1951) and Eritrea as an autonomous unit of Ethiopia (1952), show the marked influence of the Universal Declaration. The impact of the Declaration, however, is also reflected in many other instruments. In the period between 1958 and 1964 the constitutions of several States have expressly referred to the Universal Declaration. In the constitutions of Algeria (1963), Burundi (1962), Cam-

---

[42] For the text of the Human Rights provisions contained in these constitutions see the volumes of the *Yearbook on Human Rights* for 1950–1963.

eroon (1960), Chad (1960), Democratic Republic of the Congo (1964), Republic of the Congo (1963), Dahomey (1964), Gabon (1961), Guinea (1958), Ivory Coast (1960), Madagascar (1959), Mali (1960), Mauritania (1961), Niger (1960), Senegal (1963), Togo (1963) and Upper Volta (1960), the peoples of these countries affirm solemnly their devotion to the principles and ideals of the Universal Declaration. The Constitution of Somalia of 1960, in its article 7, provides that the Republic of Somalia shall comply, in so far as applicable, with the Universal Declaration of Human Rights. The Constitution of Rwanda of 1962 expressly provides that "the fundamental freedoms as defined by the Universal Declaration of Human Rights are guaranteed to all citizens".

48. Other constitutions recently enacted, although they do not expressly refer to the Universal Declaration, are clearly inspired by its provisions and very often reproduce its phraseology. Some examples are the constitutions of Afghanistan (1964), Central African Republic (1964), Cyprus (1960), Dominican Republic (1963), Gambia (1965), Guatemala (1965), Haiti (1964), Honduras (1965), Jamaica (1962), Kenya (1964), Malawi (1964), Malta (1964), Morocco (1962), Nigeria (1960), Romania (1965), Sierra Leone (1961), Singapore (1965), Syria (Provisional Constitution, 1964), Tanganyika (1962), Trinidad and Tobago (1962), Uganda (1962), United Arab Republic (1964), Yogoslavia (1963) and Zanzibar (1963).

49. The impact of the Declaration in the sphere of municipal law can be found in a number of laws and decrees enacted in various countries. In 1951 Paraguay adopted an act (No. 94) to protect scientific, literary and artistic works and to establish a public register of intellectual rights. The preamble of the act cites article 27, paragraph 2, of the Universal Declaration providing that "Everyone has the right to the protection of the moral and material interests resulting from any scientific, literary or artistic production of which he is the author".[43]

50. The Provincial Legislature of Ontario, Canada, adopted an act to promote fair employment practices in 1951 and an act to promote fair accommodations practices in 1954. The purpose of both acts is to eliminate any discrimination "because of race, creed, colour, nationality, ancestry or place of origin". The preamble of either act declares that the act is "in accord with the Universal Declaration of Human Rights as proclaimed by the United Nations".[44]

51. The Government of Argentina issued a legislative decree (No. 1664) in 1955, which declares in its preamble that provisions purporting to deprive anyone of his nationality as a measure of political persecution are

[43] *Yearbook on Human Rights,* 1951.
[44] *Ibid.,* 1951 and 1954.

contrary to human rights as proclaimed by the General Assembly of the United Nations.[45]

52. The Government of Bolivia issued a legislative decree (No. 3937) in 1955 to establish a national system of education. In its preamble the decree reaffirms the principle of equality of opportunity for all Bolivians, without any discrimination, and declares that national education shall be inspired by the Universal Declaration of Human Rights.[46]

53. Panama enacted a law (No. 25) in 1956 to implement article 21 of its Constitution, which prohibits discrimination on account of birth, race, social origin, sex, religion or political opinion. In its preamble the law says that any discrimination on account of colour or race is "a flagrant violation" of article 21 of the National Constitution and "of the Universal Declaration of Human Rights adopted by the General Assembly of the United Nations on 10 December 1948".[47]

54. The Government of Costa Rica promulgated an act (No. 2694) in 1960 prohibiting all forms of discrimination in employment. In paragraph 4 of its preamble the act makes reference to "the Universal Declaration of Human Rights, proclaimed by the United Nations General Assembly".[48]

55. The Declaration or its individual articles have been invoked with varying effect in judicial proceedings and cited in a number of judicial decisions and opinions.

56. The Universal Declaration has been referred to by judges of the International Court of Justice.[49]

57. At the level of national courts the Universal Declaration has been referred to, *inter alia,* in: *Fujii v. State of California* (California District Court of Appeals, 1950); in *Wilson v. Hacker* (New York Supreme Court, 1950); in *Lincoln Union v. Northwestern Company* and *American Federation of Labor v. American Sash and Door Company* (Supreme Court of the United States, 1949); in *Public Prosecutor v. F.A.V.A* (Penal Chamber of the Supreme Court of the Netherlands, 1951); in *Borovski v. Commissioner of Immigration and Director of Prisons* and *Majoff v. Director of Prisons* (Supreme Court of the Philippines, 1951); in several decisions (1951, 1952, 1954, 1956) rendered by

[45] *Ibid.,* 1955.
[46] *Ibid.,* 1955.
[47] *Ibid.,* 1956.
[48] *Ibid.,* 1962.
[49] Judge Azevedo in the Colombian-Peruvian Asylum Case, Judgement of 20 November 1950, [1950] I.C.J. Rep. 339; Judge Levi Carneiro in the Anglo-Iranian Oil Case (jurisdiction), Judgement of 22 July 1952 [1952] I.C.J. Rep. 168, and Judge *ad hoc* Guggenheim in the Nottebohm Case (Second Phase), Judgement of 6 April 1955 [1955] I.C.J. Rep. 63.

the Civil Court of Courtrai (Belgium); in a ruling (1954) of the Court of Taranto (Italy); in *Soc. Roy Export at Charlie Chaplin v. Soc. Le Film Rayée Richebé* (Court of Appeal of Paris (France), 1960) in *Israel Film Studies Ltd. v. Films Inspection Board* (Supreme Court of Israel, 1962) in *Gold v. Minister of Interior* (Supreme Court of Israel, 1962), in *The Queen v. Liyanage* (Supreme Court of Ceylon, 1963) and in a decision (1964) handed down by the Milan (Italy) Court of Appeal (*Foro Italiano*), 1965, II, 122 pp.).

Appendix B

Excerpt from U.N. Secretariat study entitled "Methods Used by the United Nations in the Field of Human Rights," A/CONF.32/6, at 142–49 (1967).

8. *Co-operation of the Committee on the Elimination of Racial Discrimination with competent United Nations organs in regard to petitions from Non-Independent Territories. The Saving Clause in article 7 of the Optional Protocol relating to such petitions*

463. Both the Convention on the Elimination of All Forms of Racial Discrimination of 1965 and the Optional Protocol to the Covenant on Civil and Political Rights of 1966 contain provisions relating to petitions from Territories to which the Declaration on the Granting of Independence to Colonial Countries and Peoples applies pending the achievement of the objectives of that Declaration. Article 15 of the Convention of 1965 is to the effect that the provisions of the Convention shall in no way limit the right of petition granted to these peoples by other international instruments or by the United Nations and its specialized agencies. In similar but not identical terms, article 7 of the Optional Protocol of 1966 stipulates that the provisions of the Protocol shall in no way limit the right of petition granted these peoples by the Charter of the United Nations and other international Conventions and instruments under the United Nations and its specialized agencies. The Convention of 1965 provides in addition that the Committee on the Elimination of Racial Discrimination shall receive copies of the petitions from, and submit expressions of opinion and recommendations on these petitions to, the bodies of the United Nations which deal with matters directly related to the principles and objectives of the 1965 Convention in their consideration of petitions from the inhabitants of Trust, Non-Self-Governing and other non-independent Territories. The Convention also provides that the Committee shall include in its report to the General Assembly a summary of the petitions and reports it has thus received and the expressions of opinion and recommendations of the Committee relating to the said petitions and reports. No corresponding provisions are contained in the Optional Protocol of 1966 as far as the Human Rights

Committee under the International Covenant or Civil and Political Rights is concerned.

D. PROCEDURE FOR DEALING WITH COMMUNICATIONS CONCERNING HUMAN RIGHTS

464. At its first session in January–February 1947, the Commission on Human Rights established a Sub-Committee on the Handling of Communications, the function of which was to consider how communications concerning human rights, addressed to the Commission on Human Rights or to other organs of the United Nations, may be handled, and to make appropriate recommendations to that effect to the Commission on Human Rights.[157] The report of the Sub-Committee to the Commission (E/CN.4/14/Rev.2) contained, in paragraph 3, the statement that "The Commission has no power to take any action in regard to any complaints regarding human rights." Following the unanimous adoption by the Commission of that paragraph of the report of the Sub-Committee, one member of the Commission proposed that it be amended by adding the following: "The Commission draws the Economic and Social Council's attention to the serious gap which results from the absence of this power." The member of the Commission in question did not make any proposal for bridging the gap, but hoped that the Economic and Social Council would instruct the Commission to do so. The Chairman of the Commission suggested that no mention of the gap should be made in the Commission's report but that the Rapporteur should be asked to explain the situation orally to the Economic and Social Council. This suggestion was accepted by the member concerned, who withdrew his proposed amendment.

465. The Commission on the Status of Women also considered the problem of communications at its first session. It appointed a Sub-Committee with the task (a) to deal with communications concerning the status of women already received and to bring forward to the Commission such communications as might be of special interest; (b) to consider how the Commission should deal with such communications in the future. The Sub-Committee divided the communications into two categories; namely, those which express interest, give information or suggestions or offer co-operation and those which contain protests and requests for action. The Sub-Committee summarized the latter communications and drew the attention of the Commission thereto and assumed "that the subject matter therein contained would receive further discussion in the course of the development of the Commission's programme, since all of it is truly related to such a programme."

[157] E/CN.4/SR.4, p. 4. and E/CN.4/14/Rev.2, para. 1.

466. With respect to future communications the Sub-Committee recommended and the Commission subsequently approved a procedure for handling them. Unlike the corresponding recommendations of the Commission on Human Rights, the recommendations of the Commission on the Status of Women did not contain a statement to the effect that the Commission on the Status of Women has no power to take any action in regard to any complaints relating to matters within its competence. In other respects the recommendations of the Commission on the Status of Women did not substantially differ from the corresponding recommendations of the Commission on Human Rights.

467. The Economic and Social Council considered the reports of both Commissions at its fifth session. On the recommendation of its Social Committee the Economic and Social Council on 5 August 1947 adopted resolutions 75 (V) and 76 (V) dealing respectively with communications concerning human rights and communications relating to the status of women. In resolution 75 (V) the Council approved the statement that the Commission on Human Rights "recognizes that it has no power to take any action in regard to any complaints concerning human rights". In resolution 76 (V) the Council stated that it recognizes that as in the case of the Commission on Human Rights, the Commission on the Status of Women has no power to take any action in regard to any complaints concerning the status of women.

468. The statement that the Commission on Human Rights has no power to take any action in regard to any complaints concerning human rights has, in subsequent years, repeatedly been the subject of consideration by the Commission and by principal organs. In 1949 the Secretary-General submitted to the Commission on Human Rights a comprehensive report "on the present situation with regard to communications concerning human rights" in which he made a series of technical observations including comments on the statement on the Commission's lack of power.[158]

469. At its seventh session in 1951 the Commission on Human Rights called the attention of the Economic and Social Council, in the Council's consideration of the question of petitions in connexion with the report of the seventh session of the Commission, to the fact that the Commission has been receiving communications concerning human rights since its establishment.[159]

470. At its sixth session in February 1952 the General Assembly "noting that the Economic and Social Council has taken no action with re-

[158] Document E/CN.4/165.
[159] *Official Records of the Economic and Social Council, Thirteenth Session, Supplement No. 9,* document E/1992, chap. IV, para. 94.

spect to the resolution of the Commission on Human Rights on communications concerning human rights, invited the Council to give instructions to the Commission with regard to communications and to request the Commission to formulate recommendations thereon".[160] At its eighth session in 1952 the Commission decided not to propose the reconsideration of Economic and Social Council resolution 75 (V) as amended.[161]

471. In resolution 441 (XIV) of 23 July 1952 the Economic and Social Council decided not to take action on the matter at that time in view of the action of the Commission on Human Rights that there should be no reconsideration of resolution 75 (V) and to inform the General Assembly of this decision.

472. At the eighth session of the General Assembly in 1953 one delegation proposed a draft resolution by which the General Assembly would have decided that pending the entry into force of the Covenants on Human Rights, the Commission on Human Rights should transmit to Governments concerned for their comments such communications as in the opinion of the Commission contain allegations of violations of human rights serious enough to justify such reference and should transmit to the Economic and Social Council such communications together with the replies or comments of Governments as the Commission considers should be brought to the attention of the Council. This draft resolution was rejected.[162]

473. At the eleventh session of the General Assembly in 1956–1957 one delegation proposed that, as interim measures pending entry into force of the Covenants on Human Rights, the proposal should be considered that the Commission on Human Rights instruct a committee to examine complaints of one Member State against another Member State concerning violations of human rights if, in the opinion of the Commission, the complaint should appear well founded. This proposal was not adopted; the General Assembly confined itself to transmitting the relevant documentation to the Commission on Human Rights.[163]

474. Another attempt to re-examine the rule contained in resolution 75 (V) of 1947 was made by the Commission on Human Rights in 1958 when "desiring to recommend to the Economic and Social Council to

---

[160] General Assembly resolution 542 (VI) of 4 February 1952.

[161] *Official Records of the Economic and Social Council, Fourteenth Session, Supplement No. 4,* document E/2256, chap. V, para. 295.

[162] *Official Records of the General Assembly, Eighth Session, Annexes,* agenda item 12, page 3, A/C.3/L.368.

[163] *Official Records of the General Assembly, Eleventh Session, Annexes,* agenda item 60, Report of the Third Committee, A/3524.

re-examine its resolution 75 (V) with a view to establishing a procedure for handling communications which is better calculated to promote respect for and observance of fundamental human rights" appointed a Committee to study the question.[164] The Committee's report was in the main in favour of a reaffirmation of the principle of resolution 75 (V) which in fact was maintained in what eventually became resolution 728 F (XXVIII) of 30 July 1959 of the Economic and Social Council which contains the rules for the handling of communications at present in force.[165]

475. Recommendations to modify the rule of resolution 75 (V) were also made by the Sub-Commission on Prevention of Discrimination and Protection of Minorities at its second and third sessions in 1949 and 1950.[166] The Commission decided not to sanction any change in the procedure.[167]

476. The Sub-Commission on Freedom of Information and of the Press addressed itself at its third session in 1949 to the question of procedures for the handling of communications which were of concern to the Sub-Commission. It submitted to the Economic and Social Council a series of recommendations on this question,[168] and the Economic and Social Council laid down a series of rules on communications in this field.[169] One of the recommendations of the Sub-Commission related to communications containing specific criticism or complaints against Governments in the field of information. The Sub-Commission suggested that with respect to such communications the Secretary-General be requested to inform the Governments concerned and to request them to furnish any information they might wish to on the substance of the communication and its author. The Sub-Commission contemplated that it would examine in public or private session, as it might decide, the list of communications which the Secretary-General was requested to compile in order to determine which of those communications justified discussion and

---

[164] *Official Records of the Economic and Social Council, Twenty-sixth Session, Supplement No. 8,* E/3088, para. 194.

[165] Report of the Committee in document E/CN.4/782; Report on the fifteenth session of the Commission on Human Rights, *Official Records of the Economic and Social Council, Twenty-eighth Session, Supplement No. 8,* E/3229.

[166] E/CN.4/351, Annex, draft resolution 6, and E/CN.4/358, paras. 19–21; see also document E/CN.4/361.

[167] *Official Records of the Economic and Social Council, Eleventh Session, Supplement No. 5,* E/1681, chap. IV, paras. 56 and 62.

[168] E/1369, chap. V, para. 24.

[169] E/1369, resolution of the Economic and Social Council 240 C (IX) of 28 July 1949.

merited further consideration. In resolution 240 C (IX) of 28 July 1949 the Economic and Social Council requested the Secretary-General, *inter alia,* to compile and distribute twice a year to members of the Sub-Commission a list containing a brief summary of each communication received from any legally constituted national or international Press, information, broadcasting or newsreel enterprise or association relating to principles and practices in the field of information. This rule was, however, not to apply to communications which contained specific criticism or complaints against Governments in the field of freedom of information. These were to be dealt with according to whatever procedures and principles might be laid down in the Commission on Human Rights. The Commission on Human Rights, taking note of this Council resolution at its sixth session, was of the opinion that until it had decided upon measures of implementation of the International Covenants on Human Rights, it would be premature to sanction any procedure for dealing with complaints or petitions other than that which was then in force for dealing with communications concerning human rights.[170] The Sub-Commission on Freedom on Information and of the Press held its last session in 1952, and no special arrangements for communications concerning freedom of information are at present in force.

477. The rules laid down in resolution 75 (V) of 1947 were, as far as technical questions were concerned, repeatedly amended by subsequent resolutions of the Economic and Social Council. In resolution 728 F (XXVIII) of 30 July 1959 the Council consolidated the rules relating to communications. Resolution 728 F (XXVIII) is at present in force and contains the approval of the statement repeatedly referred to that the Commission on Human Rights recognizes that it has no power to take any action in regard to any complaints concerning human rights. By virtue of the resolution, the Secretary-General is requested to compile two lists of communications: a non-confidential list containing a brief indication of the substance of each communication which deals with the principles involved in the promotion of universal respect for and observance of human rights and a confidential list containing a brief indication of the substance of other communications concerning human rights, i.e. communications which are not restricted to dealing with the principles involved, and to furnish this list to the members of the Commission in private meeting.

478. The identity of the authors of communications which are included in the non-confidential list are divulged unless the authors indicate that

---

[170] *Official Records of the Economic and Social Council, Eleventh Session, Supplement No. 5,* E/1681, chap. IV, para. 62.

they wish their names to remain confidential. In regard to communications not restricted to principles the opposite rule prevails, namely the identity of the authors is not divulged except in cases where the authors state that they have already divulged or intend to divulge their names or that they have no objection to their names being divulged.

479. The Secretary-General is further requested to enable the members of the Commission upon request to consult the originals of communications dealing with principles. He is to inform the writers of all communications that their communications will be handled in accordance with the resolution under consideration indicating that the Commission has no power to take any action with regard to any complaints concerning human rights. The Secretary-General is also requested to furnish each Member State concerned with a copy of any communication which refers explicitly to that State or to territories under its jurisdiction, without divulging the identity of its author except if the author indicates otherwise, and to ask Governments sending replies to communications brought to their attention whether they wish their replies to be brought to the attention of the Commission in summary form or in full. The members of the Sub-Commission on Prevention of Discrimination and Protection of Minorities have analogous facilities with respect to communications dealing with discrimination and minorities.

480. It may be noted that both resolution 75 (V) and resolution 728 F (XXVIII) of the Economic and Social Council suggested that the Commission on Human Rights set up at each session an *ad hoc* Committee for the purpose of reviewing the confidential list of communications prepared by the Secretary-General. The Commission has followed this practice only at its third, fifth and sixth sessions.[171] It has been the practice of the Commission on Human Rights either to recall the fact that certain lists of communications had been submitted to it or to adopt a resolution by which it takes note of the distribution of the lists of communications. The Commission on the Status of Women, on the other hand, has at every session so far set up an *ad hoc* Committee for the purpose of reviewing the confidential list of communications prepared by the Secretary-General under paragraph (a) of resolution 76 (V), as had been suggested by the Council in that resolution.

481. As far as communications concerning the status of women are con-

[171] See *Official Records of the Economic and Social Council, Seventh Session, Supplement No. 2* (E/800), para. 20; *ibid., Ninth Session, Supplement No. 10* (E/1371), para. 26; *ibid., Eleventh Session, Supplement No. 5* (E/1681), para. 54. The reports of the respective Committees are contained in documents E/CN.4/96, E/CN.4/302 and E/CN.4/460/Rev.1.

cerned, Economic and Social Council resolution 76 (V) has remained the governing resolution. Its provisions are essentially similar to those of 728 F (XXVIII).

Written statements by non-governmental organizations in consultative status

482. Under the rules governing consultative arrangements with non-governmental organizations such organizations have certain rights to submit and circulate written statements.[172]

483. In 1952 some difficulty arose regarding the circulation of written statements submitted by non-governmental organizations in consultative status which constituted or contained complaints against Governments. For that reason the Secretariat consulted the Council Committee on Non-Governmental Organizations in the matter. The Secretariat asked for guidance from the Committee as to the procedure which should be followed in regard to written statements from non-governmental organizations containing complaints, including complaints against Governments. In its report, the Committee suggested that the Secretary-General handle communications which contain complaints of violation of human rights in accordance with resolution 75 (V) (now replaced by resolution 728 F (XXVIII)). This recommendation was approved by the Economic and Social Council.[173]

---

[172] Resolution of the Economic and Social Council 288 B (X) of 27 February 1950.

[173] Resolution of the Economic and Social Council 454 (XIV) of 28 July 1952 and report of the Committee (E/2270).

Index

Abram, Morris B., 2 *n,* 13 *n,* 35, 78–80, 158
Accra, seminar in, 18
Acheson, Dean, 43
Ad Hoc Committee on Forced Labour, 132
Ad Hoc Committee on Periodic Reports, 128
Ad Hoc Groups of Experts, 95–126; nature of procedures, 96–98; origins of, 98–100; evidence before, 100–104; and International Red Cross, 101–102; South Africa's reaction to, 104–105; criteria applied to, 106–107; decisions of, 107; recommendations of, 107–108; evaluation of first performance, 108–10; South Africa Trade Union Rights Inquiry of, 110–13; and Southwest Africa prisoners investigation, 113, 122, 140, 172, 174; effectiveness of, 115; faith in, 115; on genocide in South Africa, 123; future investigations of, 124–26; publicity and, 154–55; refugees and, 163
Adjudication, non-criminal, 37–42, 170–71
African Liberation Committee, 112
African National Congress, 117
Ago, Roberto, 11
Albania, in *Corfu Channel* case, 44, 47
Albania, in Corfu Channel case, 44, 47
American Bar Association, 10, 43
American Declaration of the Rights and Duties of Man (1948), 15, 169
American Veterans Committee, 68
Anglo-Iranian dispute, judgment in, 51
Anglo-Iranian Oil Co. case, 45
Anti-Israel draft, UAR, 89, 92–93
Anti-Slavery Society, 135–36, 157

Apartheid: *Ad Hoc* Group and, 98–100; criminal adjudication against, 6, 61–64; as genocide, 123; investigation of, 84–85; publicity about, 156–57; in Rhodesia, 22–23; in South Africa, 33–36, 144, 150
Apartheid Committee, UN General Assembly, 36, 98, 107–108, 119 *n;* and UN Security Council, 23–26, 28
Arab-Israeli crisis, UN and, 81
Archer, P., 161 *n*
Armed force, use of by UN, 25
Assembly of International Covenants on Human Relations, 71
Austin, Warren, 43–44
Australia, on expulsion from ECA, 28–29
Azevedo, Judge, 53

Basic rights, protection of by adjudication, 61–69
Behr, 146
Belgium Linguistic cases, 39–40
Biafra: UN emergency relief force for, 72, 173; genocide in, 141 *n*
Bilder, R., 32, 83, 146 *n*
Biological warfare, draft committee on, 15
Bissell, T., 79 *n,* 100 *n*
Boycott, in apartheid, 32
Boye, Ibrahima, 99
Brasilia, seminar on apartheid in, 156
Brennan, William J. Jr., 37
Breugel, 146 *n*
Brohi, A. K., 17, 38, 136, 140
Brown v. Board of Education, 55
Buergenthal, T., 144 *n*
Bulgaria, peace treaties with, 53

Cairo, UN seminar in, 18

JOHN CAREY is a graduate of Yale, and holds the
LL.M. degree in International Law from New
York University. He is a partner in the firm of
Coudert Brothers and adjunct assistant profes-
sor at New York University. He served as Alter-
nate US Member and Representative of the UN
Sub-Commission on Prevention of Discrimination
and Protection of Minorities in 1966–69, and the
UN Commission on Human Rights in 1968. Mr.
Carey is a member of the Executive Council of
the American Society of International Law, the
Executive Committee of the American Branch of
the International Law Association, and of the
Committee on International Law of the New York
State Bar Association—serving as the latter's
representative to the US Mission to the UN.

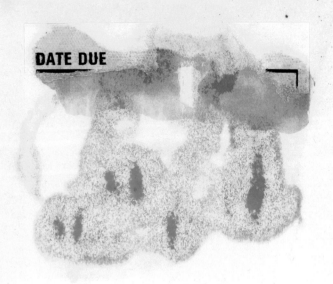